Roman Krznaric is a cultural thin̲k̲e̲r̲.
He is a founding faculty member of The School of Life in London, and also founder of the Empathy Museum and digital Empathy Library. He has been named by the *Observer* as one of Britain's leading popular philosophers. He is an internationally recognised expert on empathy, and advises organisations including Oxfam and the United Nations on using empathy and conversation to create social change. His RSA Animate video on empathy, *The Power of Outrospection*, has been watched by over half a million people.

After growing up in Sydney and Hong Kong, he studied at the universities of Oxford, London and Essex, where he gained his PhD. He has taught sociology and politics at Cambridge University, Essex University, and City University, London, and has done human rights work in Central America with refugees and indigenous people. For several years he was Project Director at The Oxford Muse, the avant-garde foundation to stimulate courage and invention in personal, professional and cultural life. His books include *The Wonderbox: Curious Histories of How to Live*; *How to Find Fulfilling Work*; *The First Beautiful Game: Stories of Obsession in Real Tennis*; and (with Theodore Zeldin) *Guide to an Unknown University*. Roman's books have been translated into twenty languages. He also writes a blog dedicated to empathy and the art of living, at www.outrospection.org.

Roman is a fanatical real tennis player, has worked as a gardener, and has a passion for furniture making.

www.romankrznaric.com

EMPATHY

Why it matters, and how to get it

ROMAN KRZNARIC

LONDON · SYDNEY · AUCKLAND · JOHANNESBURG

1 3 5 7 9 10 8 6 4 2

First published in 2014 by Rider, an imprint of Ebury Publishing
Ebury Publishing is a Random House Group company

This edition first published in 2015

Text copyright © 2014 by Roman Krznaric

Roman Krznaric has asserted his right to be identified
as the author of this Work in accordance with the
Copyright, Designs and Patents Act 1988.

The Random House Group Limited Reg. No. 954009
Addresses for companies within the Random House Group can be found at
www.randomhouse.co.uk

A CIP catalogue record for this book is available from the British Library

Penguin Random House is committed to a sustainable future for
our business, our readers and our planet. This book is made from
Forest Stewardship Council® certified paper.

MIX
Paper from
responsible sources
FSC® C018179

Printed and bound in Great Britain by CPI Group (UK) Ltd,
Croydon, CRO 4YY

ISBN 9781846043857

Copies are available at special rates for bulk orders. Contact the sales
development team on 020 7840 8487 for more information.

To buy books by your favourite authors and register for offers, visit
www.randomhouse.co.uk

Could a greater miracle take place than for us to look through each other's eyes for an instant?

Henry David Thoreau

CONTENTS

THE RADICAL POWER OF EMPATHY

The revolution of human relationships

Empathy has a reputation as a fuzzy, feel-good emotion. Many people equate it with everyday kindness and emotional sensitivity, and being tender and caring towards others. This book offers a very different view. Empathy is, in fact, an ideal that has the power both to transform our own lives and to bring about fundamental social change. Empathy can create a revolution. Not one of those old-fashioned revolutions based on new laws, institutions or governments, but something much more radical: a revolution of human relationships.

Over the past decade there has been a surge of empathic thinking and action around the globe driven by political activists and agony aunts, business gurus and religious leaders. Protesters in the Occupy Movement in Britain and the United States erected 'Empathy Tents' and ran workshops on 'Empathic Activism'. A radio soap opera in Rwanda, listened to by 90 per cent of the population every week, inserts empathic messaging into its storyline about Hutus and Tutsis living in neighbouring villages, in an effort to prevent a revival of ethnic violence. Hundreds of thousands of schoolchildren have been taught empathy skills through Roots of Empathy, a Canadian education programme that has spread to Britain, New Zealand and other countries, which brings babies into the classroom and turns them into teachers. A German social entrepreneur has established a worldwide network of museums where blind guides have taken more than seven million visitors around exhibits that are in total darkness, to give them the experience of being visually impaired. All these initiatives are part of an historic wave of empathy that is challenging our highly individualistic, self-obsessed cultures, in which most of us have become far too absorbed in our own lives to give much thought to anyone else.

But what exactly is empathy? And what does it look like in practice?

First, let's get the meaning clear: *empathy is the art of stepping imaginatively into the shoes of another person, understanding their feelings and perspectives, and using that understanding to guide your actions.*[1] So empathy is distinct from expressions of *sympathy* – such as pity or feeling sorry for somebody – as these do not involve trying to understand the other person's emotions or point of view. Nor is empathy the same as the Golden Rule, 'Do unto others as you would have them do unto you,' since this assumes your own interests coincide with theirs. George Bernard Shaw remarked on this in characteristic style when he quipped, 'Do *not* do unto others as you would have them do unto you – they might have different tastes.' Empathy is about discovering those different tastes.

If you want to grasp just what it means to make the imaginative leap of empathy, then let me introduce you to Patricia Moore, a pioneering figure for today's empathic activists. In 1979, Moore was working as a product designer at the top New York firm Raymond Loewy, who were responsible for creating the curvy Coca-Cola bottle and the iconic Shell logo. Aged twenty-six and fresh out of college, she was the only woman designer amongst three hundred and fifty men at their Midtown Manhattan office. During a planning meeting to brainstorm a new refrigerator model, she asked a simple question: 'Couldn't we design the door so that someone with arthritis would find it easy to open?' One of her senior colleagues turned to her and replied with disdain, 'Pattie, we don't design for those people.' She was incensed. What did he mean, 'those people'? Riled by his response, she decided to conduct what turned out to be one of the most radical empathy experiments of the twentieth century. She would discover what it was like to be an eighty-five-year-old woman.

'I didn't just want to be an actress pretending to be an elderly person,' she told me, 'I wanted a true immersion character, an empathic character, where I could really walk in someone else's shoes.' So with the help of a professional make-up artist, she transformed herself. She put layers of latex on her face so she looked old and wrinkly, wore clouded glasses that blurred her vision, plugged her ears so she couldn't hear well, clipped on a brace and wrapped bandages around her torso so she was hunched over, taped splints to her arms and legs so she was unable to bend her limbs, and finished off her disguise with uneven shoes so she was forced to hobble with a stick.

Now she was ready.

Patricia Moore, a young designer in her twenties *(above)*, transformed herself into an eighty-five-year-old *(right)*.

xii   The Radical Power of Empathy

Between 1979 and 1982 Moore visited over a hundred North American cities in her persona, attempting to negotiate the world around her and find out the everyday obstacles that elderly people faced and how they were treated. She tried going up and down steep subway stairs, riding on crowded buses, pushing through heavy department store doors, crossing busy streets before the lights changed, using can openers and, of course, opening refrigerators.

The result of her immersion? Moore took international product design in a completely new direction. Based on her experiences and insights, she was able to design a series of innovative products that were suitable for use by elderly people, including those with arthritic hands. Amongst her inventions was a line of potato peelers and other kitchen utensils with thick rubber handles, which can now be found in almost every home. She is credited as the creator of 'inclusive' or 'universal' design, where products are designed for people of all abilities, whether aged five or eighty-five. Moore went on to become an expert in the field of gerontology and an influential campaigner for the rights of senior citizens: she was instrumental in getting the Americans With Disabilities Act onto the statute books. Throughout her career, she has been driven more by the desire to improve people's lives than by the lures of financial success. Now in her sixties, her latest project is designing rehabilitation centres where US soldiers who have returned from Afghanistan and Iraq with missing limbs or brain injuries can go to relearn how to live independently, practising everything from buying groceries to using a cash machine.

Moore has become famous for her 'empathic model', which has enlightened a whole generation of designers who now recognise the importance of looking through the eyes of the people who will use the products they create. 'Universal design is driven by empathy,' she explains, 'an understanding that one size doesn't fit all – and that's what my whole career has been about.'[2]

Her experiment in time travel across the generations is a touchstone for the empathists of the future. Making the effort to look through other people's eyes can be personally challenging – and sometimes deeply exhilarating – but it also has extraordinary potential as a force for social change.

The Six Habits of Highly Empathic People

Patricia Moore discovered the power of empathy in the 1970s. Then why are so many people suddenly talking about it now? The idea of empathy is not new. It first rose to prominence in the eighteenth century, when the Scottish philosopher and economist Adam Smith wrote that our moral sensitivity derives from our mental capacity for 'changing places in fancy with the sufferer'. But the recent explosion of interest is largely due to ground-breaking scientific discoveries about human nature.

For the past three hundred years, influential thinkers from Thomas Hobbes to Sigmund Freud have been telling us that we are essentially self-interested, self-preserving creatures who pursue our own individualistic ends. Over time, this dark depiction of human beings has become the prevailing view in Western culture. In the last decade, however, it has been nudged firmly to one side by evidence that we are also *homo empathicus* – wired for empathy.[3] The recent discovery of our empathic selves is one of the most remarkable stories of modern science. I will be telling this story in the next chapter, but in short, there have been path-breaking advances on three fronts. Neuroscientists have identified a ten-section 'empathy circuit' in our brains which, if damaged, can curtail our ability to understand what other people are feeling. Evolutionary biologists have shown that we are social animals who have naturally evolved to be empathic and cooperative, just like our primate cousins. And child psychologists have revealed that even three-year-olds are able to step outside themselves and see other people's perspectives. It is now evident that we have an empathic side to our natures that is just as strong as our selfish inner drives.

This radical shift in our conception of who and what we are has started to filter into public life, prompting a wave of fresh thinking about how to educate our children, how to organise our institutions, and what we really need for personal wellbeing. 'Looking after number one' is becoming an outdated aspiration as we begin to realise that empathy is at the core of being human. We are in the midst of a great transition from the Cartesian age of 'I think, therefore I am', to an empathic era of 'You are, therefore I am'.[4]

Yet for all the unprecedented media coverage and public discussion of empathy, there remains a vital question that few people are talking about – and it is the one at the centre of this book: *How can we expand our empathic potential?* We may well be wired for empathy, but we still need to think about how we are going to bring our circuits to life.

I have spent the last dozen years searching for an answer to this question, exploring the research on empathy in fields from experimental psychology to social history, from anthropology to literary studies, from politics to brain science. Along the way I have delved into the lives of pioneering empathists, many of whom you will meet in these pages, including an Argentinian revolutionary, a best-selling American novelist, and Europe's most famous undercover journalist. I have also done fieldwork, speaking to people from every walk of life about their experiences of empathy, or its absence. Whether they've been trauma nurses or investment bankers, police officers or professional working mothers, people living on the streets of inner-city London or wealthy Guatemalan plantation owners, almost everyone has a story to tell about stepping into the shoes of others.

What I have discovered is that highly empathic people have something in common. They make an effort to cultivate six

THE SIX HABITS OF HIGHLY EMPATHIC PEOPLE

Habit 1: Switch on your empathic brain
Shifting our mental frameworks to recognise that empathy
is at the core of human nature, and that it can be expanded
throughout our lives.

Habit 2: Make the imaginative leap
Making a conscious effort to step into other people's shoes
– including our 'enemies' – to acknowledge their humanity,
individuality and perspectives.

Habit 3: Seek experiential adventures
Exploring lives and cultures that contrast with our own through
direct immersion, empathic journeying, and social cooperation.

Habit 4: Practise the craft of conversation
Fostering curiosity about strangers and radical listening, and
taking off our emotional masks.

Habit 5: Travel in your armchair
Transporting ourselves into other people's minds with the help of
art, literature, film and online social networks.

Habit 6: Inspire a revolution
Generating empathy on a mass scale to create social change,
and extending our empathy skills to embrace the natural world.

habits – a set of attitudes and daily practices that spark the
empathic circuitry in their brains, enabling them to understand
how other people see the world. The challenge we face, if we
hope to fully realise the *homo empathicus* that lies within each of
us, is to develop these six habits in ourselves as best we can.

There are habits to suit every temperament and personality,
whether you are an extrovert or an introvert, a risk-taking
adventurer or a connoisseur of intimacy and subtle emotions.
Making them part of your everyday life will change how you

think, how you feel, and what you do. You'll start to be fascinated by entering people's mindsets and trying to see 'where they are coming from' – their underlying motives, aspirations and beliefs. Your understanding of what makes people tick will expand beyond measure and, like many highly empathic people, you may begin to find others more interesting than yourself.

There is nothing utopian about living by these six habits: the capacity to empathise is one of the great hidden talents possessed by almost every human being. Nearly all of us have it – even if we don't always put it to use. Only a tiny proportion of people display what the psychologist Simon Baron-Cohen calls 'zero degrees of empathy'. Amongst them are psychopaths, who have a cognitive ability to enter your mind but make no emotional bond with you (think Hannibal Lecter), and people with autism spectrum disorders such as Asperger syndrome. Together they account for no more than around 2 per cent of the general population. The other 98 per cent of humanity is born to empathise and wired for social connection.[5]

We also empathise much more frequently than we would ever imagine. Most of us exercise our empathic brains every day, although we are often not conscious of doing so. When you notice a new work colleague is nervous before giving a presentation, you might try to imagine the anxiety and uncertainty she is feeling, and give her the reassurance she needs. You see someone begging under a bridge, and rather than just pitying him (remember, that's sympathy), you may think about what it feels like to sleep out on a cold winter night, or to have people walk straight past you without even bothering to look you in the eye. But empathy is not just about an awareness of the pain and suffering around us. Even when choosing a birthday present for your favourite aunt, you think about the kind of gift that would really delight her – someone with her particular tastes, and of her age and background – not what you might personally wish for as a present.

I am convinced that we cannot explain vast realms of social life without acknowledging the reality and importance of everyday empathy. Just try to imagine a world where it did not exist. It is almost impossible to do so. Mothers would ignore the hunger cries of newborn babies. Charities fighting child poverty would fold due to lack of donations. Few people would make the effort to help a person in a wheelchair trying to open a shop door. Your friends would yawn with boredom as you told them about your marriage breaking up.

This heartless world of indifference is not the one we live in. Open your eyes to it, and you will realise that empathy is all around us, it's the stuff we swim in. Yet if that is the case, what's the problem? Why should we care about cultivating the six habits of highly empathic people? Because at this moment in history we are suffering from an acute 'empathy deficit', both as a society, and in our individual lives.

Tackling the empathy deficit

In the lead-up to the 2008 US presidential election, Barack Obama made empathy one of his major campaign themes:

> There's a lot of talk in this country about the federal deficit. But I think we should talk more about our empathy deficit – our ability to put ourselves in someone else's shoes, to see the world through those who are different from us – the child who's hungry, the laid-off steelworker, the immigrant cleaning your dorm room . . . We live in a culture that discourages empathy, a culture that too often tells us that our principal goal in life is to be rich, thin, young, famous, safe and entertained.[6]

While Obama's administration may have had a mixed record on tackling the empathy deficit (the Guantanamo detention camp remained open throughout his first term in office despite his pledge to close it), he was certainly right to highlight it as a major social problem. A recent study at the University of Michigan revealed a dramatic decline in empathy levels amongst young Americans between 1980 and today, with the steepest drop being in the last ten years. The shift, say researchers, is in part due to more people living alone and spending less time engaged in social and community activities that nurture empathic sensitivity. Psychologists have also noticed an 'epidemic of narcissism': one in ten Americans exhibit narcissistic personality traits that limit their interest in the lives of others. Many analysts believe that European countries are experiencing similar reductions in empathy and increases in narcissism as urbanisation continues to fragment communities, civic engagement decreases, and free market ideologies deepen individualism.[7]

These trends are especially worrying given that the rise of social networks and online culture is believed to be making us more connected and globally aware than at any time in history. Facebook may have attracted over a billion users, but it has not served to reverse the empathic decline, and might even be contributing to it. Social networks are good at spreading information, but – at least to date – less adept at spreading empathy.

Evidence of the empathy deficit in society is everywhere we turn. In the month I write these words, over five thousand civilians have been killed in Syria's civil war. I open the newspaper and read about the scandal of Catholic priests in Ireland who have been accused of molesting young children. New figures reveal that two-thirds of high-income countries have a wider gap between rich and poor than they did in 1980, while a study at the University of California shows that the richer you are, the less empathic you are likely to be – it seems there is nothing like wealth to make you insensitive to human deprivation and suffering.[8] And don't forget the international negotiations to reduce carbon emissions that continue to stall, evidence of our inability to put ourselves in the shoes of future generations who will have to face the consequences of an ecological crisis we are collectively responsible for creating.

Political and ethnic violence, religious intolerance, poverty and hunger, human rights abuses, global warming – there is an urgent need to harness the power of empathy to tackle these crises and bridge social divides. This requires thinking about empathy not just as a relationship between individuals – which is how it is typically described in psychology textbooks – but as a collective force that can shift the contours of the social and political landscape.

I am hopeful of the possibilities. Looking back through history, there is no doubt we can see moments of mass empathic collapse, from the slaughter of the Crusades to the horrors of the Holocaust and the Rwandan genocide. But there have also been waves of collective empathic flowering, such as the humanitarian revolution in eighteenth-century Europe, which saw the rise of the movement to abolish slavery, the decline of torture in the judicial system, improved prison conditions, and growing concern for the rights of children and workers. This moral revolution, writes Steven Pinker, was rooted in 'the rise of empathy and the regard for human life'.[9] We should be turning to examples like this for inspiration – and to others that I will describe in this book – and put empathy to work to tackle the great issues of our time.

Alongside the empathy deficit that plagues contemporary society is a less obvious one that exists on the level of our individual lives. This more personal deficit takes the form of a failure to grasp the enormous opportunity that empathy offers to improve the quality of our everyday existence. We need to recognise that empathy doesn't just make you good – it's good for you too. Many wellbeing experts are beginning to recognise this fundamental truth of the art of living. Amongst them is the economist Richard Layard, who advocates 'deliberate cultivation of the primitive instinct of empathy' because 'if you care more about other people relative to yourself, you are more likely to be happy'. Similarly, personal development thinker Stephen Covey argues that 'empathic communication' is one of the keys to improving interpersonal relations.[10] So what can empathy really do for us?

For a start, it has the power to heal broken relationships. So many relationships fall apart because at least one person feels that their needs and feelings are not being listened to and understood. A healthy dose of empathy, say couples counsellors, is one of the best cures available. Empathy can also deepen our friendships and help create new ones – especially useful in a world where one in four people suffer from loneliness. Creative thinking improves with an injection of empathy too, since it enables you to see problems and perspectives that would otherwise remain hidden. And, as the stories in this book will reveal, there is nothing like looking through someone else's eyes to help question your own assumptions and prejudices, and spark new ways of thinking about your priorities in life.[11]

These are the kinds of benefits that are prompting a growing number of people to adopt empathy as a philosophy of life in its own right, turning their personal empathy deficits into a healthy surplus. They can take their lead from designer Patricia Moore, who explained to me exactly why empathy matters so much to her:

Empathy is a constant awareness of the fact that your concerns are not everyone's concerns and that your needs are not everyone's needs, and that some compromise has to be achieved moment by moment. I don't think empathy is charity, I don't think empathy is self-sacrifice, I don't think empathy is prescriptive. I think empathy is an ever-evolving way of living as fully as possible, because it's pushing your envelope and pushing you into new experiences that you might not expect or appreciate until you're given the opportunity.[12]

Empathy might well be a route to the good life, but we should also appreciate how it can make us good, shaping our ethical visions. Philosophers and social thinkers have long considered empathy to be one of the most effective means we have of expanding the boundaries of our moral universes. In the immediate aftermath of the 9/11 attacks, novelist Ian McEwan wrote: 'Imagining what it is like to be someone other than yourself is at the core of our humanity. It is the essence of compassion, and it is the beginning of morality.'[13] But perhaps the most famous and influential statement on this theme was made by Mahatma Gandhi, shortly before his assassination in 1948. It is known as 'Gandhi's Talisman':

> Whenever you are in doubt, or when the self becomes too much with you, apply the following test. Recall the face of the poorest and the weakest man whom you may have seen, and ask yourself if the step you contemplate is going to be of any use to him. Will he gain anything by it? Will it restore him to a control over his own life and destiny? In other words, will it lead to swaraj [freedom] for the hungry and spiritually starving millions? Then you will find your doubts and your self melt away.[14]

Gandhi's empathic thought experiment offers a compelling – if challenging – moral guide to live by. Just imagine if this Talisman sat framed on the desk of every political leader, banking titan and media baron. Or even on our own.

Anthropologists have also found that empathic thinking underpins moral codes in cultures around the world. A Cheyenne Native American proverb advises, 'Do not judge your neighbour until you walk two moons in his moccasins.' Most Pacific Island languages possess expressions that denote a sense of caring based on understanding other people's emotions and looking at the world from their perspective, such as the term *te nanoanga*, used by the Banaban people of Fiji.[15] In southern Africa, the humanist philosophy of Ubuntu is known for its empathic elements. 'A person with Ubuntu,' writes Desmond Tutu, 'is diminished when others are humiliated or diminished . . . Ubuntu speaks about our interconnectedness.'

Ultimately, the best reason to develop the habit of empathising is that empathy can create the human bonds that make life worth living. Once we truly recognise that we are *homo empathicus*, social animals who thrive on connection rather than isolation, it makes little sense to suppress the empathic side of ourselves. Our wellbeing depends on us stepping out of our own egos and into the lives of others, both people close to us and distant strangers. The pleasures of doing so are real and profound. Without empathic bonds we are lesser beings, only part of who we could be. Or as the poet John Donne put it in the seventeenth century:

> No man is an island, entire of itself; every man is a piece of the continent, a part of the main. If a clod be washed away by the sea, Europe is the less, as well as if a promontory were, as well as if a manor of thy friend's or of thine own were: any man's death diminishes me, because I am involved in mankind, and therefore never send to know for whom the bells tolls; it tolls for thee.

From introspection to 'outrospection'

Where have we got to so far? Put simply, empathy matters. We need to move beyond a scientific understanding of empathy, and recognise it as a powerful tool that can both create radical social change, and give greater depth and meaning to our lives. This should be cause enough to place it right at the top of our 'to do' lists. But before making a start by exploring the six habits of empathic people, there is an even bigger picture we need to see, an overarching reason why empathy deserves to be at the centre of how we approach the art of living: it is an antidote to the self-absorbed individualism that we have inherited from the last century.

I think of the twentieth century as the Age of Introspection. It was the era in which the self-help industry and therapy culture promoted the idea that the best way to understand who you are, and how to live, was to look inside yourself and focus on your own feelings, experiences and desires. This individualistic philosophy, which has come to dominate Western culture, has failed to deliver the good life to most people. So the twenty-first century needs to be different. Instead of introspection, we should create a new Age of Outrospection, where we find a better balance between looking inwards and looking outwards. By 'outrospection' I mean the idea of discovering who you are and how to live by stepping outside yourself and exploring the lives and perspectives of other people.[16] And the essential art form for the Age of Outrospection is empathy. I am not implying that we should completely reject introspection. Clearly we can learn a lot about ourselves through self-reflection, and a mindful examination of our own thoughts and actions may well help liberate us from prejudices and selfish traits that hold back our empathy. The problem is that the pendulum has swung too far towards introspection. Let me explain.

One of the consequences of the Freudian revolution was to popularise the inward gaze, especially the idea of solving personal problems by delving into the inner, unconscious world of our childhood, dreams and forgotten memories. This belief in the importance of searching inside ourselves became a core principle of the various forms of psychoanalysis and therapy that exploded in the years after Freud's death in 1939.

The rapid rise of therapy culture was striking, particularly in the United States. In 1940 around 4 per cent of the US population had tried psychotherapy but by the late 1950s this figure had grown to 14 per cent. Between 1950 and 1975 the number of practising psychotherapists multiplied eight-fold. Even more remarkable was the growing proportion of people who were going to see an analyst not to deal with mental illnesses like depression, but rather to find meaning and human connection in their lives. 'Americans were increasingly replacing traditional problem-solvers – friends and confidantes – with short-term psychotherapists,' according to medical scholar Ronald W. Dworkin, so that by the 1970s 'the therapist in American life had become a substitute friend for unhappy people'.[17]

An astute observer of this phenomenon was the Australian philosopher Peter Singer. Upon moving to New York in the 1970s, he was struck by how many of his academic colleagues were in regular therapy. They often saw their therapist on a daily basis, and some were spending up to a quarter of their annual salaries to enjoy the privilege. Singer found it strange that these people did not seem any more or less disturbed than his friends and workmates in Melbourne or Oxford. So he asked them why they were doing it. 'They said that they felt repressed,' remembered Singer, 'or had unresolved psychological tensions, or found life meaningless.'

The problem, wrote Singer, is that we are unlikely to find meaning and purpose by looking inwards:

> People spend years in psychoanalysis, often quite fruitlessly, because psychoanalysts are schooled in Freudian dogma that teaches them to locate problems within the patient's own unconscious states, and to try to resolve these problems by introspection. Thus patients are directed to look inwards when they should really be looking outwards . . . Obsession with the self has been the characteristic psychological error of the generations of the seventies and eighties. I do not deny that problems of the self are vitally important; the error consists in seeking answers to those problems by focusing on the self.

Singer thought that his colleagues would be far better off if they dedicated themselves to a cause that was greater than themselves. 'If these able, affluent New Yorkers had only got off their analyst's couches, stopped thinking about their own problems and gone out to do something about the real problems faced by less fortunate people in Bangladesh or Ethiopia – or even in Manhattan,' he wrote, 'they would have forgotten their own problems and maybe made the world a better place as well.'[18]

Singer went too far in his rejection of introspection. Most of us recognise that looking inwards, and into our pasts, can help us discover an enormous amount about who we are. Equally, good therapy has the power to transform our lives (as it has my own). Yet Singer was one of the first thinkers to notice that we may not have the balance right, and that we might need more of an outward turn – what I call 'outrospection' – to discover the good life.

He was not alone in his sceptical attitude towards introspection. Joining him was the cultural critic Tom Wolfe, who described the 1970s as the 'Me Decade', when obsession with the self reached new historical heights:

> The old alchemical dream was changing base metals into gold. The new alchemical dream is: changing one's personality – remaking, remodeling, elevating, and polishing one's very self . . . and observing, studying, and doting on it. (Me!)[19]

Wolfe argued that thirty years of post-war economic prosperity had liberated enough people from everyday material worries to create a boom in narcissism. More and more people were gazing into the mirror of their own feelings and desires. It was expressed not just in the popularity of psychoanalysis, but in communal therapy movements such as Encounter Groups and Erhard Seminars Training (est), as well as yoga circles and meditation retreats.

Introspection began to permeate Western society. Terms

such as 'self-improvement', 'self-realisation, 'self-help' and 'personal empowerment' became part of everyday conversation. The political radicalism of the 1960s was gradually giving way to a preoccupation with individual 'lifestyle'. Added into the mix was the growing influence of mass consumer culture, which fed off the enhanced obsession with the self (Buy a car that expresses the 'real you'!). Increasingly, people expressed their personal identity through luxury consumption that gave them a taste of wealth, status and privilege. It was an ideal summed up by the artist Barbara Kruger's slogan 'I shop therefore I am'.[20] The result was a whole generation drawn towards the belief that the pursuit of self-interest – especially the satisfaction of material desires – was the optimal path to personal happiness. 'What's in it for me?' became the defining question of the age.

This introspective, self-oriented approach to the art of living was evident in the new wave of 'happiness' thinking that emerged in the late 1990s. Its key figures typically framed the search for happiness as an individualist pursuit and put personal satisfaction on a pedestal. For example, Martin Seligman's book *Authentic Happiness* (2002) carries the subtitle 'Using the New Positive Psychology to Realize Your Potential for Lasting Fulfillment', while Tal Ben-Shahar's *Happier* (2007) has the subtitle 'Can You Learn to Be Happy?' These books are about 'me' not 'we'. They are direct descendants of the Me Decade of the 1970s.

Ben-Shahar, whose course on happiness at Harvard has been one of the most popular in the university's recent history, is upfront about his philosophy. 'I am no altruist,' he insists, 'the ultimate reason that I do anything – whether it is spending time with my friends or doing work for charity – is that it makes me happy.' Our actions, he writes, 'should be guided by self-interest' rather than 'the morality of duty'. Ben-Shahar's ideas reflect those of the right-wing libertarian thinker Ayn Rand – he founded an organisation at Harvard to spread Rand's philosophy – and exemplify the highly individualistic, self-centred approach favoured by many of today's happiness gurus.[21] While some happiness thinkers such as Martin Seligman have a broader perspective and discuss the importance of having empathy and compassion for others, for most such traits rarely take centre stage, and are generally considered a means to the end of personal fulfilment.[22]

The tragedy is that the Age of Introspection, with its intense focus on the self, has not led Western society into the promised land of happiness. Despite the bulging self-help shelves in bookshops and an avalanche of well-intentioned advice from happiness experts, so many people still feel that there is something missing from their lives, and that they are not gaining all they can from the rare gift of existence. The evidence is overwhelming. Levels of life satisfaction have barely risen in Western countries despite over half a century of growing material abundance. More than half of all employees feel unfulfilled in their jobs. The average rate of divorce has reached 50 per cent. And there is a rising tide of depression and anxiety: around one in four people in Europe and the United States will experience a mental health problem at some point in their lives.[23] This could hardly be described as a happy state of affairs.

Now is the moment to move beyond the Age of Introspection and try something different. Over two thousand years ago, Socrates advised that the best route to living wisely and well was to 'know thyself'. We have conventionally thought that this requires self-reflection, where we look inwards and stare into our souls. But we can also come to know ourselves by stepping outside ourselves, and learning about lives and cultures that are different from our own. It is time to forge a new Age of Outrospection, and empathy is our greatest hope for doing so.

Knowing thyself takes outrospection as well as introspection.[24]

The empathic challenge

Let's not, however, be naïve. Empathy is no universal panacea for all the world's problems, nor for all the struggles we face in our own lives. It's important to be realistic about what empathy can and cannot achieve. That is why, as I explore the six habits of highly empathic people, I will also be addressing the challenges. Is it possible to empathise too much? Can't empathy be used to manipulate people? Can we really learn to become more empathic? And what about our tendency to care far more about our nearest and dearest than people living in far away places of which we know little?[25]

These challenges also exist for me on a personal level. I am not writing this book as someone who has mastered the art of empathy and who practises all six habits with ease. Far from it.

I first became interested in empathy in my mid-twenties, after living for a short time with indigenous Mayan refugees in the Guatemalan jungle, just south of the Mexican border. I saw children dying because they had no access to medical care. I heard stories about massacres by the army. Witnessing the deprivation and insecurity these people faced in daily life opened me up to empathy. Later, as a political scientist and sociologist, I gradually became convinced that the most effective way to achieve deep social change was not through the traditional means of party politics and introducing new laws and policies, but through changing the way people treated each other on an individual basis – in other words, through empathy.

But it was only after leaving academia and researching empathy for around five years that I finally understood why it mattered so much to me. One day I was thinking about how I was affected by my mother's death, when I was ten. Not only did I lose most of my memories from before that age – as often occurs in cases of childhood trauma – but I also became very emotionally withdrawn. I found it difficult to relate to other people's sorrows, or equally to feel their joys. I rarely cried, and felt extremely distanced from people. And as I sat contemplating this, I suddenly had an epiphany. My interest in empathy was not simply due to what I had seen in Guatemala or what academic conclusions I had drawn about social change, but really stemmed from an unconscious desire to recover the empathic self that I had lost as a child.

So I am still looking for ways to engage the empathic circuitry embedded in my brain, and realise my empathic potential as fully as possible.

The concept of empathy has distinct moral overtones. But as you dive into exploring the six habits, you can think of empathising more as an original and exhilarating form of travel. Why not be daring and travel into the life of another person, and see how it affects who you are and who you want to be? Rather than asking yourself 'Where can I go next?', ask, 'Whose shoes can I stand in next?' I hope that this book will inspire you to embark on unexpected empathic journeys, leading you to destinations that cannot be found in any tourist guidebooks. If enough of us become empathic travellers, we may well find that we transform the world we live in.

HABIT 1

SWITCH ON YOUR EMPATHIC BRAIN

Science fiction or science fact?

Stardate 3196. The starship USS Enterprise, under the command of Captain James T. Kirk, has been sent to a mining colony on planet Janus VI to investigate reports of a strange creature that has recently killed fifty miners and is destroying precious equipment. Captain Kirk and his trusty Vulcan deputy Mr Spock encounter the creature, which resembles a clump of molten rock, in a deep underground tunnel. They fire their phaser guns at it, and the injured creature scuttles off. Soon after, Kirk stumbles into a chamber filled with what looks like thousands of small, round silicon rocks – and there is the creature again. But now it is hurt and poses little threat. Kirk wishes he could communicate with it to understand its violent behaviour, so Spock offers to help.

'Captain, you are aware of the Vulcan technique of joining two minds?' he says. Spock then slowly places his hands on the creature, closes his eyes, and concentrates on connecting with its mind.

'Pain! Pain! Pain!' he suddenly shouts out, staggering backwards.

From this brief moment of empathic contact, Spock learns that the creature calls itself a Horta and is in anguish because the miners have been unknowingly crushing its babies – which are soon to hatch from the round silicon 'rocks' that are found throughout the mine. The only reason the Horta had been attacking the miners was to protect its eggs.

Having discovered this, Captain Kirk tells the miners to simply leave the Horta's eggs alone, and then it will leave them alone to dig out the precious mineral they seek. And so ends *The Devil in the Dark*, a classic 1968 episode of the original Star Trek series. Spock's Vulcan 'mind-meld' abilities have saved the day.

Science fiction or science fact? While human beings may not possess the Vulcan species' empathic skill of placing their fingers on someone else's skull and understanding their thoughts and emotions, one of the most exciting discoveries of modern science is that we are much more like Vulcans than we had ever realised. Forget the traditional Darwinian idea that we are primarily motivated by self-interest and an aggressive drive for self-preservation – a vision of ourselves as *homo self-centricus*. The emerging picture of human nature is that we are just as much *homo empathicus*, with a natural capacity to meld our minds to others.

Developing our empathic abilities requires grasping this reality about who we are. We need to shift our underlying attitude – what the German sociologist Karl Mannheim called our *Weltanschauung* or 'worldview' – and recognise this part of ourselves that Western culture has been disregarding for so long. If we keep telling ourselves we are little more than egoistic creatures, there is slim chance that we will ever become any different. One of the best ways to shift our thinking is to learn about the fascinating discovery of *homo empathicus*. So this chapter reveals the little-known story of how we finally found our empathic selves. It begins with the theories of a seventeenth-century philosopher and takes us through to the latest brain research on mirror neurons, via the history of psychology, studies of orphaned babies and the emotional life of chimpanzees.

The first habit of highly empathic people is to 'switch on your empathic brain', by which I mean embracing this more sophisticated understanding of human nature. It is about recognising two things. First, that the capacity to empathise is part of our genetic inheritance, with roots deep in our evolutionary pasts. And second, that empathy can be expanded throughout our lives – it is never too late to join the empathy revolution. Implanting these ideas deep within our psyches is the perfect foundation for developing the other five habits of highly empathic people, priming our minds for stepping into other people's shoes.

Where should we begin learning about our empathic brains? By exploring the origins of one of the most powerful pieces of cultural propaganda in modern history: that human beings are essentially selfish.

It's human nature, isn't it?

We tend to be pessimistic, even cynical about other people. Survey data across Western countries shows that we typically think that 'most people can't be trusted' and 'people are mostly looking out just for themselves'.[1] The assumption that we are self-interested at our cores is so embedded in our minds that we hardly notice it. 'Oh, it's human nature,' people say – a phrase reserved to describe nasty, self-centred or otherwise negative behaviour. On the other hand, when we witness gestures of caring and generosity, we never shrug our shoulders and say, 'Well, what did you expect? It's just human nature to be generous.'[2] Empathy, kindness and other forms of benevolent behaviour are generally seen as the exception rather than the rule.

Yet it is not surprising that this view of human nature should be so pervasive. It partly reflects the reality that we do indeed have an innate selfish and aggressive side to us. But it is also a story about human nature that has been sold to us by influential thinkers for more than three centuries – it is our cultural inheritance, an ideology that has gradually seeped into our collective imaginations. Revealing who is responsible for it is the beginning of rediscovering our empathic selves. There are four prime suspects.

In modern Western thought, the self-interest narrative begins with the English philosopher Thomas Hobbes, whose 1651 book *Leviathan* argued that if human beings were left in a 'state of nature' – without any form of government – the result would be a 'warre of all against all' and life would be 'solitary, poor, nasty, brutish and short'. His conclusion was that inherently self-seeking and violent creatures such as ourselves needed an authoritarian government to keep us in check. Although Hobbes was attempting to make universal statements, his ideas were very much a product of his times: his negative portrayal of human nature was undoubtedly influenced by the fact that he wrote his book during the bloody turmoil of the English Civil War. This did not, however, prevent *Leviathan* becoming one of the most important works of Western intellectual history – it was still at the top of the reading list when I studied politics in the late 1980s.

During the eighteenth century, the ideology of self-interest found a new champion in the Scottish Enlightenment thinker Adam Smith. He is an unusual figure in this story, since he also played a decisive role in shaping how we understand empathy. Yet his ideas on this subject were almost completely eclipsed by his radical theory of self-interest that appeared in *The Wealth of Nations* (1776). Smith maintained that if buyers and sellers in an economy dedicated themselves to maximising their personal gain, goods and services would be distributed by an 'invisible hand' in the best interests of the community as a whole. 'By pursuing his own interest,' wrote Smith, an individual 'frequently promotes that of the society more effectually than when he really intends to promote it'. The power of this idea was that it offered a resounding economic and political justification for acting in accordance with one's self-interest, which helps explain Smith's popularity with business and political elites during the Industrial Revolution. The invisible hand later became a pillar of neoclassical economic thinking, which rose to prominence in the second half of the twentieth century and found its political expression in the free market ideologies of Thatcherism and Reaganomics. Its leading proponents, such as the Austrian aristocrat Friedrich von Hayek, echoed Smith by claiming that 'we will benefit our fellow men most if we are guided solely by the striving for gain'.[3]

Charles Darwin's *The Origin of Species*, published in 1859, was taken to confirm everything that Hobbes and Smith were arguing. His theory of natural selection and the 'struggle for existence' reinforced the narrative about innate human selfishness: competition rather than cooperation was the driver of our evolutionary history. This simplistic interpretation of Darwin's ideas – he actually had a more nuanced view of human nature – was popularised by 'social Darwinists' such as the English philosopher Herbert Spencer, who coined the term 'survival of the fittest'. The rich, Spencer believed, had no need to feel guilty about their wealth, since it was the inevitable result of their natural talent and superiority. His books sold spectacularly well in the United States. 'Spencer was American gospel,' wrote the economist John Kenneth Galbraith, 'because his ideas fitted the needs of American capitalism.'[4] Darwin's theories were given a different spin in the 1970s when the evolutionary biologist Richard Dawkins suggested that human beings were really 'machines for passing on genes'.[5] His metaphor of the 'selfish gene' – although never intended to imply that genes actually had wills of their own – became a celebrated pop science catchphrase that resonated with the long history of thinking that self-interest was lurking deep in our beings.

A final key figure whose work helped to cement this story in Western minds was Sigmund Freud. In books such as *Civilization and its Discontents* (1930), Freud was intent on stripping away any romantic illusions about human nature, especially in the light of the World War that Europe had just lived through. He was particularly scathing of the commandment to 'love one's neighbour as oneself', since 'nothing else runs so strongly counter to the original nature of man'. 'Men are not gentle creatures,' he wrote, but rather have an 'inclination to aggression'. Even babies, he argued, had a ruthless drive to seek their self-interest. Like Hobbes, Freud believed that without adequate controls man becomes 'a savage beast to whom consideration of his own kind is something alien'. He is driven by his libido and aggression not to love his neighbour, but 'to use him sexually without his consent, to seize his possessions, to humiliate him, to cause him pain, to torture and to kill him'.[6] There is not much room for empathy left in this eroticised – and frankly monstrous – vision of human nature.

So here we stand in the early twenty-first century, having been saturated for more than three hundred years by the overriding message that self-interest ultimately defines who we are. And there is little doubt that this message has been fully absorbed into Western culture. Our language is strewn with expressions that reinforce a dark image of humankind, from 'looking after number one' to 'nice guys finish last'. Take an economics course and the central assumption will be that human beings are rational, self-interested actors. Open a newspaper and you are much more likely to read reports of conflict rather than cooperation – acts of empathy rarely make the headlines. Hollywood films specialise in feeding us on a diet of everyday violence and human brutality, often under the euphemism of 'action movies'. Children graduate quickly from reading farmyard animal stories to playing computer games where the usual aim is to shoot and kill one another, as if they were trapped in a Hobbesian nightmare. Somehow we consider all of this quite normal.

Under the continual intellectual assault of this quartet of powerful thinkers – Hobbes, Smith, Darwin and Freud – and their followers, the idea that we may be wired for empathy just as much as for self-interest has had little chance to emerge and flower. The great tragedy is that, until now, we have been presented with only a partial account of human nature – one that focuses on our egoist selves, *homo self-centricus*. So how is it that today we are hearing so much talk of *homo empathicus*? What is the story of how we discovered our empathic brains?

Child psychology and the discovery of *homo empathicus*

Astonishingly, when we trace the roots of empathic thinking in Western culture, they go back to some of the very same authors whose writings have been used to sell us the self-interest narrative. Adam Smith may have claimed, in *The Wealth of Nations*, that the pursuit of self-interest was good for society, but in another book published seventeen years earlier, *The Theory of Moral Sentiments* (1759), he offered a more complex and complete depiction of human motivation, which was in part a direct riposte to Hobbes's pessimistic view of the state of nature.[7] 'How selfish soever man be supposed,' Smith began his book, 'there are evidently some principles in his nature, which interest him in the fortune of others, and render their happiness necessary to him, though he derives nothing from it, except pleasure of seeing it.' This is followed by the world's first fully developed theory of empathy – which at the time was called 'sympathy' – where Smith argued that we have a natural capacity for stepping into other people's shoes, which he memorably described as 'changing places in fancy with the sufferer'. His ideas were reinforced by his Scottish contemporary, the philosopher David Hume, who wrote that there is in each of us 'some particle of the dove, kneaded into our frame, along with the elements of the wolf and the serpent'.

Darwin too was well aware that everyday life was not pervaded by tooth and claw selfishness, and recognised that we have a more benevolent side to us. He noticed the sociability of many mammals – for example the way dogs and horses were miserable when separated from their companions – and believed there was also an ingrained 'social instinct' within human beings, which explained why someone might rush into a burning building to save a stranger, even if it put his own life at risk. In the years after the publication of *The Origin of Species*, Darwin became convinced that cooperation and reciprocity were as essential as competition to the evolutionary process. Unfortunately this more empathic side of Darwin's thinking, which appeared in books such as *The Descent of Man* (1871), was largely neglected at the time, and we are only beginning to recover it now.[8]

Smith and Darwin simply couldn't ignore the obvious truth that we are social animals who care deeply about other people and frequently act in their interests, often to our own detriment. They could see this in their concern for their own family and friends, but they were also witnesses to the rise of humanitarian organisations in the eighteenth and nineteenth centuries, such as those to combat child neglect. Yet powerful voices in society had little desire to hear what they had to say about *homo empathicus*. The story about self-interest was far more convenient, especially to politicians who were only minimally concerned with human welfare and industrialists who needed cheap labour to fill their factories.

It was not until the early twentieth century, when psychology was becoming an established science, that the concept of empathy started getting the attention it deserved. The roots of the English word 'empathy' can be found in the German term *Einfühlung*, which literally means 'feeling into'. *Einfühlung* was popularised in the nineteenth century by a now forgotten German philosopher called Theodor Lipps (who was greatly admired by Freud) as a concept in philosophical aesthetics that referred to our ability to 'feel into' works of art and nature, and have an emotional rather than a rational response to them. In 1909 the American psychologist Edward Titchener decided it was time for *Einfühlung* to have an English equivalent, so he invented the word 'empathy' (based on the ancient Greek *empatheia*, meaning 'in' + 'suffering'). From that moment on, the meaning of empathy underwent a series of metamorphoses, creating a complex linguistic inheritance that requires some unravelling.

Psychologists quickly shifted its use from the realm of art to denote a form of mimicry. A popular psychology textbook from the 1930s contains a photograph of a pole vaulter clearing the bar, with onlookers standing underneath unconsciously lifting their legs in the air and straining their faces, as if they were doing the vaulting themselves. The photo is captioned 'Empathy'. The author then describes how an audience will often imitate the facial expressions of a speaker standing before them – they may, for instance, involuntarily smile when the speaker smiles. This too is described as a classic instance of empathy.[9]

From the 1940s, however, these two early meanings – as a mode of appreciating art and as emotional mimicry – gave way to the two approaches to empathy that you will most commonly find in psychology textbooks today: empathy as *perspective-taking* (sometimes called 'cognitive empathy') and empathy as a *shared emotional response* (known as 'affective empathy'). So what exactly do they mean, and where do the concepts come from?

The great breakthrough in thinking about cognitive empathy came in 1948, when the Swiss child psychologist Jean Piaget published the results of an experiment known as 'The Three Mountains Task'. Children of various ages were presented with a three-dimensional model of a mountain scene, then asked to describe what a doll would see from different positions around the model. Those aged under four tended to choose their own perspective of viewing the model, rather than that of the doll, whereas older children were able to step into the doll's shoes. Piaget's interpretation of this was that the younger children were as yet unable to consider another person's point of view.

The current consensus in empathy research, which builds on Piaget's pioneering studies of visual perception, is that children as young as two or three have a rudimentary ability to imagine perspectives other than their own.[10] I've seen it in my own twins. When they were around eighteen months old, if my son was crying, his sister would try to comfort him by giving him her toy dog. But once they reached twenty-four months, if he was crying she would no longer offer him her own little dog, but realised he would be much happier if she passed him his favourite toy cat. This is what cognitive empathy or perspective-taking (sometimes also known as 'theory of mind') is all about. It

Cognitive empathy is about seeing the world from the perspective of others, just like in this 1950s architecture experiment. Students designed giant furniture to understand how a child might perceive and experience an adult-sized room.

involves making an imaginative leap and recognising that other people have different tastes, experiences and worldviews than our own. The very fact that cognitive empathy develops naturally in early childhood – just at the time when the distinction between self and other begins to emerge – tells us that human beings are inherently social creatures that are wired for empathy. It is not just Mr Spock who is able to read another person's mind.

The second kind of empathy, 'affective empathy', is less about the cognitive ability to understand 'where a person is coming from' than about sharing or mirroring another person's emotions. So if I see my daughter crying in anguish and I too feel anguish, then I am experiencing affective empathy. If, on the other hand, I notice her anguish but feel a different emotion, such as pity ('Oh, the poor little thing,' I might think), then I am showing sympathy rather than empathy. Sympathy typically refers to an emotional response that is not shared. You may have noticed that the definition of empathy I used at the beginning of this book combines both the affective and cognitive elements: empathy involves stepping into someone's shoes, gaining an understanding of their feelings (the affective aspect) and perspectives (the cognitive aspect), and using that understanding to guide our actions. In practice, both forms of empathy are closely intertwined.

This dual definition that recognises both the cognitive and affective forms of empathy helps clear up two common confusions. First, a frequent criticism of empathy is that it can be used to 'manipulate' people. The concern here is that a serial killer might try to understand his victims' minds in order to lure them to their deaths. But what the psychopathic killer is doing is just taking the cognitive step into another person's shoes, without any affective sharing of their emotions or concern for their welfare. Using cognitive insights to manipulate people for self-interested ends cannot be construed as empathy by any sensible and complete definition of the word.

A second confusion is that people often use the terms empathy and compassion interchangeably. While they overlap in some ways, they are distinct concepts. The Latin origin of the word 'compassion' means 'to suffer with another'. This is different from empathy, which can include sharing the joys of another as well as their suffering. Additionally, the emphasis in compassion is on affective connection with others – feeling their emotions – and does not usually include making a cognitive leap to understand how their beliefs, experiences and views might be different from our own. Compassion is also often used to refer to sympathetic emotional responses such as pity or mercy, which are outside the realm of empathy. Despite these differences, in some cultural and religious traditions empathy and compassion are closely intertwined. Buddhist notions of compassion, for example, usually stress the importance of empathically understanding other people's perspectives and worldviews. Overall, though, we should resist using empathy and compassion as synonyms.

The distinction between cognitive and affective empathy can help us think about the much-debated issue of whether women are more naturally empathic than men. The psychologist Simon Baron-Cohen thinks so. After finding that women generally score higher than men on standard empathy tests, he boldly declared: 'The female brain is predominantly hard-wired for empathy. The male brain is predominantly hard-wired for understanding and building systems.' In his view, women are good at relationships and emotions, while men are relatively better at analytical and mechanical tasks. This gender divide is evident from early childhood, and cannot be fully explained by cultural forces such as the barrage of gender-stereotyped toy advertisements, or parental behaviour and expectations.[11]

Does this mean that you should toss aside the book you are currently reading, since if you are a man there's no point trying to empathise, and if you are a woman you are naturally skilled at it anyway? Certainly not. For a start, studies like Baron-Cohen's are not saying that all women are better than all men at empathising, but that this is the case on average: across the spectrum there are some men who are highly empathic, just as there are some women who are not. Moreover, most measures are designed to rate affective empathy more than cognitive empathy. Their focus is on our ability to respond to one another's feelings, so they ask questions like, 'Can you tell if someone is masking their true emotions?' or 'Do you get upset if you see people suffering on news programmes?'[12] There is little evidence that men and women differ substantially on their cognitive ability to step into other people's shoes. A final reason to approach gender differences cautiously is that the real issue is not how much empathy you are born with, but the extent to which you are willing and able to develop it. Enhancing your capacity to see the world through the eyes of others is much more about the steps you take than what sex you happen to be.

Returning to the story of how the concept of empathy developed in modern psychology, at around the same time that Piaget was experimenting with dolls, researchers were making startling – and disturbing – discoveries about how emotions and sociability developed in early infancy, especially the capacity for affective empathy. In 1945, the Austrian-American psychoanalyst René Spitz conducted one of the world's first studies of maternal and emotional deprivation, in two very different children's homes in the United States. The first was an orphanage where the babies were kept clean and well fed, but – as was common in foundling homes at the time – they had minimal physical and emotional contact with their caregivers. The nurses rarely picked them up, and sheets were even hung between the cots to prevent the spread of germs. They spent the day in almost complete isolation, with virtually no human stimulation. And this is what happened: despite having good physical care, thirty-four of the ninety-one babies died before they turned two. The other children's home was in a prison, but each day the convicted mothers were allowed to visit their babies, and hold and play with them. Hygiene standards may not have been as high in the prison, but none of the babies died. Two years later, Spitz made his point even more graphically in a film showing babies who were giggling when they first arrived at an orphanage, but within weeks had become dazed and forlorn, gnawing strangely on their hands and losing weight, and after just a few months had been reduced to emaciated, expressionless and motionless shells.[13]

Spitz's shocking research revealed that human affection may be even more critical to survival than food and shelter, or was at least of equal importance in our hierarchy of needs. His work was taken a step further by the British psychiatrist John Bowlby, whose 'Attachment Theory' attempted to explain what Spitz had discovered. In the 1950s Bowlby showed that a child's early relationship with its mother (or primary caregiver) was critical for emotional and mental development. If an infant does not receive deep affection, particularly in its first year of life, 'there is risk for his future happiness and health'.[14] This is a foundational period when a baby starts learning the basic skills of human communication, such as reading facial expressions, and also how to identify and regulate its own feelings. When an infant is deprived of secure attachment – or if there is a fear of losing an attachment figure such as a parent – in later years they can develop a range of problematic behaviour patterns, from anxiety and emotional detachment to aggression and sociopathic traits. So if a person has had unresponsive or emotionally unavailable parents in infancy (for instance parents who let the baby 'cry it out' when distressed) this may impact on their sensitivity to stress, resulting in outbursts of violent behaviour.[15]

Bowlby's work was a direct challenge to the Freudians, many of whom remained obsessed with the idea that we are primarily driven by our individual material and sexual desires. In contrast,

Bowlby shifted thinking about human nature, suggesting that the need for companionship and sociability was at the core of our beings, or as the psychotherapist Sue Gerhardt describes it, 'every human being is born seeking an emotional connection, an attachment to a protective adult who will tune into him and respond to him'.[16] Bowlby's research, together with that of other psychologists such as Mary Ainsworth, also offered two vital insights into our understanding of empathy. First, lack of secure attachment stunts the development of empathy, especially the ability to make the emotional connection with other people's feelings, which is the basis of affective empathy. Second, one of the most effective ways to nurture emotional capacities such as empathy in children is to show them empathy as a parent. As the psychologist Alan Sroufe explains:

> How do you get an empathic child? You get an empathic child not by trying to teach the child and admonish the child to be empathic, you get an empathic child by being empathic with the child. The child's understanding of relationships can only be from the relationships he's experienced.[17]

Bowlby's ideas on attachment, despite being highly controversial at the time, have become widely accepted today amongst child psychologists and parenting experts. But for anybody interested in developing their empathy, they might come as disappointing news. If we were not doused with affection and empathy as infants, does that mean we have little chance of expanding our empathy as teenagers or adults? Is it too late to become *homo empathicus* for the estimated one in three people who grew up without secure attachment relationships?[18]

Fear not. Even though the first years of life are an intense and concentrated time for wiring together the circuits in our brains, it is certainly still possible to extend our empathy as we get older. It just gets that bit harder, since we have developed habitual ways of responding, thinking and behaving that are resistant to exercising our empathic imaginations. As Bowlby observed, 'change continues throughout the life cycle' – in the right circumstances, with the right stimulus, we can overcome the limits of insecure attachment.[19] Running in our favour is that we all have a latent empathic potential that has been built into us by our evolutionary history and genetic make-up. And that leads us to the next stage in the story of how we discovered *homo empathicus*. Following the advances made in psychology in the 1940s and 1950s, in the last two decades evolutionary biologists and neuroscientists have been at the forefront of explosive new insights into the origins and nature of empathy.

Get in touch with your inner ape

In 1902, Peter Kropotkin – who was both an anarchist revolutionary and a noted scientist – wrote a book called *Mutual Aid: A Factor of Evolution*. A counter to orthodox Darwinian ideas about the competitive struggle for existence, Kropotkin argued that cooperation and mutual aid are just as important as competition in the evolutionary process. He showed how most animal species, from ants to pelicans, from marmots to humans – exhibit cooperative tendencies such as sharing food and protecting one another from predators, which enable them to survive and flourish. Wild horses and musk oxen, for instance, form a ring around their young to shield them against attacking wolves.[20]

When *Mutual Aid* was first published, Kropotkin was considered an eccentric, but he was just a century ahead of his time. Today his views have become mainstream amongst evolutionary biologists, many of whom believe that empathy is one of the keys to understanding the cooperative story he identified. Prominent amongst them is the Dutch primatologist

Frans de Waal, who has been voted one of the 100 World's Most Influential People Today by *Time* magazine. But why should a chimp expert have received such an accolade? Because his research since the mid-1990s has turned the old Hobbesian and Darwinian picture of human nature on its head by showing that empathy is a natural capacity in a range of animals such as gorillas, chimps, elephants, dolphins – and human beings. De Waal has done more than almost anyone on the planet to alert us to the existence of *homo empathicus*.

I asked de Waal why he was so interested in the evolution of empathy. 'No one denies that humans are aggressive – in fact I consider us one of the most aggressive primates,' he told me.[21] But he believes we should equally beware thinking about ourselves simply as killer apes. 'We have been fed a lot of nonsense about being inherently aggressive and predestined to wage war,' he said. Indeed, he points out that we are genetically very close to the peaceful, hippy-like bonobo, which exhibits stronger empathic traits than other primates such as chimpanzees. 'Empathy is second nature to us,' according to de Waal, 'so much so that anybody devoid of it strikes us as dangerous or mentally ill.'[22]

De Waal argues that empathy is so basic to the human species and develops at such a young age – as the psychology research by Bowlby and Piaget revealed – that it is unlikely that it only emerged when our lineage split off from apes. Because of our shared ancestry, we can learn about the long evolutionary history of empathy in humans by studying it in our primate relatives.

The evidence for empathy in other species is now overwhelming, de Waal explained to me. 'Since the 1990s, so many studies have been conducted by others and by my own team that it is getting hard to keep up. We have collected thousands of observations of so-called consolation behaviour in chimpanzees. As soon as one among them is distressed – has lost a fight, dropped out of a tree, encountered a snake – others will come over to provide reassurance. They embrace the distressed chimp or try to calm him or her with a kiss and grooming.' This is just the kind of emotional sensitivity that was observed by primatologist Dian Fossey when she spent thirteen years in the 1970s and 1980s living with gorillas in the misty rainforests of the Virunga Mountains in central Africa.

But how do we know these responses are really based on empathy, rather than some other emotion? De Waal has little doubt that empathy is at work, a point he makes with a story about a bonobo chimp named Kuni, who found a wounded bird that had hit the glass wall of her enclosure in Twycross Zoo in England. Kuni took the bird up a tree to set it free, taking special care to spread its wings wide open before throwing it towards the barrier of the enclosure. The bird fell short and so Kuni guarded it until the end of the day, when it finally flew to safety. For de Waal, it was a perfect demonstration of putting yourself in another's shoes. 'Having seen birds in flight many times, she seemed to have a notion of what would be good for a bird, thus giving us an anthropoid illustration of Adam Smith's "changing places in fancy with the sufferer".'[23]

De Waal also described to me one of his latest lab experiments revealing evidence of altruistic behaviour driven by empathy. Two capuchin monkeys were placed side by side. One of them needed to barter with the researchers using small plastic tokens. The critical test came when it was offered a choice between two differently coloured tokens with different meanings: one token was 'selfish', the other 'pro-social'. If the bartering monkey picked the selfish token, it received a small piece of apple for returning it, but its partner got nothing. The pro-social token, on the other hand, rewarded both monkeys equally at the same time. The monkeys gradually began to prefer the pro-social token, showing how much they cared about each other's welfare. This was not based on fear of possible repercussions, de Waal explained, because they found that the most dominant monkeys – who have least to fear – were actually the most generous.

This experiment resembled one of the most famous early demonstrations of animal empathy. In 1964, psychiatrist Jules Masserman reported that rhesus monkeys refused to pull a chain that gave them food if it also gave an electric shock to a companion. One monkey stopped pulling the chain for twelve days after seeing another monkey receive a shock – it literally starved itself to prevent harm to one of its fellows.[24]

From his decades studying primates, de Waal argues that empathy probably developed in humans for two reasons. First, to ensure that we respond to the needs of our offspring: if a mother did not react appropriately to the hunger cries of her child, the infant's life would be put in jeopardy. 'During the 180 million years of mammalian evolution,' says de Waal, 'females who responded to their offspring's needs out-produced those who were cold and distant.' Second – echoing Kropotkin – to sustain the mutual assistance required for individual and group survival: in harsh primitive environments, for example, empathy enabled humans to cooperate to make sure everyone in the community had enough to eat. 'Effective cooperation requires being exquisitely in tune with the emotional states and goals of others,' observes de Waal.[25] His ideas on the importance of cooperation in the evolutionary process have been bolstered by the growing evidence that cooperation even exists on the cellular level. Some of the earliest bacteria formed strings where certain cells in each filament would die in order to nourish their neighbours with nitrogen.[26]

De Waal is not content, however, with burying his findings in academic journal articles. Like his predecessor Peter Kropotkin, who thought that society should be organised on a more communal and cooperative basis to reflect the cooperative tendencies in human nature, de Waal too believes that his work has implications for how to design the kind of society that can make us thrive:

> I can't stand the many references to biology by conservatives in the United States. They use biology as a convenient justification for their policies, saying that since nature is based on a 'struggle for life' we ought to build our societies around selfishness and competition. They read into nature what they want to, and I feel it is my task to point out that they got it all wrong. There are many animals that survive through cooperation, and our own species in particular comes from a long line of ancestors dependent on each other. Empathy and solidarity are bred into us, so that our society's design ought to reflect this side of the human species, too.

In his view, it is a mistake to consider the free market economy as somehow 'natural'. In fact, 'you need to indoctrinate empathy out of people in order to arrive at extreme capitalist positions,' he contends.[27] De Waal also believes that empathy has the power to erode our cultures of violence and racism, and expand the boundaries of our moral concern. 'Empathy is the one weapon in the human repertoire that can rid us of the curse of xenophobia,' according to de Waal. 'If we could manage to see people on other continents as part of us, drawing them into our circle of reciprocity and empathy, we would be building upon, rather than going against, our natures.'[28]

De Waal's research is the stuff of paradigm shifts. In the seventeenth century, Galileo shocked European society by demonstrating that the earth was not at the centre of the universe, with the sun and planets revolving around us. De Waal has revealed something just as revolutionary: that human nature does not simply revolve around self-interest. Empathy is at the centre of who we are. *Homo empathicus* has roamed the earth for hundreds of thousands of years. Our task is to create the kind of world that enables, rather than hinders, the flourishing of our empathic selves.

Dissecting the empathic brain

Thanks to insights from child psychologists and primatologists, we have taken huge strides in our understanding of empathy during the last century. The conventional Hobbesian depiction of human nature no longer looks tenable, or even sensible. But there is one source of evidence we have yet to tap into: the neural activity inside our brains. Since the turn of the millennium, neuroscience has been the most creative field of empathy research. It is now clear that even Thomas Hobbes's brain was wired for empathy. What have scientists actually found happening inside our craniums? And what do their discoveries reveal – or fail to reveal – about how empathy really works in human beings?

The place to begin is in a laboratory at the University of Parma, Italy, in August 1990. A team of neuroscientists led by Giacomo Rizzolatti were conducting experiments on macaque monkeys, whose brains had been implanted with a hair-thin electrode. They recorded that a particular region of the pre-motor cortex was activated when a monkey picked up a peanut. Then, in one of those bizarre moments of scientific serendipity, they noticed that the same region lit up when the monkey happened to see one of the researchers pick up a nut – even though the monkey had not moved an inch. The brain responded as if the monkey had grasped the nut itself. Rizzolatti and his colleagues simply didn't believe it. But subsequent experiments on macaques, and also humans – using functional magnetic resonance imaging (fMRI) – produced exactly the same results.

They had accidentally discovered 'mirror neurons'. These are neurons that fire up both when we experience something (such as pain) and also when we see somebody else going through the same experience. People with lots of mirror cells tend to be more empathic, especially in terms of sharing emotions. According to Rizzolatti, 'mirror neurons allow us to grasp the minds of others not through conceptual reasoning but through direct simulation'. Eminent neuroscientist Vilayanur Ramachandran has compared the discovery of mirror neurons to Crick and Watson's double helix revelation: 'I predict that mirror neurons will do for psychology what DNA did for biology.'[29]

One of the most important figures in contemporary mirror neuron research is Christian Keysers, head of the Social Brain Lab at the Netherlands Institute for Neuroscience, who has worked as part of Rizzolatti's team in Parma. I asked him to explain what makes mirror neurons so significant:

> The question that fascinates me is how we understand others. I often just look at my wife in the face, and instantly know how she feels (and thus whether I'm in trouble or not . . .). Hollywood movies are a good example too: your heart beats faster as you watch a tarantula crawl on James Bond's chest in the movie *Dr No*, your hands sweat and your skin tingles under the spider's legs. Effortlessly, you feel what Bond feels. How? This is what we have found in our discovery of mirror neurons: our brain mirrors the state of other people. Understanding what they feel then becomes understanding what you now feel in their stead. Neuroscience has discovered empathy.
>
> Let me be bold and say that this tells us a new story about human nature. As Westerners in particular, we are brought up to centre our thinking on individuals – individual rights, individual achievements. But if you call the state of your brain your identity (and I would), what our research shows is that much of it is actually what happens in the minds of other people. My personality is the result of my social environment. The fate of others colours my own feelings, and thus my decisions. I is actually we. Neuroscience has put the 'we' back into the brain. That is not a guarantee (and my wife will agree) that some of my actions are not egoistic and selfish, but it shows that egoism and selfishness are not the only forces that direct our brains. We are social animals to a degree that most didn't suspect only a decade ago.[30]

Can you feel this spider crawling across your own skin?

The existence of mirror neurons suggests a radical redefinition of what it means to be human: the boundaries of the self extend far beyond our skin and bone physicality. If Keysers and his colleagues are right, we are in a perpetual state of Vulcan mind-meld without even realising it, our brains constantly mirroring what we sense in the world around us, whether it is the face of a crying child or a spider crawling across James Bond's chest. Our neurological wiring also shapes our ethical behaviour, such as our capacity to follow the Golden Rule. 'Neuroscience shows us the limits of our natural empathy,' argues Keysers, 'so ethics that suggest "treat others as they would like to be treated" are harder to follow than ethics that suggest "treat others as you would like to be treated".'

While mirror neurons are undoubtedly fascinating, they are just the beginning of our understanding of the empathic brain. Indeed, some researchers believe they are receiving more attention than they deserve. This is in part because mirror neuron studies generally focus on how we share emotions (affective empathy) more than perspective-taking (cognitive empathy), giving us a lopsided account of how empathy functions at the neurological level. But it is also because, in the words of Harvard psychologist Steven Pinker, the discovery of mirror neurons has created 'an extraordinary bubble of hype'. Neuroscientists and science journalists, he points out,

> have touted mirror neurons as the biological basis of language, intentionality, imitation, cultural learning, fads and fashions, sports fandom, intercessory prayer, and, of course, empathy. A wee problem for the mirror-neuron theory is that the animals in which the neurons were discovered, rhesus macaques, are a nasty little species with no discernible trace of empathy.[31]

Cambridge psychologist and autism expert Simon Baron-Cohen is less critical than Pinker, yet nevertheless urges caution. 'Some people are quick to assume that mirror neurons alone can be equated with empathy,' says Baron-Cohen, but in reality the mirror neuron system 'may simply be the building blocks for empathy'. Mirror neurons, for instance, are involved in mimicry – like when someone yawns, we involuntarily do so too, or when we are feeding an infant, they open their mouth and we may open ours as well. But 'empathy seems to be more than just this automatic mirroring,' suggests Baron-Cohen. Rather, it involves an active engagement in understanding someone's emotions and mental states, and how they relate to our own.

Baron-Cohen's big idea – and one that is becoming the consensus in the field – is that mirror neurons are one part of a much more complex 'empathy circuit' comprising at least ten interconnected brain regions. If any of these regions get damaged or do not develop properly, then our natural empathic capabilities may become impaired. One famous neurological patient known as S.M., who has very specific amygdala damage, is unable to recognise the emotion of fear in other people's faces, despite having otherwise normal intelligence. Similarly, people with borderline personality disorders, who typically have low levels of empathy, may have smaller than average amygdalas, a lack of binding of neurotransmitters to one of the serotonin receptors, and relatively little neural activity in the orbital frontal cortex and the temporal cortex.[32]

Neuroscientists at the University of Washington have extended our understanding of the circuit. They have found core brain areas closely associated with cognitive or perspective-taking empathy, which stimulate activity in regions known as the posterior cingulate/precuneus and the right temporo-parietal junction. In practice this means, for example, that particular parts of the brain are active when we think about getting one of our fingers pinched in a door, but when we think about this happening to another person, alongside some of the same pain-processing regions being active, there are other cognitive empathy hotspots that are switched on. According to the researchers, these distinctive ways in which our brains respond to our own and other people's pain reveals that 'empathy does not involve a complete Self-Other merging', and may be 'what allows us to distinguish empathic responses to others versus our own personal distress'.[33]

Neurologist and economist Paul Zak fills out the picture further with research showing that the hormone oxytocin (the one that mothers release when their baby is breastfeeding, but which is also present in men) can generate empathic action. Oxytocin is well known for its social effects. Studies of prairie voles, which mate for life, show that they release more oxytocin during sex than other vole species that do not mate for life; blocking the hormone in prairie voles prevents the formation of long-lasting pair bonds. When it comes to human beings, particular situations, such as seeing someone in moderate distress, trigger the release of oxytocin in the brain – together with the neurochemicals serotonin and dopamine – which then prompts us to social engagement. He calls this the Human

Oxytocin Mediated Empathy (HOME) circuit. High stress can block oxytocin release, a response that makes complete sense, argues Zak, since 'if we are in dire straits ourselves, we can't easily afford to invest time and resources in helping another'. But in normal circumstances 'oxytocin generates the empathy that drives moral behaviour'. People without oxytocin show a high degree of selfishness and self-interest, and low levels of empathic concern. While oxytocin and empathy appear closely related, some scientists stress that the relationship between them is highly context- and person-specific, so don't imagine that spraying a little oxytocin on your aggressive boss will immediately transform him or her into a beacon of empathy.[34]

So where does all this research lead? We need to recognise the complexity of empathy processes in the brain. Phenomena such as mirror neurons are only one part of a larger 'empathy circuit' that enables us to connect with other people's minds. Neuroscience has certainly made great progress: it would have been impossible to imagine, just a couple of generations ago, that we could pinpoint parts of the human brain that were responsible for empathising. But the truth is that we are still at the earliest stages of knowing how it all really works and relates to everyday behaviour.[35] Armed with our brain-scanning machines, we are like the first astronomers in the seventeenth century, who were able to see new stars with their powerful telescopes but were far from having a complete understanding about what they were made of, or why and how they moved. Our greatest discoveries about *homo empathicus* may be yet to come.

Can we learn to be more empathic?

Adding together this accumulation of evidence and insights from psychology, evolutionary biology and neuroscience, there is little doubt that we are social creatures defined by our capacity to empathise. Accompanying our self-seeking Hobbesian side is our Vulcan other half. We are both serpents and doves.

But there may be a niggling worry at the back of your mind, which is whether it really is possible to become *more* empathic, and expand your ability to look through other people's eyes. Might your empathic capabilities be fundamentally limited by the kind of brain you happened to be born with? Or what if you didn't receive enough nurturing care as an infant to develop deep empathic sensitivity?

On these questions there is overwhelming agreement amongst the experts that our personal empathy quota is not fixed: we can develop our empathic potential throughout our lives. Our brains are surprisingly malleable or 'plastic', enabling us to rewire our neural circuitry.[36] Empathic ability is a little like musical ability – part nature and part nurture. Some people just seem to be born with innate musical skills – they've got perfect pitch or can pick up almost any instrument and play it beautifully. But musicality is also learned. It is best if we start young, yet most people could still learn to play the guitar pretty well at forty-five, as long as they put in the effort to practise. And that is how it is with empathy.

Psychologists have repeatedly shown that adults can tap into their latent empathic abilities by making a conscious effort to focus on the minds of others. In one experiment designed by Adam Galinsky and Gordon Moskowitz, a group of US college students were shown a photograph of a young African-American man and told to write a short narrative about a typical day in his life. One third of them – the control group – were given this instruction and no more. One third were additionally told to actively suppress any stereotypical preconceptions they might have about the person. And the final third were given an empathic perspective-taking instruction: 'Imagine a day in the life of this individual as if you were that person, looking at the world through his eyes and walking through the world in his shoes.' The result was that the perspective-takers showed the most positive attitudes towards their subject, followed by the suppressor group, then the control group. The experiment was repeated with a photo of an elderly white man, with the same outcome.[37]

In another famous study of the transformative power of perspective-taking empathy, C. Daniel Batson asked two groups of students to listen to a tape recording of a young woman in distress because her parents had recently been killed in a tragic car accident. The first group were given the instruction to listen objectively to the facts in the recording, while the second group were asked to imagine the experiences and feelings of the woman involved. The second group were shown to have higher levels of reported empathy for her than the first. Moreover, when subsequently asked to help her raise funds to care for her surviving younger brother and sister, members of the second group gave much more generously. In over three decades of research, Batson has consistently found that 'perspective-taking has proved effective in inducing empathy not only for total strangers ... but for members of stigmatised groups', and that it tends to produce moral or 'pro-social' helping behaviour, rather than leaving people unmoved.[38]

This kind of research suggests that it is a mistake to believe we are the prisoners of the empathic abilities we were born and raised with in our early years. Rather, most people are able to expand their capacity for empathy throughout their lives – especially their cognitive or perspective-taking empathy – by practising mindful attention towards other people's feelings and experiences.

Our capacity for doing so has been confirmed by studies of empathy training for doctors, who are often criticised for being too clinical and emotionally detached from their patients. In 2010, doctors at a Boston hospital took part in a programme in which they were advised to pay greater attention to the changing expressions on their patients' faces (for instance whether they showed anger, contempt, fear or sadness), to take note of voice modulations, and to make simple changes such as facing the patient rather than their computer screens during a consultation. After just three one-hour training sessions, doctors who went through the programme showed vastly improved empathy levels. Their patients said these doctors made them feel more at ease, showed greater care and compassion towards them, and had a better understanding of their concerns. The doctors too could see the benefits. After spending a day putting the programme's methods into practice, one hospital doctor reported that while it was initially difficult to empathise with the patient while simultaneously making her diagnosis, eventually it 'became fun' and embodied the kind of personal interaction that had initially drawn her into medicine.[39]

There is also a growing body of neuroscience research showing that 'compassion training' – which is partly focused on enhancing empathy – can shift the neural configuration of certain brain regions and lead to increased pro-social behaviour. In one study co-designed by Matthieu Ricard, a world-renowned French Buddhist monk with a PhD in molecular genetics, participants took part in a training broadly based on Buddhist meditation techniques. The workshop included practices such as sitting in silence and mentally focusing attention and positive feelings first on themselves, then on a beloved person, a neutral person, a person they have difficulties with, and finally all human beings. The result of the training was to increase brain activation in areas typically associated with social connectedness. It was also found to reverse feelings of emotional distress after the test subjects had watched news and documentary videos of people suffering in situations such as natural disasters or due to personal injury. This kind of research remains in its initial stages: it is only in the last decade that neuroscientists have been willing to team up with Buddhist monks and take their practices seriously. Moreover, the studies tend to focus on women, which skews the results as women are generally more responsive to compassion training than men. Nevertheless, it is clear that our brains are surprisingly malleable when given appropriate stimulus.[40]

So there is nothing to stop us from turning our personal empathic development into a life-long practice. Yet there is little doubt that – as with music – we are most open to learning when we are young. There are plenty of methods out there for teaching violin or piano to children, but how do you go about teaching them empathy?

Picture a state primary school in Lewisham, South London. The eight-year-old pupils are sitting on the floor, fixated by a baby on a mat in the middle of their classroom. They are observing her closely and talking about what she might be feeling or thinking at that moment, and why she suddenly started crying. Afterwards they do an activity about reading emotions by imitating the facial expressions people make when they are upset, happy, afraid or shy. This leads on to a role-play about bullying, before the baby leaves with a gift made by the children.

This is what happens in a Roots of Empathy class, the world's most successful and innovative empathy teaching programme. It was founded as a charity in Canada in 1995 by parenting expert Mary Gordon and, so far, over half a million children aged five to twelve have taken part, and the numbers are growing fast.

The originality of Roots of Empathy is this: the teacher is a baby. Each class 'adopts' a baby, who visits them regularly over the course of a school year with its mother or father. Together with an instructor from the programme, the pupils watch the baby's unfolding development, discussing its emotional responses and changing view of the world, as well as the relationship it has with its parents. They also do empathy-based art and drama, which helps them make the leap from trying to understand the baby's feelings and perspectives, to trying to understand those of their classmates and the wider community.

A Roots of Empathy class. The teacher is on the mat.

'It's very easy to look at Roots of Empathy and think it's cute,' says Gordon, 'but let me assure you it's beyond cute.' While the baby-centred teaching model is unique, the real point about Roots of Empathy is that it works. Multiple studies have shown that it dramatically reduces playground bullying, encourages cooperation, improves pupils' relationships with their parents, and even boosts their grades. Studies in Scotland in 2010 found that the programme increased children's 'pro-social behaviour' – such as sharing and helping – by 55 per cent, prompting the Scottish government to expand Roots of Empathy across the nation, especially into schools in low-income areas and those facing problems with bullying and aggression. The key to the programme's success, Gordon tells me, is the emphasis on experiential learning: it is based on real human-to-human contact rather than traditional book learning.[41]

Education experts increasingly recognise that teaching empathy skills is not just a 'nice-to-have' added extra, but deserves to be at the core of the curriculum alongside reading, writing and arithmetic. Mary Gordon believes that empathy education is vital for children's wellbeing, and is a cornerstone of emotional intelligence. Yet she also has a more ambitious vision, and thinks that it is essential for creating a new generation of global citizens who will care about tackling the world's social and political problems, from child poverty to armed violence. 'During the Nuremberg Trials,' she points out, 'one of the judges described the war crimes as a failure of empathy. Empathy is integral to solving conflict in the family, schoolyard, boardroom and war room. The ability to take the perspective of another person, to identify commonalities through our shared feelings, is the best peace pill we have.'[42]

Re-framing your mind

Most of us were not lucky enough to have a baby teach us empathy at school, so we have to find other ways to spark our empathic potential. The first step is to make a habit of switching on our empathic brains. And that means tuning into a new understanding of human nature. Yes, *homo self-centricus* is alive and kicking within us, but it is time to catch up with the science and recognise that *homo empathicus* is just as much a part of who we are. We possess complex brains that are wired for both individualism and empathy. Our individualistic wiring has been emphasised, encouraged and pushed into the foreground for three long centuries. Let's now give our empathic circuitry the opportunity it deserves to stand alongside its rival, acknowledging that we are the proud possessors of social brains.

The task before us is to change what the cognitive linguist George Lakoff calls our mental 'frame'. Frames are structures in our minds that shape the way we look at the world. They are buried deep in our cognitive unconscious, writes Lakoff, and influence 'the goals we seek, the plans we make, the way we act, and what counts as a good or bad outcome of our actions'.[43] In Western society, the dominant frame for thinking about human nature has been the idea that we are fundamentally self-interested. Its influence is so pervasive that we can hardly see it. Schoolchildren are immersed in a culture of competitive individualism and rewarded much more for their personal achievements than their capacity to cooperate with others. Companies assume that their employees will work harder if given greater financial incentives, despite evidence to the contrary.[44] Governments argue that public services will improve if they are open to market competition. As individuals, we believe that our wellbeing hinges on satisfying our personal ambitions and lifestyle desires far more than on dedication to social causes and community projects.

We now need to absorb and internalise a different frame, which is the idea that empathy lies at the core of our beings cheek-by-cheek with self-interest. The question is how to alter our frame of thinking, or worldview, so that this more scientifically accurate picture of human nature becomes embedded in our brains. Learning about the science is a good start. But it is also useful to sharpen our daily awareness of its reality. An effective way to do this is to draw on a method used in cognitive behavioural therapy, which is to make a mental note every time you notice an instance of empathic thinking or action in yourself or others. Maybe you will spot your boss managing to see someone else's point of view, or observe empathic cooperation between your children. Think of it as becoming an 'empathy detective'. Over time, your observations will build up to a picture of humankind that defies the dominant cultural message. The more we look for empathy with our social antennae, the more we will be able to see it, and erode the narrow mental frame we have inherited from the ideas of Hobbes, Smith, Darwin and Freud. We can also develop an awareness of what kinds of contexts bring out empathy in ourselves and others. Are we less likely to empathise with people when we are stressed or in a rush? Are we more empathic with family, friends or strangers? This kind of detective work can help us understand that empathy is not a fixed personality trait: it can rise and fall depending on the situation, and we can train ourselves to get better at it.

Switching on our empathic brains is just the beginning. With a new story about human nature planted firmly in our psyches, we are poised to develop the other five habits of highly empathic people. The moment has come to step outside the research labs of psychologists, biologists and neuroscientists, and into the everyday world of human relationships.

HABIT 2
MAKE THE IMAGINATIVE LEAP

If empathy is so good for us, why don't we do it more?

Empathy is now acknowledged as an essential ingredient of human wellbeing. It helps to create the human relationships that give our lives meaning, and expands our mental landscapes so we have new perspectives on the world and our own lives. 'A sign of health in the mind,' wrote the psychoanalyst Donald Winnicott, 'is the ability of one individual to enter imaginatively and accurately into the thoughts and feelings and hopes and fears of another person; also to allow that person to do the same to us.'[1]

Yet if empathy is so good for us, and if it is wired deep into our brains, why don't we do it more? The reason is that we face four fundamental social and political barriers that block the full expression of our empathic imaginations. Their names? Prejudice, authority, distance and denial. If we are to stand a chance of getting beyond them, we first need to grasp how they prevent us from stepping into others' shoes. We can then turn to highly empathic people and discover what it takes to jump the barriers. Their secret is this: to consciously strive to make the imaginative leap into other people's mental worlds, whether it is that of a sulking child, a surly supermarket cashier, or an old man in an Afghan village glimpsed on the evening news.[2] I would like to explain exactly how they do it with assistance from three people who underwent surprising empathic transformations: a heavy-drinking and womanising industrialist, a mother who suffered a terrible personal tragedy, and a lawyer who shed his privileged background and took up nursing. They will be our guides, inspiring us to expand our imaginations and tune into the feelings and thoughts in other people's heads.

Before meeting them, however, we must explore the four barriers to empathy, and prepare ourselves to defy them.

Prejudice

Have a look at this photograph and give yourself thirty seconds to take in all you can about it. What can you say about the man it depicts? When and where was the photo taken? How is he feeling? What kinds of interests and views might he have?

Have you got the measure of him now? Then let me reveal the photograph's original caption. The image was taken by the British photojournalist Thurston Hopkins in 1951 and was titled 'Emrys Jones, miner and principal tenor of the Welsh National Opera Company'.

That caption surprises most people. My point is simple: the vast majority of us have assumptions and prejudices about others. We are prone to stereotyping, making snap judgements based on first impressions, and casually project our biases and preconceptions onto people while knowing very little about the reality of their lives. We make clichéd associations, for instance that miners are 'uncultured', that hedge fund managers are arrogant and selfish, or that Jews are tight with their money – a prejudice that has survived over five hundred years. We also frequently use collective labels that mask people's individuality, like 'yobs', 'toffs', 'hoodies', 'fundamentalists', 'nerds'. These labels tend to denigrate others, placing them in a convenient box that makes it difficult to appreciate their humanity and uniqueness, or the personal stories behind their circumstances.

One result of such stereotyping is that we are so often mistaken in our judgements about others. Take this example from the Australian novelist Nikki Gemmell, recalling an encounter in a London car park.

> We've all, I suspect, been guilty of a lack of empathy at some point. I have. I'm not proud of it . . . London, five years ago. December, 3 pm, sky glooming down. Running late, and cold. Grumpy? Oh yes. A Muslim man walking towards me, bearded and robed. The papers were full of warnings that al-Qa'ida was planning a Christmas terror campaign focusing on people travelling through the festive season. Let's just say I wasn't feeling particularly . . . open at that moment. My whole being was one huge flinch; there may even have been a scowl. 'Would you like my parking ticket, madam?' 'Pardon?' 'I've got several hours left on it and I'm going.

Please. Have it.' Well, stun me with kindness. I looked right
into that good man's face, properly this time. Saw not a Muslim
but a fellow human being beaming nothing but compassion,
friendliness.[3]

Think to yourself how often you have been plain wrong
about someone because you were looking at them through the
distorting lens of prejudice and stereotype. I used to regularly
see a dishevelled homeless man who spent his days muttering
crazily to himself and picking up cigarette butts – it never
occurred to me that our lives might connect. But one day I
spoke to him (his name was Alan Human) and found out he
had studied philosophy at Oxford University, and we embarked
on a friendship based on our mutual interest in Nietzsche, Marx
and pepperoni pizza.[4] It was a friendship that I had, for years,
been walking straight past in ignorance. I could fill this page
with plenty more examples.

Some popular psychology books, such as Malcolm Gladwell's
Blink: The Power of Thinking Without Thinking, argue that we
are actually very skilled at making quick judgements about
others – such as whether we are compatible with someone
we met for just two minutes while speed dating – and ought
to more readily trust our instincts. But our instincts can easily
be infected by assumptions inherited from society and culture
that have penetrated deep into our psyches. Gladwell admits
that 'our unconscious attitudes may be utterly incompatible with
our stated conscious values'. This helps explain phenomena
such as the fact that while few white people acknowledge they
have prejudices against black people, the evidence defies this:
whether consciously or not, white job interviewers regularly
discriminate against black applicants in a range of employment
fields.[5]

Perhaps the most insidious stereotyping has been a product
of political ideologies. The British Empire was built on the
colonialist notion that 'civilised' whites were superior to

'barbarian' non-whites, whether in Africa, India or Australia. The Nazis notoriously created the racial category *Untermensch* – subhuman – in which they placed Jews and Gypsies. Stereotyping remains a staple of contemporary politics. In Australia, politicians from across the spectrum frequently refer to asylum seekers as 'illegals', despite the fact that the Australian Refugee Council and the UN point out that this is an inaccurate term since there is nothing illegal about seeking asylum. According to Don Watson, an Australian expert on political language, the reason politicians use words such as 'illegals' is to denigrate asylum seekers and refugees in the eyes of the public:

> If you wanted to disenfranchise refugees, and leave the public thinking they have no rights, then call them 'illegal' over and over again. If the first thing that enters your head is a cliché or some kind of prejudice or some line that has been drummed into you, you can guarantee that there's no room for anything else until you get that cliché out. So if you're constantly being told that these people are 'illegals', then that will do you for thinking about refugees. It also helps keep any kind of empathy at bay, so people don't have to imagine it were their family in the situation of an asylum seeker.[6]

What all stereotyping has in common, whether it is a product of politics, religion, nationalism or other forces, is an effort to dehumanise, to erase individuality, to prevent us from looking someone in the eye and learning their name. The consequence is to create a culture of indifference that empathy finds difficult to penetrate.

Unfortunately we cannot switch our prejudices and assumptions about others off like a light switch, for they are typically far too embedded in our personal psychological histories. But we can certainly erode their power over us, a subject I will return to when discussing how to make the imaginative leap of empathy.

Authority

Aside from prejudice, one of the greatest obstacles to empathy is the human tendency to obey authority. Throughout history, those involved in massacres, genocides and other rights violations have defended themselves with the claim that 'I was just following orders'. The most famous of them, Adolf Eichmann – one of the chief architects of the Holocaust – claimed at his trial in 1961 that he bore no responsibility for his actions because he was simply 'doing his job'. In her study *Eichmann in Jerusalem*, the political theorist Hannah Arendt pointed out that he was no psychopath or monster but rather a fairly typical individual who 'did his *duty*' and 'not only obeyed *orders*, he also obeyed the *law*'. According to Arendt, 'The trouble with Eichmann was precisely that there were so many like him, and that the many were neither perverted, nor sadistic, that they were, and still are, terribly and terrifyingly normal.' This attitude embodied what she called 'the banality of evil'.[7]

Was Nazi Germany an exceptional era? Or is obedience to authority a more universal human trait? Psychologist Stanley Milgram wanted to find out. In the same year that Eichmann was put on trial, he conducted one of the most controversial experiments in the history of social psychology. Milgram invited students and local residents around Yale University in New Haven, Connecticut, to take part in what they were told was a study of the effects of punishment on improving memory and learning. Under the guidance of an 'experimenter' in a grey lab coat, each participant took on the role of the 'teacher' and was asked to read out pairs of words like 'strong arm' and 'black curtain', which could be heard by a 'learner' situated in another room. If the learner made an error when repeating back the word pairs, the teacher was instructed to administer them an electric shock. With each incorrect answer, the strength of the shock was increased. The whole experiment was actually a complete fabrication: the learner was an actor, who did not receive any electric shocks, but this was not revealed to the participants until later. When a participant hesitated in flicking the electric switch, the experimenter would say things like, 'It is important that you follow the procedure exactly' or 'You have no choice, you *must* go on.'

Milgram could not believe the results: 65 per cent of people kept administering the shocks, even when they heard the learner crying out in pain and pleading for the test to stop, saying things like, 'Experimenter! That's all. Get me out of here. I told you I had heart trouble.' Only two months after the experiments began, Milgram was clear about his conclusions:

> The results are terrifying and depressing . . . In a naïve moment some time ago, I once wondered whether in all of the United States a vicious government could find enough moral imbeciles to meet the personnel requirements of a national system of death camps, of the sort that were maintained in Germany. I am now beginning to think that the full complement could be recruited in New Haven. A substantial proportion of people do what they are told to do, irrespective of the content of the act, and without pangs of conscience, so long as they perceive that the command comes from a legitimate authority.[8]

The 'Milgram test' is often cited as definitive evidence that empathic concern is easily overpowered by obedience to authority.[9] Yet we should we wary about jumping so quickly to this conclusion. For a start, flipping around the result, a full 35 per cent of participants actually defied the experimenter and walked out of the lab before the test was finished, even though they had been paid to take part, and were under the instruction of a very official-looking research scientist at the august institution of Yale University. Moreover, when Milgram adjusted the experiment slightly, the results changed dramatically. By doing the test at offices in a nearby town rather than in the imposing Yale lab, the obedience figure fell from 65 per cent to 48 per cent. When the learner was visible in an adjoining room, 60 per cent of people broke off the test, a figure that rose to 70 per cent when the punishment required physically placing the learner's hand on an electric shock template. When the participant was accompanied by two actors playing fellow teachers, and who both disobeyed the experimenter, 90 per cent of those participants also disobeyed – solidarity appeared to give them the confidence to defy authority. Few participants followed without misgivings – many bit their lips and even groaned as the experiment progressed. Others made their empathic concern more explicit: when told by the instructor to increase the voltage, one person replied, 'I don't think I'd like to take that myself, what he's taking right now,' and promptly broke off the experiment.

Subsequent attempts to replicate the test by other psychologists should also make us cautious about Milgram's results. While some have obtained similar obedience levels, others have not. Several US studies have revealed an obedience rate not of 65 per cent but as low as 30 per cent, while a test in Australia generated only 28 per cent obedience, a figure that fell to just 16 per cent when the test subjects were all women.[10]

All this variation tells us that obedience to authority is not simply an innate trait embedded in human nature, but is rather highly sensitive to context and culture. This was, in fact, Milgram's own belief. 'The social psychology of this century,' he wrote, 'reveals a major lesson: often, it is not so much the kind of person a man is as the kind of situation in which he finds himself that determines how he will act.'[11] On the other hand, we must accept that the disposition to obey authority lies within most of us. We learn it at an early age from parents and teachers, and slowly absorb a culture of obedience as we grow up, telling ourselves that we should 'obey the law', 'follow the rules', or simply 'behave', whether it is in the workplace or on the football pitch. We all too easily internalise submission to authority and abandon our empathic instincts. What makes highly empathic people unusual is their desire and capacity to defy authority when empathic action calls for it.

Distance

The planet seems to be shrinking. There are, according to the urban myth, only six degrees of separation between each of us. We have been unified like never before by a global network of internet connections, mobile phones and satellite receivers. A young woman is killed on a demonstration in Cairo and within hours, thanks to Twitter and other online platforms, hundreds of thousands of people around the world have seen her photo and know her name.

And yet spatial distance remains a barrier to the spread of empathy. When we do not know people, when their lives are far away and unfamiliar, our capacity to care about them is more difficult to ignite. Many philosophers, amongst them Peter Singer, argue that distance should not affect our moral judgements: we ought to feel just as obliged to help a starving child in Africa as to rescue a child drowning in front of our eyes at the local park.[12] But other thinkers recognise how, in reality, distance diminishes our moral concern. Adam Smith was aware of this in the eighteenth century:

> Let us suppose that the great empire of China, with all its myriads of inhabitants, was suddenly swallowed up by an earthquake, and let us consider how a man of humanity in Europe, who had no sort of connection with that part of the world, would be affected upon receiving intelligence of this dreadful calamity. He would, I imagine, first of all express his sorrow for the misfortune of that unhappy people, he would make many melancholy reflections upon the precariousness of human life . . . And when all this fine philosophy was over, when all these human sentiments had

been once fairly expressed, he would pursue his business or his pleasure, take his repose or his diversion, with the same ease and tranquillity as if no such accident had happened. The most frivolous disaster which could befall himself would occasion a more real disturbance. If he was to lose his little finger tomorrow, he would not sleep to-night; but, provided he never saw them, he would snore with the most profound security over the ruin of a hundred million of his brethren, and the destruction of that immense multitude seems plainly an object less interesting to him than this paltry misfortune of his own.[13]

Not much has changed. Whether it is an earthquake in China or millions on the edge of starvation in the Horn of Africa, the majority of people find it hard to be moved to action by news reports of tragic events in faraway places. Equally, when distance shields us from the consequences of our actions, we seem capable of almost anything: the pilot who dropped the first atomic bomb on Hiroshima in August 1945 never saw the faces of the 140,000 victims, and later said that he performed his task without any feelings of guilt or remorse.[14]

For most of us, our strongest moral and empathic ties are with family and members of our immediate community (though, of course, some people have little love for their siblings or parents). I readily admit that I care far more about my young twins than about any number of victims in China's latest earthquake. This may be why the Confucian ethic of *ren*, or benevolence, appears so intuitively attractive. The idea is that our greatest ethical obligations should be to our kin, and then graduate outwards to our friends and neighbours, then society at large, then all of humankind, in ever-expanding circles. Those at the periphery have less claim on our compassion. While I do not agree with this as a principle, I do believe it is a reasonably accurate empirical description of how many people's ethics function in practice.

Yet distance is not merely a spatial phenomenon: *social distance* is just as much a barrier to empathic connection. We may, for instance, have a bias towards empathising with people who socially resemble us in some way, such as educational background, ethnicity or religion. 'Far from being a guide to what is right, empathy often leads us astray,' writes the historian of science Mark Honigsbaum, 'as when judges go easier on white-collar criminals who share their social background.'[15] Mirroring this phenomenon, we might fail to empathise with those who are socially distant, even if they live nextdoor. That is why highly empathic people strive to overcome this barrier, and make a sustained effort to look through the eyes of strangers and people who are outside their 'in-group'.

Apart from spatial and social distance, a third form, *temporal distance*, also weakens the possibilities for empathy. We worry about the welfare of our children or grandchildren. But the bonds start becoming weaker with respect to our great-grandchildren, and become almost completely absent when we consider the prospects for people a century from now to whom we are not related. How easily can we imagine how a teenager living in Belfast or Mumbai in 2100 might think and feel about global warming, and how much do we really care? It is so difficult to project ourselves into their lives and to experience a profound emotional connection. The evolutionary biologist J.B.S. Haldane acknowledged the problem of temporal distance when he quipped, only half joking, 'I would happily die for three of my children or six of my grandchildren.' Our ability to empathise through time remains rudimentary, stuck in the earliest stages of psychological evolution. This may be one of humankind's greatest moral failings.

The empathic challenge we face, therefore, is to close this distance as much as possible so that those who are far away from us across space, time and social background are drawn into our circle of caring, enabling us to touch them more easily with our imaginations.

Denial

How often have you looked at a newspaper photo of a starving child in a distant country, or civilian victims of war, and had little emotional or empathic response? A common explanation for this phenomenon is that we suffer from 'compassion fatigue' or 'empathy fatigue', a state of psychological exhaustion brought about by the barrage of depressing news stories and images from every corner of the planet.[16] Cultural critic Susan Sontag described something akin to this when she wrote that 'images anesthetize': we have now seen too many photos of hungry, gaunt children for them to make much of a difference any more. We have become, in the words of Pink Floyd, comfortably numb.[17]

A deeper explanation of empathy fatigue is given by sociologist Stanley Cohen in his book *States of Denial*. He argues that we are products of a 'culture of denial' that allows most of us to know about atrocities and suffering yet also block them out and do nothing, 'turning a blind eye' as we say. 'People, organizations, governments or whole societies are presented with information that is too disturbing, threatening or anomalous to be fully absorbed or openly acknowledged,' he writes. 'The information is therefore somehow repressed, disavowed, pushed aside or reinterpreted.' We live in a twilight between knowing and not knowing.[18]

Why do we often retreat into a state of denial that curtails empathy? Perhaps we do not want to know because of the shame or guilt we feel for having, by contrast, such privileged lifestyles. Sometimes we turn away because we do not wish to admit that we might be somehow responsible, either through our acts or omissions. Human beings are particularly skilled at protecting themselves by inventing convenient reasons why they need not take action to relieve the suffering of others. For example, we might feel for flood victims in Bangladesh, but tell ourselves that there is little point doing anything about it since our individual actions would not make any difference to such a huge problem, or because any money we donate could be misused by aid agencies and corrupt local officials. Highly empathic people are acutely aware that such reasoning may well be a form of denial designed to relieve them of a sense of guilt or moral responsibility, and which poses the danger of eating away at the core of their empathic selves.

The four barriers I have described – prejudice, authority, distance and denial – are formidable obstacles. Yet I am hopeful that most of us can defy them and turn ourselves into highly empathic people. Why such optimism? It is essential to recognise that the barriers are primarily inventions of culture, society and politics, rather than traits deeply embedded in human nature. This means we can, as individuals and societies, find ways to challenge them. We may have been educated with prejudices but it is possible to reject the dehumanising labels we were implicitly taught to apply. Empathy must contend with the power of authority, but the history books are full of dissent as well as obedience. We can overcome distance when we hear the personal stories of strangers living in other lands. We can choose to engage with suffering rather than deny it, drawing on our inner strength, integrity and curiosity to avoid the lures of denial.

Having looked squarely at the barriers, we are now set to find ways to get past them. I think it takes three steps to make the imaginative leap of empathy: we must humanise the 'other', then discover what we share – and what we don't – with people, and finally we need to empathise with our enemies.

Humanise the 'Other'

Empathy withers and dies when we fail to acknowledge the humanity of other people – their individuality and uniqueness – and treat them as beings of less than equal worth to ourselves.

That sounds obvious. But what does it really mean to treat someone with humanity, or what philosophers describe as humanising the 'other'?[19] And how exactly do you do it? Answers emerge from the life of Oskar Schindler, who metamorphosed from being a boisterous Nazi businessman with a taste for fine cognac and voluptuous secretaries (he was a serial adulterer), into one of the most renowned of all Holocaust rescuers.

What makes Schindler's case so fascinating is that his transformation was utterly unexpected. At the beginning of the Second World War he was a fully paid-up Nazi. As a loyal party member he wore the *Hakenkreuz* (swastika) pinned to his lapel and was an informant for the *Abwehr* (military intelligence). Schindler took advantage of the expropriation of Jewish businesses in occupied Poland by starting up an enamelware factory in Krakow, which produced equipment for German soldiers. He had no qualms about using forced Jewish labour, whose 'wage' was paid directly into the hands of the SS, since it was far cheaper than employing Polish workers. Schindler spent his evenings schmoozing with top Nazi commanders and bureaucrats, plying them with drink, getting them girls, and offering them bribes to obtain the military contracts that kept his profit margin healthy and allowed him the luxury of fat cigars and fine double-breasted suits.

Schindler was not a vicious anti-Semite like Hitler or Goebbels but rather – like so many others – had an indifferent attitude towards Jews and saw them as an anonymous mass who he could easily exploit for his own ends. Nobody in 1940 could have predicted that by the end of the war, he would be risking his own life and paying huge bribes to save his Jewish factory workers from extermination in Auschwitz. What explains his radical conversion? Something very interesting happened to Schindler in the intervening years: he began to see Jews as human beings.

It all started with his Jewish accountant, Itzhak Stern. What was originally a formal business relationship slowly turned into a friendship. 'Stern was the only father confessor Oskar had ever had,' according to Thomas Keneally in his meticulously researched documentary novel *Schindler's Ark*. Through their daily conversations, Schindler found out about Stern's life and traumatic experiences living in the Cracow ghetto – the starvation, the fear, the random shootings by German soldiers. The result was to transform Stern, in Schindler's eyes, from being just one amongst many employees into a unique individual. It was an individuality that he began extending to his other workers, learning their names and discovering their own stories of persecution.

Schindler experienced a moment of empathic epiphany on 8 June 1942, when he was horse riding with his mistress Ingrid on a hillside outside Crakow. Looking down into the ghetto they could see an SS *Aktion* in progress – a systematic effort to clear the ghetto of Jews. People were being herded out of their homes, mauled by dogs, beaten and shot at point-blank range in the streets. It was not just that this gross slaughter sickened Schindler, but that he noticed a young girl dressed in a red coat and cap, wandering amongst the mayhem, somehow defying the SS guards on the rampage. He saw the red girl stop and watch while a soldier jammed his foot onto the skull of a boy and shot him in the back of the neck. Somehow this girl, for Schindler, came to represent the individuality and humanity of Crakow's Jewish population, helping to scorch the horror of Nazi violence onto his mind. 'Beyond this day,' he later claimed, 'no thinking person could fail to see what would happen. I was now resolved to do everything in my power to defeat the system.'

And that is exactly what he did. When the city's Jews were moved in autumn 1942 to a new labour camp in nearby Płaszów, under the control of the sadistic commandant Amon Goeth, Schindler bribed officials to let him keep his factory outside its gates. He made sure his workers secretly received extra rations, and that there were no dogs or beatings by SS guards. To help keep families together, he argued with SS officials that he needed child workers whose nimble fingers could clean the inside of shell casings, and told tall stories of how a man with one arm was a valuable machinist.

Towards the end of the war, when Płaszów was being closed down and its inmates transferred to death camps such as Auschwitz, Schindler bribed Goeth and others – at enormous financial cost to himself – so that his workers and their families would be sent to a new munitions factory that Schindler was building across the border in Brinnlitz, Czechoslovakia. These were the 1,100 people whose names were placed on the list made famous in Steven Spielberg's film *Schindler's List* (which was based on Keneally's book *Schindler's Ark*). On Schindler's instructions, the shells and rocket casings they made were defective. When Nazi officials complained in a telegram, he exclaimed to Stern, 'It's the best birthday present I could have got. Because I know now that no poor bastard has been killed by my product.'[20]

The dramatic and dangerous transfer to Brinnlitz yielded the ultimate result: when peace was finally declared, most of those on the list were still alive. While there are fewer than five thousand Jews left living in Poland today, there are more than six thousand descendants of the Schindler Jews worldwide.

Why did Schindler sacrifice his fortune to save those on the list? Why did he risk imprisonment and execution to help Jewish families from the Crakow ghetto? For some his actions are perplexing. 'His motives you couldn't guess,' remarked one *Schindlerjuden* survivor.[21] Could he have been driven by religion, like so many other Holocaust rescuers?[22] Unlikely: Schindler was, like his father, a negligent Catholic. I think his essential motive was summed up in a remark he made when asked to explain his actions: 'I knew the people who worked for me. When you know people, you have to behave towards them like human beings.'[23]

Therein lies the deceptively simple answer: knowing people. Schindler's story tells us that the act of empathising begins with looking someone in the eye, giving them a name, and recognising their individuality. It is about acknowledging their humanity in defiance of prejudices and stereotypes; it is about refusing to obey authorities who command us to denigrate them. The power of treating an individual with humanity is that it can be a stepping stone to empathising with a wider circle of people, as happened to Schindler, whose personal relationship with Stern and other workers helped bond him to the suffering of Jews more generally.[24] Schindler also reminds us that our ability to empathise is not fixed but can change and develop throughout our lives: even the most unlikely people can, in the right circumstances, make the imaginative leap, and be inspired to take action as a result.

None of this means that Schindler was an unalloyed saint – a tag often applied to Holocaust rescuers such as Raoul Wallenberg. Especially early in the war, he had more selfish motives, and was using Jewish labour and protecting workers because they were essential to the profitability of his business, and he may have 'saved' some young Jewish women because he was attracted to them. In that sense, his 'humanitarian' actions started out as a very realistic mixture of both personal and altruistic motives.

Oskar Schindler was an extraordinary person living in extraordinary times. But the message of his life is now more pertinent than ever. Across Europe today a resurgence of right-wing populism is raising the old spectre of anti-Semitism, and discrimination against Gypsies (Roma) and Muslims. Moreover, neoliberal individualism and the erosion of public services is creating a culture of uncaring that has not been seen since the nineteenth century, where we are increasingly immune to social tragedies such as child poverty. The danger is that we become bystanders to human suffering. Oskar Schindler, for all his faults and contradictions, was no bystander.

One of the many humanitarian accolades Schindler received after the war was the Martin Buber Prize, named after the

Austrian-born Jewish theologian and philosopher who had fled Nazi Germany in the 1930s. Buber's ideas, more than any other twentieth-century thinker, capture the essence of the imaginative, empathic act of humanising the 'other'.

In his book *I and Thou*, Buber describes two forms of relationship we can engage in. One he refers to as 'I–It', which is when we treat other people as objects, as an 'it' without humanity or individuality. This occurs especially when we use derogatory stereotypes to label people, or in instances of prejudice. A second form of relationship Buber calls 'I–Thou'. This involves treating another person as a unique being equal to yourself, and attempting to look at the world through their eyes and to comprehend their thoughts and feelings. He speaks of an I–Thou dialogue as an effort to 'come into relation' with others and discover who they really are. We can only become fully human, says Buber, when we have 'genuine conversations' that embody the I–Thou ideal, and make an effort to imagine other people's realities:

> I imagine to myself what another man is at this very moment wishing, feeling, perceiving, thinking, and not as a detached content but in his very reality, that is, as a living process in this man . . . The inmost growth of the self is not accomplished, as people like to suppose today, in man's relation to himself, but in the relation between one and the other, between men.[25]

How can we bring the lessons of Buber's philosophy into our own lives, so we are able – like Schindler – to humanise others and develop an I–Thou relationship with them? One route is through face-to-face conversations that help us break through the I–It barrier (a subject I discuss in an upcoming chapter). But there are three other ways we can kick-start the process.

A first step is to humanise our imaginations by developing an awareness of all those individuals hidden behind the surface of our daily lives, on whom we may depend in some way. The religious thinker Karen Armstrong suggests we do this by undertaking a Buddhist-inspired practice, where we spend a day becoming mindful of every person connected to our routine actions:

> When you get up in the morning, remember those who planted, picked and spun the cotton of your sheets and who collected, treated and exported the beans you grind for your morning coffee. You enjoy their product, so you have a responsibility for them, especially if they were working in poor conditions . . . As you set off to work, reflect on the thousands of workers and engineers who maintain the roads, cars, railways, planes, trains and underground transport on which you rely. Continue this exercise throughout the day.[26]

Engaging in this practice is a way of deepening universal human concern, argues Armstrong. It can 'help you appreciate how dependent you are on other people you have never met and who may live far away', and ultimately lead to you taking action on their behalfs.

A second approach is to play imaginative 'character games'. You are at a conference and meet a seemingly unemotional, hard-hearted businessman – the kind of person you might naturally treat as an 'it'. The game is simply to imagine him in a different, more human guise, for instance when he is playing hide and seek with his three-year-old son or singing to his elderly mother to cheer her up. Doing this might subtly alter the way you speak to him, and what you decide to talk about – behind the frosty and formal exterior, he may well be more like the person you are imagining. Equally, you might see an apparently sullen, slouching teenager smoking on a street corner and your prejudice rises up; so consider that she could be an amazing youth leader, or a talented poet. This exercise – a form of creative storytelling – can help give people a human face, expose our stereotyped views of them, and open us to new opportunities for connection and conversation.

I developed a variation of such character games after working in telesales in Sydney when I finished university. My short and unsuccessful career included selling children's encyclopaedias, laser printer toner, tax advice kits and photocopying machines. I absolutely hated the jobs. The duty managers were always pacing around, gesturing to us to 'close' the sale and berating us for failing to reach our sales targets. Most people I called were irritated by the interruption to their lives, and I was regularly subject to serious verbal abuse. So now when I receive a telesales call in my own home, I try to imagine the caller facing the same challenges and harsh treatment I did twenty years ago. Rather than spending their evenings cold calling people, they would probably rather be studying for a master's degree in Systems Engineering or visiting their sister and her new baby. Trying to imagine the life of the person at the other end of the phone line prompts me to treat them with respect rather than hang up rudely and abruptly. It is the least I can do to bridge our faceless digital divide.

A final strategy for humanising our imaginations is to ask ourselves some penetrating questions concerning the assumptions we make about people, to boost our self-awareness and enable us to identify prejudices that might be quietly lurking in our minds:

- What assumptions do you think people make about the kind of person you are? How accurate are they?
- Think of three instances when you were mistaken in your assumptions and judgements about others. What were the consequences of your error, and why did it matter?
- How often do you make assumptions, and about which kinds of people?

To help us think about the last question, we can try to catch ourselves making assumptions and judgements about people throughout the day – be it the security guard at your office, or your sister's heavily tattooed new boyfriend. Maybe you will find yourself presuming that a work colleague who remains silent during meetings has nothing interesting to say, which might then prompt you to strike up a conversation where you discover their real views and the cause for their silence. Proving ourselves wrong is one of the fastest forms of empathic education.

Humanising other people is only the first step in developing the habit of making the imaginative leap into their lives. We might come to see them as individuals equal to ourselves, yet we may still be lacking a detailed portrait of their inner worlds, their hopes, fears, beliefs and ambitions. If we wish to respond appropriately to their feelings and needs, we should aim for greater empathic accuracy. We must take a second step, which is to find out both what we share with others, and what we don't.

Discover what you share . . . and what you don't

Adam Smith's *The Theory of Moral Sentiments* was probably the first handbook on the art of empathising. He repeatedly stressed that we need to let go of our own egos and work hard to attune ourselves to the subtle contours of other people's emotions and experiences.

> [T]he spectator must first of all endeavour as much as he can to put himself in the situation of the other, and to bring home to himself every little circumstance of distress which can possibly occur to the sufferer . . . When I condole with you for the loss of your only son, in order to enter your grief, I do not consider what I, a person of such a character and profession, should suffer, if I had a son, and if that son was unfortunately to die; but I consider what I should suffer if I was really you; and I not only change circumstances with you, but I change persons and characters. My grief, therefore, is entirely upon your account, and not in the least upon my own. It is not, therefore, in the least selfish.[27]

What Smith does not mention here is that our capacity to put ourselves in other people's shoes is enhanced when we are able to identify points of common experience that sensitise us to their mental landscapes. Highly empathic people are engaged in a constant search for what they share with other people, even when those people appear alien to them. Our own suffering is one of the most effective conduits into the lives of other people. Certainly empathy can be found in collective joy – it happened at the raves of the 1990s to many of those who popped Ecstasy pills, a drug giving them a shared, euphoric feeling of empathic connection with others on the dance floor (curiously enough, the early developers of Ecstasy wanted to call it Empathy due to its empathy-generating properties, but thought this name insufficiently catchy).[28] There is little doubt, however, that some of the most profound forms of empathy are built on the common experience of pain, anxiety and loss. That's just what happened to the nineteenth-century novelist Harriet Beecher Stowe.

Beecher Stowe was born in 1811 into a family of evangelical and intellectual Protestant preachers. Growing up in New England, and then moving out west to Cincinnati, she had a privileged upbringing, living in well-appointed homes and, typical of her class, was accustomed to being waited upon by black servants.[29]

The great political issue of her age was slavery. There was increasing dissent in the north of the country against the cruelty and inhumanity of the slave economy that prevailed in the southern states, especially on the cotton plantations. Some of Beecher Stowe's brothers were abolitionists, but even in the 1840s, when the newspapers were full of debates on the issue, she displayed little interest in the growing movement against slavery, and was more concerned with expanding women's access to education and bringing up her bevy of children.

Beecher Stowe was propelled into the public spotlight in 1852, when she published *Uncle Tom's Cabin*, a vibrant and moving story that was effectively a political tract against slavery. By 1861, on the eve of the American Civil War, it had sold an astonishing four million copies. When she met Abraham Lincoln the following year, he is said to have greeted her with the words, 'So you're the little woman who wrote the book that started this great war!'

It is, undoubtedly, one of the most widely read and influential novels ever written. While today many people ridicule its sentimental depiction of African-Americans and excessive melodrama, its power lies in relating the historical reality of slavery – the buying and selling of human beings, the back-breaking servitude, the violence and bloodshed. That is why George Orwell described it as a 'good bad book', one that is valuable not for its literary merits but because 'it is trying to be serious and deal with the real world'.

But there is a mystery. What drove Beecher Stowe to write *Uncle Tom's Cabin*? Why did this genteel white woman whose contact with African-Americans was largely limited to her own servants, and who had barely travelled into the southern states, pen a novel that made much of a nation empathise with the plight of an oppressed minority?

More than anything else, it was because of a child. Charley was her sixth and favourite, born in 1848. Beecher Stowe referred to him as 'my pride and joy', and she openly gave him more love and attention than any of her other children. But at the age of just a year and a half, he died in an outbreak of cholera that swept Cincinnati, killing nine thousand people. Her grief was extreme. It consumed her, haunted her. She could not escape the vision of him dying in agony before her eyes as she watched helplessly, unable to mitigate his suffering.

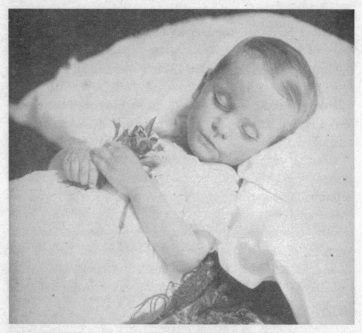

Harriet Beecher Stowe's son Charley, killed by cholera in 1849.

Charley's death, however, was the motivation for her transformation into an abolitionist and for the story of *Uncle Tom's Cabin*. It was the singular event that broke down the barriers and opened her to empathy, for she could now understand how black slave women might feel when their children were taken from them to be sold, a common occurrence throughout the slave states. She wrote, 'It was at his dying bed, and at his grave, that I learnt what a poor slave mother may feel when her child is torn away from her.' In a related entry in her journal she noted, 'I wrote what I did because as a woman, as a mother I was oppressed and brokenhearted with the sorrows and injustice I saw.'[30]

The death of her son provided a sharp, excruciatingly painful moment of empathic insight, and it is unsurprising that the theme of the separation of mother and child is so prevalent in her novel. It was through her own experience of suffering that Beecher Stowe was able to step into the lives of people whose daily existence, in so many ways, was the opposite of her own, and to play such a crucial role in the struggle against slavery.

If we reflect on our own lives, we all possess deep wells of pain and sorrow that we can draw on to help bridge social divides and create empathic bonds. We may be able to console a friend whose mother has just died because we have gone through our own trauma of parental death. We can step into the shoes of someone who is feeling rejected and unconfident after having been sacked from their job if this has happened to us too.

Shared experiences like these offer us the insights that help us put into practice one of the best known moral axioms in human history, the Golden Rule: 'Do unto others as you would have them do unto you.' During the Axial Age (800–300 BC), the world's major spiritual traditions, including Buddhism, Confucianism and Judaism, all developed some version of the Golden Rule. It also appears in Hindu classics such as the Mahabharata and is a central tenet of Christian thought.

The Golden Rule is often described as an 'empathic principle'.[31] But should it be? While it may work admirably well when our emotional lives and experiences coincide with other people's – especially through a recognition of shared suffering – what happens when others' experiences, culture and worldviews are very different from our own? Here the Golden Rule is not enough, since we might end up treating people in a way that would suit ourselves, but which could be wholly inappropriate from their perspective. We need to go beyond the Golden Rule and turn to what has become known as the Platinum Rule: '*Do unto others as they would have you do unto them.*'[32]

The scholar and journalist Robert Wright explains why it can be so important to treat others how they, rather than you, would like to be treated.

The world's biggest single problem is the failure of people or groups to look at things from the point of view of other people or groups – i.e. to put themselves in the shoes of 'the other'. I'm not talking about empathy in the sense of literally sharing people's emotions – feeling their pain, etc. I'm just talking about the ability to comprehend and appreciate the perspective of the other. So, for Americans, that might mean grasping that if you lived in a country occupied by American troops, or visited by American drone strikes, you might not share the assumption of many Americans that these deployments of force are well-intentioned and for the greater good. You might even get bitterly resentful. You might even start hating America.[33]

Wright's reflections are a reminder that the perspectives of subjugated peoples have long been ignored by their overlords. When I was in high school in Australia in the early 1980s, for example, we were taught in our history classes that Britain had benignly 'colonised' Australia in the late eighteenth century. But Australia's Aboriginal peoples typically describe this same event as an 'invasion' – a word that never appeared in my school textbooks. It is only in recent years that non-indigenous Australians have begun to see the arrival of the First Fleet in 1788 through Aboriginal eyes, an expansion of the empathic imagination that has been very late in coming.[34]

We cannot assume that others will share our moral codes, our tastes, our interpretations of the world. That is why highly empathic people do not simply try to discover what they share with others, but also actively attempt to understand what they don't. This two-fold step to ensure empathic accuracy lies at the core of making the imaginative leap into other minds. So when it comes to acting on their insights, highly attuned empathists do not just employ the Golden Rule, but complement it with its Platinum counterpart.

The Platinum Rule presents us with a greater imaginative challenge than its golden cousin, for it asks us to resist the temptation of projecting our own experiences and views onto others. Yet it is certainly worth practising them both, and learning to recognise in which contexts each is appropriate. The easiest way of doing so is to conduct a one-month experiment, where every time you act with empathy, you make a note of whether you were following the Golden Rule or the Platinum Rule. So one day you might give your elderly mother a call because you are aware she feels lonely, and you would probably want someone to phone you too in similar circumstances (Golden Rule).[35] But on another day, you refrain from smoking on your friend's balcony since you know she doesn't like the smell wafting into her apartment, even if you wouldn't mind it yourself (Platinum Rule).

By the end of the month you will have started to develop the habit of tuning into both what you share with others, and where your perspectives diverge, and you will be the proud owner of a brain that is wired with golden and platinum circuitry worthy of *homo empathicus*.

Empathise with the enemy

'My life is my message,' said Mahatma Gandhi, perhaps the most radical empathist in modern history. What does his life teach us about stepping into the shoes of other people? Gandhi's empathic instincts were first visible in his passion for nursing, which emerged soon after he moved to South Africa, aged twenty-six, to start working as a lawyer. When the Boer War began in 1899, he organised a Volunteer Ambulance Corps of over a thousand Indians for the British Army, sometimes walking more than twenty miles to fetch soldiers wounded on the battlefield. During the Zulu rebellion in Natal, he nursed Zulus who had been flogged and left by the British, whose regular field nurses refused to attend them – for Gandhi, there was no relevant distinction between the two sides in the conflict.

His more explicit experiments with empathic living began upon his return to India in 1915. His first act was to swap his lawyer's suit and starched collars for a dhoti, or loincloth, the traditional clothing of the poor. Two years later Gandhi founded the Sabarmati Ashram near the city of Ahmedabad, where his ambition was 'to live the life of the poorest people', as an act of solidarity and empathic understanding. In between giving political speeches and spearheading the movement for Indian independence from Britain, he and his wife and followers spent years living and working like subsistence peasants, eating only the simplest meals, dwelling in sparse shelters, growing their own food, and spinning their own cloth. He abolished the caste system on the ashrams, so even he had to clean the latrines, a job that was normally confined to Untouchables (Dalits). Gandhi was not a man without flaws: he could, for instance, be incredibly stubborn. But there is no doubt about his empathic credentials.[36]

Gandhi's desire to experience for himself the daily life of the poorest Indians was by many seen as a harmless eccentricity. Far more controversial was his insistent advocacy of the need to empathise with one's political adversaries. Trying to look at the world through their eyes – and so appreciating their values, motives, aspirations, and suffering – was, he believed, essential for building a culture of peace and tolerance. This issue became increasingly pertinent as tensions between Hindus and Muslims grew in the lead-up to Independence in 1947. Many Muslims wanted their own state, while Gandhi abhorred the prospect of partition and supported the ideal of a united India. A devout Hindu, he called for brotherhood and mutual understanding: 'I am a Muslim! And a Hindu, and a Christian and a Jew.' His words reflected an unwavering belief in the need to empathise with one's enemies – who were not really enemies but simply other human beings whose lives and values were of equal worth to one's own.

The half a million deaths that occurred during partition in violence between Hindus and Muslims showed that the moral demands of empathising with enemies were too great in that turbulent moment of history. So was Gandhi overly idealistic? Should he have admitted the darker sides of human nature that prevented the empathic understanding he valued so highly?

I think he was right to advocate empathising with our supposed enemies. In fact, I consider it a third and essential step in making the imaginative leap into other minds. We should try to extend our empathy beyond the usual suspects – the poor and marginalised, the voiceless and powerless – and be more adventurous in our efforts to step into other people's shoes. In situations of violent conflict, whether in Palestine, Syria or Sudan, long-lasting peace and reconciliation requires not just political agreements by leaders, but empathic bonds amongst everyday people so they can live side by side as neighbours. Equally in our personal lives, empathy with 'the enemy' can play a crucial healing role and resolve the deadlocks that beset our relationships. It might help reduce antagonism with your boss, revive communication with a sibling you have not spoken to for years, or ease tensions with a neighbour with whom you have been on perpetually frosty terms. This approach to empathy has been championed in an international Charter for Compassion, drawn up in 2009 by representatives of six different faith groups (Judaism, Christianity, Islam, Hinduism, Buddhism and Confucianism), which calls on people 'to cultivate an informed empathy with all human beings – even those regarded as enemies'.[37] We can each ask ourselves this question: Who are my three greatest 'enemies', and how could I use empathy to start bridging the divide between us?

For some people, the idea of empathising with an enemy, such as a manager who has been making your life hell, might seem like going too far. Isn't *she* the one who should be making the effort to empathise with *you*? And what's the point of bothering anyway, since she's unlikely to change her ways? According to a stream of thinking in Buddhism, a good reason to make the effort to understand how she might be feeling is that it is a step towards living a more compassionate and contented life. The Zen Buddhist monk Thich Nhat Hanh tells a story about a letter he received concerning a young girl who, as a refugee crossing the Gulf of Siam in a small boat, was raped by a Thai sea pirate. She was only twelve years old, and jumped into the ocean and drowned herself. Although we might immediately want to take a gun and shoot the sea pirate, says Hanh, we must step into his shoes and show compassion for him, because if we had grown up in similar circumstances, there is good chance we may have become a violent pirate ourselves.[38]

I find this example almost too confronting: trying to empathise with the pirate makes my stomach turn. But another Buddhist thinker, Stephen Batchelor, suggests that we can find the courage to engage in this kind of extreme compassion through a progressive empathic meditation, where we imagine ourselves first into the lives of a friend, then an enemy, and then a stranger:

> Start with a friend. Imagine her as a newborn baby, covered in blood. Slowly follow her as she grows from a toddler to a child to an adolescent to a young adult to the moment you first met her. Try to picture what her hopes and longings were before she even suspected your existence. Think of her now as someone who values her own ideas and feelings in the same inscrutable way you hold on to yours. Then look into the future and watch her age, fall ill, grow old and die . . . Turn to the enemy and stranger and do the same, until three human beings sit before you: equal in birth and equal in death.[39]

In my own experience, attempting to empathise with enemies has been extraordinarily challenging – yet ultimately rewarding. This was particularly the case when I travelled to Guatemala in the late 1990s to conduct research for my doctoral dissertation.[40] I had decided to study the country's oligarchs – the thirty or so families of European origin who dominated the economy and politics, and who kept Guatemala impoverished. They owned the big coffee and sugar plantations, the banks and major industries. They lived luxury lifestyles, flying around in private helicopters and shopping in Miami, while the majority of the population, 60 per cent of whom were indigenous Mayans, lived in extreme poverty. The oligarchs had also collaborated with the military in Guatemala's recently ended civil war, in which the armed forces had killed an estimated 200,000 civilians, mostly Mayans, in their attempt to root out leftist guerrillas.

I certainly had no empathy for the oligarchy when I began my research. Quite the opposite: I despised them. To me they were a faceless ruling elite who were responsible for terrible crimes, such as funding paramilitary death squads to assassinate trade unionists, peasant leaders and journalists during the civil war. I thought, however, that if Guatemala was ever going to become a more equal and less violent society, it was vital to speak with the oligarchs and understand their psyche and mental outlook, to discover what really made them tick. How did they think about issues such as poverty, the civil war, and indigenous land rights? Without understanding the oligarchy's worldview, I thought, it would be impossible to develop effective strategies to erode their power.

Once I began interviewing them, I was immediately confronted by their racism against indigenous people. One woman told me a story about 'a very small, swarthy, ugly-looking, flitty-eyed Indian'. Another complained about the 'ignorance' and 'lack of ambition' of the Mayan workers on her plantation. They were repeatedly described as backward, deceitful, filthy, stupid and lazy. Part of me wanted to retort upon hearing such statements, but I forced myself to remain silent and to try to step into the oligarchs' shoes. Their racism was hardly surprising: most had grown up within a small, inward-looking, elite community where such views were entirely normal, having been nurtured for centuries. But my attempts to empathise with them did not bring on a wave of Gandhian tolerance and mutual understanding: I considered their views detestable.

This situation embodied the problem of what I call 'empathic dissent' – how do you empathise with someone whose views or values you deeply disagree with? It is an issue we face in our daily lives. You might be having dinner at a friend's house and one of the guests tells an anti-Semitic joke. Should you respond by pointing out that the joke is offensive to you? Or instead call on your empathy, and attempt to look through the eyes of the misguided comic to understand his mindset?

I think the answer is that we can do both. And this raises a crucial point about empathy that is often misunderstood. No matter what a person's politics, religion or moral code might be, the process of empathising does not destroy the possibility for moral judgement. You can gain an understanding of someone's worldview without having to agree with their beliefs or principles. I never condoned the oligarchy's racism, but the more I learned about how closed their world was – how they had barely any contact with Mayan people apart from their maids and drivers – the more I could comprehend it.

Over time, my ignorance about the oligarchy was gradually eroded, and the seeds of empathy began to flower. With each interview, they became more individual, more human, less of a uniform caste that I could simply label as 'exploiters' or 'the ruling class'. My prejudices against them were most strikingly challenged when I began hearing accounts of how their children had been kidnapped and sometimes murdered by the guerrillas and renegade paramilitary groups in an effort to extract ransom money from them during the war. I remember one aristocratic woman, speaking to me in her palatial home in a gated compound, weeping as she described how her son was abducted. I was completely unprepared for such revelations: I had never considered how the war had affected Guatemala's powerful families on a personal level. Although they had not faced violence on nearly the same scale as the Mayan population, they had undoubtedly suffered. And in a kind of epiphany, I suddenly realised that Guatemala was not as divided as I had always imagined: both the wealthy oligarchs and the impoverished indigenous population craved something very simple, which was personal security. In other words, there was common ground on which the country could be united and rebuilt following the civil war.

I could never have developed this perspective on the political possibilities for Guatemala if I had not been willing to talk to the oligarchs, hear their stories, and empathise with those who I had long thought of as enemies. I certainly do not think of myself an apologist for the oligarchs, and still consider the erosion of their economic and political power to be of paramount importance, but I believe I am now less ignorant about them, and a much better judge of their motivations and actions. And that may well be the best reason to step into the arena and empathise with our enemies: although the conflicts and tensions may not all get fully resolved, we will almost certainly come out of the process more informed, less quick to judge, and wiser about both other people and ourselves.

What is it like to be a bat?

In the 1970s, the philosopher Thomas Nagel wrote a classic article called 'What is it like to be a bat?' He argued that 'our own experience provides the basic material for our imagination, whose range is therefore limited', so we are unable to imagine what it may be like to spend a day hanging upside down by our feet in an attic or to have webbing on our arms. All we can imagine is 'what it would be like for *me* to behave as a bat behaves', but we can never understand 'what it is like for a *bat* to be a bat'.[41] The point he was arguing is that it is impossible for us to step into the shoes of other people to the extent that we can understand their minds. We can never escape the limits of our own subjectivity.

I don't agree. By taking the three steps of humanising the 'other', discovering what we share and what we don't, and empathising with our enemies, it becomes possible to get a good grasp of the feelings, beliefs, values and experiences of other people. Human beings are not so different from each other that they cannot attempt to journey – albeit incompletely – into one another's lives, and overcome the barriers to empathy in the process. Harriet Beecher Stowe never had a child stolen from her by a white slave trader, yet the emotional wrench caused by her son's early death no doubt offered some insight into the pain. Gandhi never *became* an Untouchable (Dalit), but spending years living as a peasant farmer and cleaning toilets with his own hands at least brought him closer to the reality of their lives. Oskar Schindler would have been the first to admit that he did not know what it felt like to be a persecuted Jew in the Cracow ghetto, but he could still feel a common humanity with his workers. Some people's lives do seem almost incomprehensible to us, almost bat-like. I find it difficult to project myself into the worldview of a Guatemalan shaman, or a dying child in Rwanda, or a Rockefeller heiress, but this realisation does not deter me from trying as best I can to imagine their inner lives. Even without absolute success I will have been transformed by the effort, and my personal empathy deficit eroded in the process.

Where have we reached so far? Our empathic brains should be well and truly switched on, and our minds tuned for making the imaginative leap into other people's worlds. The next step in the quest to release our empathic potential: start limbering up for the extreme sport of experiential empathy.

HABIT 3
SEEK EXPERIENTIAL ADVENTURES

Being Daniel Day-Lewis

During the filming of *My Left Foot*, Daniel Day-Lewis, playing the Irish artist and writer Christy Brown who had cerebral palsy, spent almost the entire shoot in a wheelchair, refusing to come out of character, even on tea breaks. He not only had to be pushed around the set, but insisted that everyone call him Christy and spoon-feed him at mealtimes. He prepared for the role by teaching himself to paint with his left foot, just as he learned to hunt and trap using eighteenth-century tools for his part as a frontiersman in *The Last of the Mohicans*. While making *In the Name of the Father*, Day-Lewis readied himself for a scene where a confession is beaten out of him for a crime he did not commit by replicating his character's experiences, forcing himself to stay awake for three days and nights, and hiring real policemen to interrogate him. For *The Ballad of Jack and Rose* he lived apart from his wife so he could understand the isolation of a dying man, while for *Lincoln* he maintained his persona's high-pitched Kentucky accent off-camera and requested to be addressed as Mr President at all times.

Day-Lewis is a leading practitioner of method acting – an approach made famous in the 1930s by the Russian theatre director Constantin Stanislavski – and believes that the successful practice of his craft requires immersing himself, as far as possible, in the life and spirit of his character. He attempts to completely embody his role, both physically and psychologically, 'because that is where the work is, that's where the discoveries are – you're not discovering anything when you're having a cup of tea and a laugh with the grips, as tempting as that would be'. The aim is not just to gain insights into his stage character, so he can perform with authenticity, but also to make discoveries about himself. 'I've been mostly interested in lives that seem very far removed from my own, and the mystery of that life is what draws me towards it,' says Day-Lewis. 'In an underground sense, you're choosing to explore yourself through another life.'[1]

Method acting embodies one of the principal habits of many highly empathic people, which is their willingness to dive into the extreme sport of experiential empathy. Like Day-Lewis, they think that one of the best ways to step into someone else's shoes is to have direct experience of their life, so it becomes etched onto their skin and psyche. This process does not involve a merging of personalities that totally eradicates their identity – a state of being that is neither possible nor desirable to achieve – but is rather a way to think outside the limits of their own experiences, beliefs and emotions. It is common in acting for men to play women, rich to play poor, young to play old. An empathist strives to become as sensitive, versatile and imaginative as the finest actors.

Experiential learning may be the most demanding approach to empathising – more confronting than having a conversation or watching a film – yet has the potential to yield the greatest rewards. There are several ways of trying it for yourself, each with its challenges. At the extreme end of the spectrum is physical *immersion*, similar to Daniel Day-Lewis's effort to recreate Christy Brown's life by spending months in a wheelchair. Another option is *exploration*, where we become like anthropologists who search out and closely observe lives and cultures that are different from our own, engaging in empathic travel. A final form is *cooperation*, in which working together with others – often in testing or traumatic circumstances – brings us into empathic union with them: think of it as being in the same boat rather than the same shoes as other people. Our companions on this experiential leg of our journey include pioneering undercover journalists, an aspiring Argentinian doctor, and the members of your local choir.

Immersion, or how to be an undercover empathist

How do we learn? Our education systems are geared towards learning via the second-hand modes of words and images. Yet for over five hundred years there has been a recognition in Western culture that the most effective learning may take place through experiential encounters with reality. Leonardo da Vinci described himself as a 'disciple of experience'; he developed his knowledge of anatomy not by studying medical texts but by dissecting bodies. In the eighteenth century, Jean-Jacques Rousseau argued that 'true education consists less in precept than in practice. We begin to instruct ourselves when we begin to live', while the twentieth-century philosopher John Dewey believed that 'all genuine education comes about through experience'.[2]

As a way of learning about ourselves and other people, experience has few parallels. In the history of empathy, one of the first figures to understand this was St Francis of Assisi. After a visit to St Peter's basilica in Rome in the early thirteenth century, he was so disgusted by its opulence that he swapped clothes with a beggar he spotted at the door, and spent the day begging in rags. Living in poverty became the distinctive mark of the brotherhood he later founded.

In modern times, St Francis' experiment in Rome has been emulated by undercover investigative journalists and writers who have disguised themselves and for a period attempted to live on the social margins by staying in slums, working in low-paid factory jobs, and trying to survive on the streets. Also known as 'role reporting', this genre of empathic immersion dates to the late nineteenth century, and most of its exponents have been motivated by a desire to expose social injustice, inequality and exploitation. At the same time, they have often been highly educated, middle-class individuals who have wished to confront their own privilege and prejudices by delving into lives that seem, at least on the surface, alien to them.[3]

Here I wish to chronicle the adventures of four of the most important and original of these undercover empathists, who I hope can inspire us to try out experiential immersion for ourselves.

First amongst them is the British social reformer Beatrice Webb, who was born in 1858 into a family of successful businessmen and politicians. Largely self-educated, her early ideas were influenced by the social Darwinist Herbert Spencer, who encouraged her belief in the Victorian philosophies of self-help and individualism, and the view that poverty was largely due to a failure of character, a moral flaw of those who suffered from it. Such beliefs were typical amongst people sharing her upper-middle-class background.

In the late 1880s Webb's ideas underwent a fundamental transformation, largely due to her experience as a researcher for Charles Booth's social survey of poverty in London's slums. Webb started out investigating conditions amongst dock workers, spending time at the wharves where they bid for scarce casual work, and mingling with them at working men's clubs, aided by her unusual habit of being a woman smoker. In 1887, her research took a more experiential turn when she dressed up in a bedraggled skirt and buttonless boots in search of work as a seamstress in an East End textile sweatshop. After knocking on countless doors she was taken on as a 'plain hand' in a small, Jewish-owned clothing business. Crammed in with thirty other women and girls, she did piecework on twelve-hour shifts, but was more incompetent than most, constantly making mistakes and working too slowly.

Webb lasted only four days, yet the account of her experiment, which she wrote up in a magazine article called 'Pages From a Work-Girl's Diary', caused a sensation. It was unheard of for a respectable member of bourgeois society, especially a woman, to have first-hand experience of life amongst the destitute. She described the exploitative pay levels and physical hardship of the work – 'my fingers are horribly sore, and my back aches as if it would break' – and combined this with a some-what paternalistic commentary on the loose morals of her companions, remarking on their 'promiscuous lovemaking' and 'frank enjoyment of the low life'. As a result of her venture, in May 1888 she was called to testify before a House of Lords Select Committee on sweat shops.

The immersion also caused Webb to rethink her political beliefs. 'My own investigations into the chronic poverty of our great cities opened my eyes to the workers' side of the picture,' she wrote in her autobiography. She could now see that from their perspective, the Industrial Revolution was 'a gigantic and cruel experiment' that was 'proving a calamitous failure'. Webb turned against the individualist ideology of self-help, expressed her 'ethical revulsion' of capitalism and 'profit-making enterprise', and declared herself to be a socialist. She spent the rest of her life campaigning for improved factory conditions, and supporting the cooperative and trade union movements. She also became a leading figure (with her husband Sidney Webb) in the socialist Fabian Society, and later co-founded the *New Statesman* magazine and the London School of Economics. For a former London 'society girl', it was an extraordinary legacy.[4]

The East End of London has attracted a succession of undercover empathists since Webb toiled there with needle and thread. In 1902, the American adventurer Jack London stayed for eight weeks in the guise of a stranded sailor, which he chronicled in *People of the Abyss*. The most renowned explorer, however, was George Orwell. After a privileged upbringing, including school at Eton – an experience which turned him, in his own words, into 'an odious little snob' – Orwell spent five years in the colonial police force in Burma. While abroad, he became so disgusted with the part he was personally playing in imperialism, that he returned to Britain in 1927 determined to discover the realities of life amongst the poor in his own country. 'I wanted to submerge myself, to get right down among the oppressed,' he wrote, 'to be one of them and on their side against the tyrants.' He did not want to condemn poverty from the sidelines like so many Bloomsbury intellectuals, but to live it for himself. So he decided to become a tramp on the streets of East London, swapping his suit for dirty dungarees and a cloth cap, living off bread and margarine, and sleeping in bug-infested dosshouses with drifters, beggars and unemployed labourers.

Orwell took a more uncompromising approach than Beatrice Webb: rather than tramping for just a few days, over a period of several years he went on multiple underground excursions, sometimes for weeks at a time. He was never tempted to have a stash of spare cash in his pocket or to run away to his parents' comfortable home in Suffolk. Yet he always recognised that his tramping was just a temporary assignment, a matter of choice rather than necessity that could never touch the true bitterness, disappointment, and inescapable hardship of the lives he sought to understand. Still, it was a huge education in life. As he concludes in *Down and Out in Paris and London*:

> I shall never again think that all tramps are drunken scoundrels, nor expect a beggar to be grateful when I give him a penny, nor be surprised if men out of work lack energy . . . I am not saying, of course, that most tramps are ideal characters; I am only saying that they are ordinary human beings.[5]

While challenging his prejudices and assumptions, Orwell's journeys also helped him make new friendships, develop his curiosity about strangers, and gather superb literary material that would serve him in his career as a writer. In other words, the benefits of empathy were both ethical and personal.

Most examples of undercover empathy are, like Orwell's, attempts to cross class boundaries. John Howard Griffin decided to do something more unusual: to cross the divide of race. Griffin, who was born in Texas in 1920, was a remarkable character. During the Second World War he joined the French underground, helping smuggle Jewish children out of Germany to England. In 1945 a bomb explosion left him blind, but he still managed to write a bestselling novel before miraculously recovering his sight a decade later. Having experienced discrimination when blind and witnessed Nazi anti-Semitism, he became acutely aware of racial discrimination in the segregated Deep South of the United States, and was determined to publicly expose its injustice. 'Black men told me that the only way a white man could hope to understand anything about his reality was to wake up some morning in a black man's skin,' wrote Griffin. So that is what he did. In November 1959, Griffin dyed his skin black with pigment-darkening medication, and spent six weeks travelling and working in Louisiana, Mississippi, Georgia and South Carolina as an African-American.

He started out as a shoeshine boy in New Orleans, and was immediately struck by the casual inhumanity of his white customers, who were completely taken in by his disguise. 'When they paid me, they looked as though I were a stone or a post,' he recalled, 'they looked and saw nothing.' Griffin suffered the everyday indignities of segregation, walking miles to find anywhere that a black man was permitted to go to the toilet or sit down for a cup of coffee. He experienced not just verbal racist abuse and the threat of physical violence, but the 'hate stare' when he walked past white men and women:

I learned within a very few hours that no one was judging me by my qualities as a human individual and everyone was judging me by my pigment. They could not see me or any other black man as a human individual because they buried us under the garbage of their stereotyped view of us. They saw us as 'different' from themselves in fundamental ways: we were irresponsible; we were different in our sexual morals; we were intellectually limited; we had a God-given sense of rhythm; we were lazy and happy-go-lucky; we loved watermelon and fried chicken.

Griffin wrote about his experiences in a series of articles for the black monthly magazine *Sepia*, and also in a book, *Black Like Me*. Today we might consider that a white man speaking on behalf of African-Americans is unnecessary, condescending or possibly unethical – surely black people are able to speak for themselves. But at the time white Americans would scarcely listen to black voices campaigning against segregation, which is why *Sepia* had agreed to publish Griffin. It was a smart move: his revelations had enormous impact. He gained widespread media attention for the cause of racial equality, and became a prominent civil rights spokesman, working with Martin Luther King and lecturing on college campuses across the country. Yet there was a cost. He and his family received death threats from white supremacists and were hounded out of the United States. They returned a year later, but the Ku Klux Klan eventually caught up with Griffin, beating him with chains and leaving him for dead on a Mississippi back road. He was lucky to survive and resolutely continued his political activism.

Today *Black Like Me* remains a standard text on high school and college syllabuses across America. At its heart is Griffin's resounding message about the value of empathy: 'If only we could put ourselves in the shoes of others to see how we would react, then we might become aware of the injustice of discrimination and the tragic inhumanity of every kind of prejudice.'[6]

If there were a prize for the extreme sport of empathic immersion, it would probably have to go to the German investigative journalist Günther Wallraff. In March 1983 he placed the following newspaper advertisement: 'Foreigner, strong, seeks work of any kind, including heavy and dirty jobs, even for little money. Offers to 358458.' Wallraff intended to expose the harsh, low-paid and often illegal working conditions suffered by the tens of thousands of immigrant Turkish workers in West Germany – by becoming one of them himself. He had gone undercover before, working in a chemical factory and also posing as an alcoholic in a mental hospital, but this was to be his most audacious experiment yet. Rather than spending just a few days in character, this time he disappeared into it for two years.

Wearing dark contact lenses, a black hairpiece and having perfected broken 'foreigners' German', Wallraff threw himself into a succession of back-breaking immigrant jobs. He unblocked toilets on building sites that were ankle-deep in urine, shovelled coke dust hour after hour without a protective mask, and was made to work in areas filled with noxious gases at a steel factory, all the while putting up with racist jokes and comments from his German bosses and co-workers. He also flipped burgers in McDonald's and was a guinea pig in medical experiments that caused his gums to bleed. At times he chose to provoke, such as his visits to Catholic churches to see if they would baptise a Turk (he was turned away by almost every priest despite displaying expert knowledge of the Bible). Gradually, his character Ali began to become part of him. 'I identify more and more with the part,' wrote Wallraff in his book *Lowest of the Low*. 'At night, when I'm asleep, I often talk aloud in broken German. I now know what strength it takes to bear just for a short time, what my foreign colleagues have to suffer all their lives.'

'There is a bit of apartheid happening right here among us – in our *democracy*,' concluded Wallraff after leaving his last job. 'I experienced conditions which are usually only described in history books about the nineteenth century. The work was dirty, crushing and drained one's last reserves; but worse, was the humiliation that I had to bear and the contempt in which I was held.' His book was explosive. It sold more than two million copies in thirty languages, led to criminal investigations of firms using illegal labour, and resulted in improved protection for contract workers in several German states. Earnings from the book funded the establishment of a free legal aid foundation for immigrant workers. For Wallraff, the experience may have secured his reputation as Europe's most enterprising investigative reporter, but his work in the coke plant left him spitting out black saliva for months, and permanently scarred with chronic bronchitis.[7]

Thanks to the inspiration of figures such as Webb, Orwell, Griffin and Wallraff, experiential empathy has become an

Günther Wallraff cleaning toilets during his two-year empathy experiment as an immigrant Turkish worker in West Germany in the early 1980s.

established means of uncovering social inequities. More recently, for instance, journalists such as Polly Toynbee in Britain and Barbara Ehrenreich in the United States have revealed the realities of surviving in the low-wage economy by working in it themselves. It is true that these are often temporary sojourns, allowing the practitioners to escape back to more comfortable lives afterwards. Yet they retain the virtue of being based on experience rather than hearsay or books, and involve far more commitment and sacrifice than the superficial efforts of tourists who 'go local' by viewing shanty towns in developing countries from the comfort of air-conditioned coaches.

When it comes to our own lives, few people would be willing to work for months in a steel mill like Wallraff did in order to expand their empathic selves. So we might consider less drastic – though still challenging – ways of directly experiencing lives that contrast with our own. You could take part in one of the fundraisers organised by homelessness charities where you sleep out on the streets for a night, or sign up alongside tens of thousands of others for Oxfam campaigns such as 'Live Below the Line', which asks you to spend five days living on one pound per day, the amount that 1.4 billion of the world's population have to survive on.

Some people prefer a DIY immersion. If you are used to a middle-class lifestyle, you could try living off the minimum wage or the equivalent of unemployment benefit for a time. This is just what Tushar Vashisht, an investment banker who had worked in Silicon Valley, and Matthew Cherian, an engineering graduate from MIT, decided to do. In 2012 they returned to their native India and attempted to get by for several weeks on the average national income of 100 rupees ($2) per day. Cherian admitted to me that their effort to live poor in Bangalore was somewhat artificial, since they were only 'temporary visitors', but he felt they nevertheless learned an enormous amount, such as how physically and mentally fatigued you become when you cannot afford an adequate diet. They also discovered, said Cherian, that 'empathy is essential for democracy'. It is vital to put ourselves in the shoes of people living in poverty, otherwise 'the rights of the minority or the less vocal will always be neglected'.[8]

Such 'wealth-swap' experiments might not be to your taste, so you could test yourself with a 'God swap' instead. If you happen to believe strongly in a particular religion, then spend a month attending the services of faiths different to your own, including a meeting of Humanists. By doing so, you would be following in the footsteps of Nelson Mandela, who went to the services of every religion while imprisoned on Robben Island, despite having been brought up as a Methodist.[9] You could also fast for Ramadan alongside your Muslim neighbours, or for Lent together with your Christian ones. Alternatively, try a 'job swap' with a friend whose work is very different from yours, perhaps shadowing them for a few days to give you experience of being a car mechanic or a puppeteer. If you have toddlers and your partner does most of the childcare, why not give them a break and spend a whole week looking after the children totally alone? You may be shocked by how stressful and exhausting it can be, and decide that it is only fair that you start taking on a greater share of the domestic work.

As a final challenge, you could opt for a 'sense swap'. What might it be like to be deprived of your full sensory faculties? To find out, go to Dialogue in the Dark, a global network of public exhibitions founded by the German social entrepreneur Andreas Heinecke. Visitors are immersed in complete darkness, and led by a visually impaired guide around experiential galleries. You might fumble about with coins as you attempt to buy food from a market stall, panic slightly as you try crossing a busy street with only a long white cane for protection, then sip your drink with extra care in the pitch-black cafe. Almost every visitor describes it as a confronting, exhilarating and unforgettable experience.

Dialogue in the Dark is leading the way in bringing empathic immersions to a mass audience. Since being founded in 1988, the travelling exhibitions have appeared in more than 130 cities in thirty countries, provided work for six thousand blind people, and have received over seven million visitors. The aim, says Heinecke, is to encourage people 'to think differently about ability and disability', and to generate tolerance and understanding about 'otherness'. It is no surprise to discover that he is an official 'Empathy Fellow' of Ashoka, the global organisation for social entrepreneurs. When explaining the fundamental concept behind Dialogue in the Dark, Heinecke quotes the philosopher of empathy Martin Buber: 'The only way to learn is by encounters.'[10]

Exploration, or how empathy journeys can change you

Romantic revolutionary. Champion of social justice. Fanatical ideologue. Murderer and terrorist. Or just a cool poster on your college dorm wall.

Ernesto 'Che' Guevara means many things to many people. But he is rarely invoked as an icon of empathy. Yet when he was a young medical student in Argentina – before he converted to Communism in 1954 and joined Fidel Castro's rebel forces in Cuba – Guevara took a life-changing journey around South America that shook him out of his narrow upper-middle-class worldview and opened his eyes to the continent's endemic poverty and inequality. It was a trip revealing how empathy can emerge not just from a direct immersion in other people's lives, as John Howard Griffin discovered, but from the experience of travel, where we explore and observe other cultures and ways of being. As we will see, however, Guevara's story is a complex one, raising difficult questions about the relationship between empathy and violence.

In 1952, aged twenty-three, Guevara set out from Buenos Aires on a year-long motorcycle trip with his friend Alberto Granado, a doctor and biochemist. At the time, he was far from being the revolutionary he would later become. 'None of his friends or relatives thought Ernesto a Marxist,' writes his biographer Jon Lee Anderson, 'and indeed, neither did *he*.'[11] Guevara had been born into a family with aristocratic connections, and was more interested in rugby than proletarian revolution. He was an eclectic reader: he had dipped into Marx, but had also read Freud, Sartre, Whitman, Frost and Huxley. Perched on the back of 'La Poderosa', a 500cc Norton motorbike (that would later fall apart and be abandoned), Guevara was like so many young men setting out on a gap year: he wanted to meet girls, have adventures, and satisfy his wanderlust.

By the end of the trip, however, he had also undergone a series of experiences that amounted to an empathic epiphany. In Valparaíso in Chile, he was deeply affected by his encounter with an elderly servant woman, who was dying because she could not afford the medicines she needed. He tried to treat her using his half-trained medical knowledge, and gave her some tablets, but knew it was already too late. One night they met an out-of-work miner and his wife, 'frozen stiff in the desert night, hugging one another', and shared their blankets with the marooned couple. 'It was one of the coldest nights I've ever spent,' recalled Guevara, 'but also one which made me feel a little closer to this strange, for me anyway, human species.' He was shocked by the poverty of indigenous peasants he saw in the Peruvian and Bolivian Andes, and equally enraged by the power that local landlords wielded over them.[12]

Although Guevara and Granado were travelling for fun, they also had a medical project driving their journey, which was to study leprosy along the way and volunteer for a few weeks at a leper colony in the Peruvian Amazon. Their time at the San Pablo colony had a profound impact on Guevara. In part he was

Che Guevara (right) and Alberto Granado floating down the Amazon in 1952. The raft was a gift from the lepers at the San Pablo colony.

appalled at the inadequate facilities and the unfeeling way the patients were treated by many of the staff. Yet he also revelled in his work tending to the patients, and enjoyed joking around and playing football with them.

Looking back at his travels through South America, Guevara wrote:

> I came into close contact with poverty, hunger and disease; with the inability to treat a child because of lack of money; with the stupefaction provoked by the continual hunger and punishment, to the point that a father can accept the loss of a son as an unimportant accident, as occurs often in the downtrodden classes of our American homeland . . . I wanted to help those people with my own personal efforts.[13]

Nothing in his privileged background had prepared him for these harsh realities. It was his travel experiences – not reading books or having intellectual political discussions – that opened him to the plight of the continent's people. According to historian Carlos Vilas, 'his political and social awakening has very much to do with this face-to-face contact with poverty, exploitation, illness and suffering.'[14] Or as Guevara put it after his motorcycle expedition, 'I am not the same as I was before. That vagabonding through our "America" has changed me more than I thought.'[15]

There is little doubt that Guevara's travels were an empathic revelation that fired in him a strong desire to alleviate people's suffering. Yet is it legitimate to describe him as an exemplar of empathy? Some reject this, pointing out how he later engaged in what can hardly be described as empathic conduct. He not only took up arms as a guerrilla fighter and developed a strong authoritarian streak, but also – most notoriously – was ruthless in his role as 'supreme prosecutor' when the Cuban revolutionaries took power in 1959, ordering the execution by firing squad of several hundred 'war criminals'.[16]

I am nevertheless cautious about erasing Guevara's name from the annals of empathy, for two reasons. First, the main impact of his youthful travels around South America was to inspire him to dedicate himself to what he called 'social medicine', not guerrilla warfare. He decided to return to Argentina to finish his medical studies, planning to use his knowledge to bring healthcare to an impoverished continent. It was not until two years after his trip, when he witnessed the CIA-backed military coup in Guatemala in 1954, that he consciously decided to become a Marxist revolutionary. The violent overthrow of a democratically elected left-wing government convinced him that armed struggle was the only viable path to social and political change. As he once said, 'I was born in Argentina, I fought in Cuba, and I became a revolutionary in Guatemala.'[17]

A second, and perhaps more provocative point, is that Guevara was not alone in thinking that it might be legitimate to use unempathic methods to achieve what he considered to be empathic ends. At particular moments in history, it has been common for people who are fuelled by a deep personal desire to reduce human suffering and confront injustice to believe that the only effective way to do so is with a gun in their hands, especially when all other options have been tried and failed. In the 1930s, for instance, over thirty thousand writers, poets, and political activists – amongst them George Orwell – joined the International Brigades to fight with the Republicans against the Fascists in the Spanish Civil War, in support of Spanish workers and peasants. A less talked-about example of someone who shared this approach is Nelson Mandela.

Today we think of Mandela as an archdeacon of empathy. Perhaps no other political leader has made such a concerted effort to step into the shoes of his adversaries and treat them with humanity. Since his release from prison in 1990, he has unfailingly preached reconciliation with white South Africans. During the 1995 Rugby World Cup, for example, he called on black South Africans to support their national rugby team, despite the fact that its members were almost all white and the team had long been a hated symbol of Apartheid.[18] Mandela understood that empathising with the white population was essential to create national unity and political stability in the post-Apartheid era, and possibly to prevent a descent into civil war.

But wind back the clock and a different story emerges. From a young age Mandela was filled with a profound empathy for the suffering of his own people under Apartheid, and a sense of injustice about the legal system that upheld it. He trained as a lawyer, and initially viewed the law as a 'sword of justice' that could be used to tackle racial discrimination. In 1946, however, Mandela and other members of the ANC Youth League became disillusioned with the possibility of legal and legislative reform, and shifted to supporting non-violent direct action, based on Gandhi's protests in India. Mandela argued that they 'had to be willing to violate the law, and if necessary go to prison for their beliefs'.

Within a few years he saw that this approach too was failing, and a more radical solution was required. From the early 1950s,

Mandela became the leading figure making the case for using armed violence to achieve the ANC's political goals. He started reading the works of Marx, Lenin and Mao, and alongside his African nationalist ideals, dreamed of creating a classless society. He even had a picture of Stalin hanging on his living room wall (Roosevelt, Gandhi and Churchill were up there too). By 1955 he was convinced that guerrilla warfare was the only answer. As he wrote in his autobiography, *Long Walk to Freedom*:

> For me, non-violence was not a moral principle but a strategy; there is no moral goodness in using an ineffective weapon . . . In the end we had no alternative to armed and violent resistance. Over and over again, we had used all the non-violent weapons in our arsenal – speeches, deputations, threats, marches, strikes, stay-aways, voluntary imprisonment – all to no avail, for whatever we did was met by an iron hand. A freedom fighter learns the hard way that it is the oppressor who defines the nature of the struggle, and the oppressed is left no recourse but to use methods that mirror those of the oppressor. At a certain point, one can only fight fire with fire.[19]

So Mandela, driven by frustration, anger and a sense of impotence, became a revolutionary. He went underground and formed Umkhonto we Sizwe (The Spear of the Nation, or MK), the armed wing of the ANC. He studied guerrilla tactics, including the writings of Che Guevara, and travelled to Ethiopia, where he learned how to make bombs and 'think as a soldier thinks'. As Mandela stated at his trial, he was a key figure in MK until his arrest in August 1962. MK continued to operate into the 1980s while Mandela was imprisoned, and was responsible for sabotage and bombing attacks throughout South Africa, some of which killed civilians, despite its efforts to minimise loss of human life. As a result, Amnesty International never campaigned for the release of Mandela because it does not represent anyone who advocates or uses violence.[20]

By the late 1980s, though, Mandela was beginning to see that it was empathy, not guns, that would be the most effective political tool for constructing a post-Apartheid South Africa. He realised that he needed to build trust with the government, and work with them rather than against them. He had also developed a deeply humane, empathic attitude towards his former adversaries, which guided his actions in the years following his release: 'In prison, my anger towards whites decreased, but my hatred for the system grew. I wanted South Africa to see that I loved even my enemies while I hated the system that turned us against one another.'[21]

Nelson Mandela and Che Guevara were very different people, with distinct temperaments and visions of social justice: Mandela, for example, believed in representative democracy, whereas Guevara favoured a top-down socialist state, and Mandela certainly never presided over the kinds of political executions that brought Guevara such infamy. What they shared, though, was a pragmatic approach to politics, believing that armed struggle was a legitimate and necessary route to achieving their objectives for justice. While both men were motivated by empathy, they were willing to use tactics that most highly empathic people today would reject. Those of us – including myself – who are opposed to the use of violence, and who do not believe that the end justifies the means, might challenge themselves to step into the shoes of political figures such as Guevera or Mandela. If thrust into similar extreme circumstances, might we too have felt no option but to take up arms in defiance of our empathic instincts, and at risk to our own and other people's lives?

Exploring the world through travel does not normally raise such dilemmas. The trouble with most travel is not so much that we may be tempted to become revolutionaries, but that it so often fails to provoke any significant empathic response at all. On my own early trips around Indonesia, China and Nepal, I was doing little more than following the well-worn tourist trails offered by my Lonely Planet and Rough Guides, which typically directed me to idyllic beaches or mountain trekking adventures. Such guidebooks contain no advice on how to understand the everyday lives of the inhabitants; the word 'empathy' does not appear in any index. There was little that was challenging or life-changing about these journeys, and at the time I never fully appreciated what Thomas Cook, the visionary nineteenth-century tour operator, saw as the greatest benefit of travel: 'To travel is to dispel the mists of fable and clear the mind of prejudice taught from babyhood, and facilitate perfectness of seeing eye to eye.'[22]

So how can we ensure that travel is a way of expanding our empathic vision? Che Guevara provides the answer: we ideally need a project to direct us. Guevara's project was to volunteer for a few weeks at the leper colony in Peru, and to visit leprosy experts and hospitals *en route*. He still spent plenty of time getting drunk and dancing badly in pursuit of female attention. But his project brought him into contact with local people and their lives, enabling him to see far more than the Inca remains at Machu Picchu.

It was only when I tried a similar approach that travelling began to shake me out of the narrowness of my own worldview and erode my empathy deficit. In the mid-1990s I volunteered for a summer as a human rights observer in a village in the Guatemalan jungle (this was a few years before I went there to study the oligarchy). I was struck not just by the extreme deprivation faced by the inhabitants, most of whom were indigenous Mayans who had been caught in the midst of the country's civil war, but by what I learned from my daily encounters with them. I remember, on one of my first days, a little boy named Bernabé coming to my hut and showing me a drawing he had done. At the bottom was a typical green jungle scene, but the sky above resembled no child's picture I had ever seen before. He had drawn an egg, which hatched into a bird in the image next to it, which in turn became a little plane, which was followed by a large, menacing army helicopter with bullets being fired out of it. This macabre evolutionary tale offered my first insight into the minds of the people around me. Their mental landscape, even that of the children, was pervaded by the violence of the civil war (which, at the time, was in its final months). Although Bernabé then burst into a song about butterflies, his artwork, on a scrappy piece of paper, revealed a different narrative. It was, in part, the impact of this drawing that inspired me to dedicate several years to working on human rights and social justice issues in Guatemala and other developing countries.

There are many organisations that can help us evade the standard itineraries, offering volunteering opportunities and other projects to transform a getaway holiday into an empathic journey. Sure, you might want to put up your feet and laze around a beach resort in Thailand, but why not spend at least some of your time teaching English conversation to students at a nearby school? Or how about joining a tour with a company called Traveleyes? Their speciality is organising trips for visually impaired people, but they invite sighted tourists to come along too, who do not just assist those who are blind but get to discover the riches of travelling with people who possess exquisite sensitivity to touch, sound and smell.

I would love to see an Empathy Travel Agency on every High Street and in every shopping mall. What to expect when you walk through the door? You begin by spending an hour talking to one of the friendly attendants about your approach to life, the kinds of people you would like to meet but have never had the chance, and the areas of curiosity or ignorance that you wish to explore. From this discussion they assess your empathic needs and desires, and offer you a tailor-made experiential package. Your travel adventures could be right on your doorstep. If you express an interest in North African culture, they might send you to work for a week in the kitchen of a local Moroccan restaurant, or to volunteer in a refugee

The next revolution in holiday travel

and immigrant support centre. I've already got a name and strapline for this innovative travel company, in case you wanted to set up a franchise: Empathy Escapes – Unpack Your Personal Baggage.

Cooperation, or why it may be time to join your local choir

While experiential empathy can emerge through direct immersion or exploring diverse cultures on our travels, it can also grow out of cooperation. There are times when working together towards common goals and sharing experiences with others can draw them into our circle of concern and create – often unintentionally – empathic fusion. According to sociologist Richard Sennett, cooperation has the power to 'join people who have separate or conflicting interests, who do not feel good about each other, who are unequal, or who simply do not understand one another'.[23]

A good place to begin exploring the relationship between cooperation and empathy is through the human response to disasters. When the cultural thinker Rebecca Solnit began interviewing people in North America and Mexico who had lived through both natural and man-made disasters, such as Hurricane Katrina and 9/11, she noticed something very strange: they frequently 'lit up with happiness' as they told their stories.[24] Rather than describing trauma and tragedy, they recalled the sense of community when neighbours who were usually too busy to speak to each other joined forces to clean up after a hurricane, or the feelings of personal worth and solidarity when working in an improvised soup kitchen, or the empathy with which strangers helped those in need, often at risk to their own lives.

Solnit spoke to a young Pakistani Muslim immigrant who had fallen as he was running from the collapsing Twin Towers, and a Hasidic Jew grabbed his hand and pulled him to safety. 'He was the last person I would ever have thought to help me,' he told her. 'If it weren't for him, I probably would have been engulfed in shattered glass and debris.' A young architect remembered the mass of volunteers who coordinated the donation of food, boots and other supplies to emergency workers at Ground Zero in the aftermath of 9/11. 'People were really working well together,' he said. 'There was a tremendous cross-section of people. You had people who very clearly English wasn't their first language, working with people who spent their Sundays doing the *Times* crossword.' Others noticed that the atmosphere in New York resembled a sombre carnival: 'No one went to work and everyone talked to strangers.'[25]

Over and over again, Solnit found that the standard media depiction of disasters – of people running around in panic and busily trying to save their own skins – was not borne out in reality. More typical was that they quickly banded together to help each other out, successfully organising relief efforts in their community in a decentralised and non-hierarchical way, long before official assistance arrived from emergency services:

> In the wake of an earthquake, a bombing, or a major storm, most people are altruistic, urgently engaged in caring for themselves and those around them, strangers and neighbours as well as friends and loved ones. The image of the selfish, panicky, or regressively savage human being in times of disaster has little truth to it . . . The prevalent human nature in disasters is resilient, resourceful, generous, empathic, and brave.[26]

In the course of her research, Solnit discovered what I think of as 'the principle of empathic cooperation': thrust people together in an intense shared experience or to pursue a common enterprise, and empathy is likely to flower. Naturally, I am not advocating that we go around searching for disaster zones where we can stretch our empathic muscles. What we can do, though, is get involved in collaborative projects with strangers, where empathy-building may not be the primary objective, but where it can creep up on us unawares, and find unexpected ways through our carapace of assumptions and ignorance about others. We may gradually realise that our aspirations and lives intertwine with people whom we might never normally meet or even consciously avoid.

One of the most famous examples of this principle in action took place in 1971 in the town of Durham, North Carolina. A notorious Ku Klux Klan leader, Claiborne Paul Ellis, was coaxed during a public meeting into joining an education committee to tackle racial problems in local schools. He was forced to work alongside an African-American civil rights activist, Ann Atwater, whom he hated with a purple passion. But in the course of doing so, he discovered that he shared much more with her than he had ever expected, such as the fact that they were both poor and struggling financially in cleaning jobs – he as a janitor at Duke University, and she as a domestic servant. The scales began to fall from his eyes, changing his views not just of Ann, but of her whole community: 'I was beginning to look at a black person, shake hands with him, and see him as a human bein' . . . It was almost like bein' born again.' After ten days he stood up in a community meeting in front of a thousand people and tore up his KKK membership card. He later became a civil rights activist and leader of a janitors' union, 70 per cent of whose members were African-American. He and Ann became friends for the rest of their lives.[27]

A more recent case is the West-Eastern Divan Orchestra, a pioneering ensemble formed in 1999 by the cultural critic Edward Said and the conductor Daniel Barenboim. The Divan brings together young musicians from across the Middle East, so there might be a Jewish cellist from Tel Aviv playing alongside a Muslim violinist from Ramallah. According to Barenboim, 'It has very flatteringly been described as a project for peace. It isn't. It's not going to bring peace, whether you play well or not well. The Divan was conceived as a project against ignorance. A project against the fact that it is absolutely essential for people to get to know the Other, to understand what the Other thinks and feels, without necessarily agreeing with it.'[28] The trick has been not to have the members take part in empathy workshops to overcome their cultural differences, but simply to play music together.

Has it worked? Not always. Some critics have suggested the orchestra is less a utopia of social harmony than an opportunity for ambitious young musicians to play professionally under the esteemed Barenboim, while others have pointed out clashes amongst the musicians, such as a heated debate where some Arabs argued that the Israelis had no feel for playing Arab music. It is a realistic assessment: collaboration can bring out intra-group conflict as much as generate cooperation.[29] But the overwhelming picture is one of musical collaboration creating mutual understanding. Barenboim recalls a moment when an Israeli and a Syrian were sharing a music stand and attempting to play the same note on their cellos, with the same dynamic and expression: 'They were trying to do something together. It's as simple as that . . . Having achieved that one note, they already can't look at each other the same way, because they have shared a common experience.' One of the Israeli members, viola player Amihai Grosz, has described the orchestra as 'a human laboratory that can express to the whole world how to cope with the Other'.[30] In defiance of easy listening, the Divan even performs Wagner, the music that was played by the Nazis as Jews were being sent to the gas chambers.

Although you probably don't have the training to be a concert musician, you may well be able to sing – or at least enjoy doing so. In Britain, group singing, especially in community choirs, is currently undergoing its greatest revival since the nineteenth century. One of the catalysts has been *The Choir*, a BBC television series first broadcast in 2006. The programme format is that the young, charismatic and slightly eccentric choir master Gareth Malone goes into unusual places and creates a scratch choir out of amateur singers, which he then trains up for a major public performance. He has worked with groups including postal workers, schoolchildren, wives and girlfriends of military personnel, and residents of a housing estate, and the choirs have found themselves singing anywhere from the Albert Hall in London to the Choral Olympics in China. Those taking part frequently describe it in transformative terms. The choir offers them self-confidence, personal and civic pride, a sense of community belonging, and some good songs. But what also emerges from the experience, often unexpectedly, is empathy.

Many of Malone's choirs bring together people who do not know each other or who may live and work side by side yet have diverse social and professional backgrounds, and rarely interact. The Manchester airport choir had a Sikh aviation officer singing alongside baggage handlers and security guards with African-Caribbean and Welsh heritage. At the Severn Trent Water company, senior managers were struggling to hit their notes next to site workers with perfect pitch who laid the pipes. At the Royal Mail, Malone began to notice how 'as a result of rehearsing and performing together, a bond was forming . . . people they had never met before from their own company could now be called friends'.[31] The most striking impact was at Lewisham Hospital, where the choir began to break down some of the assumptions that employees had about people from very different positions in the workplace hierarchy. As Malone recounts:

> I spoke off-camera to a pharmaceutical porter called Aaron who told me that through being in the choir he had a new appreciation of how much pressure those further up the chain were under. Eddie, a tough-talking vascular surgeon, always entered rehearsals looking slightly flustered and had probably just come from cutting some poor soul apart with a very sharp scalpel. Sitting together in the choir humanised them both.[32]

None of this should surprise us: that's how the principle of empathic cooperation works. Yes, there might be internal tussles in the choir over who gets to sing the solos, but the general effect of the intense effort to work as a group with a shared, challenging goal is to break down barriers and forge bonds of friendship and understanding. Although the TV show may have been emphasising the feel-good nature of the experience for the participants, the evidence suggests that the camaraderie and empathy were very real. As a Lewisham nurse put it, 'One of the best things about the choir was that it brought together different people from different parts of the NHS. I work with neo-natals, tiny babies, and ordinarily would have nothing to do with the surgeons or porters or speech therapists. It gave me the opportunity to interact with them, to get to know what they do, to socialise. Every hospital should have a choir.'[33]

So where might we find opportunities for this kind of cooperation and collaboration in our own lives? We humans are sociable creatures, so despite our individualist culture and the disintegration of communities in the West over the past century, there remains an abundance of possibilities all around us. Many of them are familiar, everyday activities. You might join a community choir or a group campaigning to keep the local library open. You could play five-a-side football every Sunday afternoon in the park or start up a unisex knitting circle. Alternatively, get yourself an allotment, which are hotbeds of collaboration, generating empathy between people from different backgrounds and generations. You may tend your own plot, but before long you will be will sharing seeds with a stockbroker and helping an elderly nun with her weeding.[34]

The only proviso is that you should be wary of projects and organisations that fortify boundaries between communities. Religion, nationalism and political ideologies all have dark histories of creating social division and turning people against one another. They must be treated with caution. 'We' is a 'dangerous pronoun', says the sociologist Richard Sennett, because it reinforces the distinction between 'them' and 'us'. 'The social bond,' he continues, 'arises most elementally from a sense of mutual dependence.'[35] It is precisely when we have to work together – as in a choir or in the wake of a disaster – that we are immersed in the kind of interdependent communities that are likely to generate empathy and social harmony rather than intolerance. The nineteenth-century Anarchist thinker Peter Kropotkin argued that human beings, like all animals, have a natural tendency to engage in mutual aid.[36] We should strive to create more interdependent societies, where mutual aid and social cooperation can help our empathic selves to flourish.

Learning the language of empathy

When teaching Islamic Studies at McGill University, the Canadian scholar of comparative religion, Wilfred Cantwell Smith, used to make all of his students fast during Ramadan, observe Islamic holidays, and perform the prayers at the correct times – even getting up to pray at dawn. Why? Because he believed that they could never understand another faith merely by reading books about it.[37] In so many fields of learning, it is experience that really makes the difference. Carpenters don't hone their skills by studying texts on how to use a plane. Pianists don't perfect their technique by reading musical scores. They practise, practise, practise.

So too when it comes to developing empathy. It is by stepping into the world of experience – through immersions, exploration and cooperation – that we can make huge leaps in our ability to understand the lives of others. You might have the courage of a George Orwell or Patricia Moore, who approaches experiential empathy as an extreme sport that rivals ice-climbing or skydiving. Perhaps, though, you feel more at ease embarking on travel expeditions into unfamiliar cultures, or just turning up for choir practice on a Wednesday evening after work.

Learning to empathise is like learning a language. You may be able to make some linguistic headway by poring over a textbook and repeating all the right phrases, but if you really want to master another tongue, there is no substitute for hanging out with the natives and having to speak it every day. You will probably stumble with the words at first, but gradually the language will become second nature – you will develop the habit of thinking in it, and maybe even dreaming in it. The practice of empathy is no different: we can learn it best when we leave the manuals behind and set out on experiential adventures.

HABIT 4
PRACTISE THE CRAFT
OF CONVERSATION

The crisis of conversation

The newspapers may not be reporting it, but we are currently facing a crisis of conversation. On the one hand, there is a famine of quality conversation in our relationships. Communication breakdown has become a major cause of divorce in Western countries, while the average couple in Britain spends more time watching television together – around fifty minutes per day – than directly talking to each other.[1] On the other hand, there is a plague of superficial talk, much of it due to the incessant chatter created by new technologies. Around 10 trillion text messages were sent globally in 2012, but how many of them involved conversations that inspired, consoled or touched people?

This crisis matters for the future of empathy. Why? Because conversation is one of the essential ways in which we come to understand the inner emotional life and ideas of others. 'The hidden thoughts in other people's heads are the great darkness that surrounds us,' observes the historian Theodore Zeldin.[2] Conversation enables us to penetrate that darkness. It shines a light into the minds of the human universe we encounter every day – lovers, strangers, adversaries or friends. Conversation and empathy are intimately intertwined: making the effort to comprehend another person's perspective can help bring an otherwise unremarkable dialogue to life, while conversation itself has the power to forge empathic connection. Together they can generate a virtuous circle, building upon and reinforcing one another. That's good news for confronting the crisis in conversation, and also for tackling our empathy deficits.

The challenge is to rethink how we talk to people so we can gain greater insights into their thoughts, feelings and worldviews, and deepen our emotional bonds with them. And for this we can learn from the experiences of highly empathic people. I have noticed that they bring six unusual qualities to their conversations: curiosity about strangers, radical listening, taking off their masks, concern for the other, a creative spirit, and sheer courage.

Beware: these qualities should not be thought of as 'techniques' or 'tools'. The idea of conversational technique goes back to the etiquette books of the eighteenth century, which instructed people on how to correctly address a duke or a cardinal (if you happened to meet one). In the 1930s, the self-help writer Dale Carnegie popularised communications techniques in his book *How to Win Friends and Influence People*: his advice included smiling a lot and repeating people's names as you speak, so they think you like them and are really listening to them. His tips and tricks can still be found amongst the long shelves of communication guides on sale today. The problem with such strategies is that they can make conversation mechanical and stilted, introducing a self-consciousness and artificiality that actually get in the way of empathy.

Instead of thinking about conversation as a technique, highly empathic people tend to view it as a *craft*. While crafts typically require an element of technical prowess and practice for you to be good at them, they also offer the scope for introducing your own creativity, personality, and spontaneity. Every bowl thrown by a potter is slightly different, and revealing of their unique aesthetic, just as every conversation we embark on should have its own character and individuality, rather than being constructed from a set of rules.

How should we begin practising the craft of conversation? Having spent over ten years running workshops on conversation and empathy – for everyone from business executives and BBC journalists, to schoolchildren and professional oral historians – I have found that the single most striking habit of highly attuned empathists is their insatiable curiosity about other human beings.

Curiosity about strangers

Curiosity had a bad press before the eighteenth century. Early Christians such as St Augustine classified curiosity as one of the three major sins, alongside carnal pleasure and pride, since it revealed a lack of self-restraint (Eve should never have given into her curiosity and eaten that apple from the Tree of Knowledge). In the first century, the Greek thinker Plutarch similarly labelled curiosity as a vice, equating it with being a gossiping busy-body who pokes about in other people's business.[3] During the Enlightenment, however, curiosity was transformed into a virtue. It was considered the driving force behind scientific advancement and technological progress. Scientific revolutionaries like Isaac Newton and Alexander von Humboldt were possessed of a healthy curiosity, an inquisitiveness that enabled them to see beyond conventional ideas and make extraordinary discoveries.[4]

Curiosity remains valued in the arts and sciences today. But it is limited by our Enlightenment inheritance, which assumes that curiosity should be applied to ideas and objects, rather than people. One recent study, for instance, defines curiosity as an exploratory inquisitiveness about 'what we don't know', omitting any reference to *who* we don't know.[5] We should move beyond this inheritance and elevate curiosity about others into a supreme virtue, because it is a key to opening the door to empathy. We live surrounded by strangers – many of us hardly know our neighbours, we see the same shop assistants every day but understand little about their lives, we can work alongside people for years while their inner selves remain a mystery to us. Curiosity can help us discover who they are and how they see the world. As sociologist Richard Sennett writes, we can think about empathy as 'the sentiment of curiosity about who other people are in themselves'.[6]

Does curiosity about strangers come naturally to us? Not according to many anthropologists. Jared Diamond points out that in traditional societies, such as the tribes of New Guinea, people have been generally considered to fall into one of three groups. 'Friends' are members of your own band or village, who you can trust. 'Enemies' are members of neighbouring bands or villages with which your band is on hostile terms. And then there are 'strangers', unknown individuals from distant bands. 'If you do happen to encounter a stranger in your territory,' says Diamond, 'you have to presume that person is dangerous', since they are likely to be scouting in order to raid your group or kidnap your womenfolk. In other words, any stranger is a potential enemy, and should be treated with extreme caution.[7]

Contemporary culture reflects this attitude, and we are often wary of engaging strangers in conversation. While we don't think they are likely to stick a spear through our chests, we might worry that they are not interested in talking to us, that they will think we are nosey, or that what we have to say is facile or unintelligent. Or we may just find talking to strangers plain embarrassing.

Curiosity is more socially acceptable in some cultures than others: it is easier to get chatting to a stranger on a park bench in small-town America than to do so in Finland, a country famous for its reserved and untalkative inhabitants.[8] Yet there is one social group unafraid of expressing their curiosity: children. It is astonishing how they will go up to strangers and start talking to them, asking the bus driver how the motor works, or another child what they are holding in their pocket. 'Children are alive, curious, sensitive,' said the Italian educator and social activist Danilo Dolci, and 'growing up is a process of becoming calloused'. We need to find ways of rediscovering the childhood curiosity about strangers that most of us once possessed.

One person whose curiosity never became calloused, but remained refreshingly childlike, was the Chicago radio journalist and writer Studs Terkel. During a five-decade career (which lasted until his death in 2008, aged ninety-six), Terkel interviewed at least seven thousand people about their lives for his radio show and books, from famous politicians and musicians to unknown steelworkers and hairdressers. Terkel was a gifted conversationalist. He put people at their ease, so they felt able to talk openly about their emotions and life stories. He had a photographic memory, which meant he could always recall the names of their children or ask them whether their mother was still unwell. But his greatest gift was a natural curiosity. He was simply fascinated by people from every walk of life – what they thought about politics or education, how they faced the struggles of work and having families, what they had learned about life itself. In the words of one of Terkel's long-time radio colleagues:

> What drives him on still, and so remarkably at his age, is his genuine curiosity about other people, no matter who or what they are. And it's matched somehow with his almost total lack of interest in himself . . . His curiosity is endless, and it's an honest curiosity into who people are, it's never motivated by jealousy or envy.[9]

This curiosity about strangers was what made him such an extraordinarily empathic human being. It enabled him to step into their skin for a while and walk around in it. Terkel was hungry to understand other people, and to learn from them. 'I think everyone has a story to tell,' he said, 'what your childhood was like, what your own memories are like, your own dreams . . . everyone is an expert on their own experience.'[10] He was unusually non-judgemental about people, and believed that 'you need to empathize with them if you want to find out what they're like'. When asked how he could have possibly talked to a Ku Klux Klansman (who appears in one of his books), without wanting to argue with him or walk away, Terkel was truly surprised, responding:

> But I couldn't understand him, I couldn't understand how anybody could think like he did and not even be aware I could possibly be offended by what he was saying. I was fascinated and I really got hooked on trying to find out.[11]

That's empathic curiosity in action. The essence of his approach – the key to his ability to make such strong connections with people and get them to speak so candidly with him – is summed up in one main piece of advice: 'Don't be the examiner, be the interested enquirer.' Wise words for any aspiring empathist.

Terkel always wanted his readers and listeners to empathise with 'the anonymous millions who make the world go round'. He tried to give voice to the voiceless, those who are ignored by the history books – the shoeshine boys, the dockers, the elderly trapped in care homes, the immigrants trying to make a new life. He was perpetually intrigued by the question, 'What is it like to be a certain person – ordinary so-called – living at a certain moment in history, in a certain circumstance?'[12]

We might all lead more interesting lives – and reduce the global empathy deficit – if we became a little more like Studs Terkel. In practice, that means stepping out into the world and talking to strangers, focusing not on the small talk of weather and sports results, but on the big talk of priorities in life, ideas, hopes and dreams. It means ruling nobody out: everyone, no matter what they look like or where they come from, could be a unique and captivating conversational partner, if you can find a gentle way to tap into their souls. It means listening hard, without constantly interrupting their thoughts, and having the confidence to let them pause and think without rushing in to fill every silence. 'Listen, listen, listen, listen,' insisted Terkel, 'and if you do, people will talk. They *always* talk. Why? Because no one has ever listened to them before in all their lives. Perhaps they've not ever even listened to themselves.'[13] It means refraining from interrogating them like a journalist digging for a story, who cares little about encroaching on private or painful ground, and being willing to share your own ideas and experiences to create a two-way dialogue, a 'conversation' rather than an interview. Ultimately, though, it is about recognising that conversations with strangers can be an adventure in personal learning and enlightenment, a way to challenge your own ideas and discover new ones. In other words, grasping that conversation can be good for you.

Terkel once claimed that he would like his tombstone to be inscribed with 'Curiosity never killed this cat'.[14] If he were still with us, what might he suggest we do to ignite our curiosity about strangers? I think his basic prescription would be to have a conversation with a stranger at least once a week, and really make an effort to understand the world inside their head. It could be the person who sells you a newspaper each morning, or the guy in the accounts department at work who always eats his lunch alone, or the sprightly elderly woman sitting next to you on the bus (Terkel would *always* talk to people on the bus on his daily commute).[15] There are some playful ways to meet strangers too. One woman I know named Sarah, who works in a large multinational organisation, found the email addresses of all the other Sarahs in the building and invited them to lunch in the cafeteria. It was such a success that the Sarahs – some of them receptionists, others senior managers – started a regular get-together.

Studs Terkel, perhaps the twentieth century's greatest conversationalist.

Some people find talking to complete strangers intimidating. They may feel inhibited, and think it better suited to gregarious extroverts who are brimming with conversational self-confidence. This I can comprehend. Yet it is a myth to think that nurturing curiosity about strangers requires an extrovert personality. As Susan Cain shows in her book *Quiet*, it is precisely the more introverted types who often develop into especially skilled listeners, and who make others feel at ease by not overwhelming them with force of character. They also tend to avoid the superficial chatter of parties and favour one-to-one conversations, which are much more likely to result in interesting and empathic discussion.[16] But whatever your personality type, it is essential to realise that most people actually want to talk about the things that matter to them. Offer them the space, and they will open themselves to you.

While we can nurture our curiosity as individuals, we need to invent new social institutions to spread conversational curiosity far and wide. Luckily some of them already exist. Have you ever been to a Human Library? The Human Library movement was founded in Denmark in 2000, to erode prejudices and create dialogues across social divides, and has now spread to over twenty countries. Here is how it works. The 'libraries' typically take place at a local public library, for example one Saturday morning per month. If you go along, instead of borrowing a book, you can borrow a person for conversation. The Human Library is full of volunteers who you can take out for around half an hour of discussion on any topic you like – they might be a naval officer, an asylum seeker, or a nightclub bouncer. The point is to talk to people who you would never normally come into contact with in your everyday life.

I spent several years working with one of the world's leading conversation experts, Theodore Zeldin, at an organisation he founded called The Oxford Muse, which shares the Human Library movement's faith in the power of talking to strangers. Zeldin's belief – one that I fully subscribe to – is that if you can bring two people together from different backgrounds, and encourage them to have a one-to-one conversation in which they take off their masks, share parts of their lives, and look through each other's eyes, then you have created a small moment of equality and mutual understanding. And by multiplying these kinds of conversation, you can produce a microcosmic yet potent form of social change. Think of it as changing the world one conversation at a time.

The main way we transformed this philosophy into practice was by holding Conversation Meals, which resembled the conversational feasts or 'symposiums' held by the Ancient Greeks. I remember one meal I organised, held in the gymnasium of an Oxford state primary school, where I invited around sixty people from diverse backgrounds across the city: corporate executives, homeless people, university professors, car factory workers, students, elders from the Chinese community, and Pakistani curry-house waiters. They were seated in pairs with a stranger at long tables. And between them, instead of a menu of food, there was a Menu of Conversation, containing questions like, 'What have you learned about the different varieties of love in your life?'

A Conversation Meal at an Oxford primary school. The first question on the menu on the table is 'How have your priorities changed over the years?'

and 'In what ways would you like to be more courageous?' There were around twenty questions on the menu, which each pair explored freely, in their own way, as they were served a simple meal to accompany their discussion. The questions had been designed to help people get beyond superficial talk, and engage with the big issues of life that matter to individuals of every culture and generation.[17]

The Oxford Muse meals are the opposite of speed dating – you talk to someone for one hour, not one minute – and also very different from conversational models such as 'interfaith dialogues', which generally dwell on topics specific to those participating (such as the role of religion in state education) rather than subjects of universal human concern. The Conversation Meals, which have been held in the UK, France, China, the Czech Republic and other countries, have been a catalyst for change, leading to new friendships, community projects, exploded prejudices and, inevitably, the occasional love affair. Their success lies not just in the unusual format, but in creating a shared space where the diners are given permission to talk openly about themselves. There is nothing odd about discussing your philosophy of love with a stranger if you are sitting amongst dozens of other people who are doing exactly the same thing. Actually, it is quite exhilarating.

The Conversation Menu idea has now spread to other organisations, such as The School of Life in London, as a way of fostering curiosity about strangers and creating empathy across the fissures of society. While it can be inspiring to attend one of these meals, there is nothing to stop you developing your own menu of questions to try with friends around the dinner table, acquaintances from the office, new neighbours, or other strangers you happen to meet. You will be surprised by the discoveries you make even about people who you thought you already knew well. To get you started, here is a sample of questions to use that might help rekindle the childhood curiosity that lies hidden inside all of us. Just remember, don't rush, otherwise you may end up with conversational indigestion.

A Conversational Entrée

What, in your experience, are the best and worst ways
of being good?

What would you most like to change about
your philosophy of love?

How have your ambitions affected your humanity?

Do you feel more at home in the past, the present, or the future?

Are you better at laughing or forgetting?

What is your personal history of self-confidence,
and what has it taught you?

Do you think we can empathise with animals, plants
and the planet itself?

What is your ideal way of growing old, and who might
help you do it?

Radical listening

There are plenty of obstacles to empathic conversation. Some people have a tendency to become combative when a discussion gets tense or heated, while there are those who move fast to blame others and make them feel guilty. Another common malady is narcissistic one-upmanship: when a friend reveals their tale of unrequited love, many people cannot help outdoing it with their own even more sorrowful tale ('If you think that's bad, just hear what happened to me . . .').

One of the most useful skills for getting beyond these obstacles is listening. Studs Terkel was a great fan of it. So is personal development guru Stephen Covey, who points out that while we spend years learning to read, write and speak, most of us dedicate little time to becoming better listeners.[18] But *how* should we listen? Apart from curiosity about strangers, highly empathic people have a habit of engaging in what I think of as 'radical listening', a very particular way of tuning in to what others are saying.

One of the most radical listeners of them all is Marshall Rosenberg, inventor of Non-Violent Communication (NVC), an approach to conversation that is especially designed to resolve conflicts – in anything from a rocky marriage to gang warfare – and that 'allows our natural compassion to flourish'.[19] He initially trained as a psychotherapist with Carl Rogers, a founder of 'humanistic' or 'client-centred' psychology in the 1950s, which encourages the psychotherapist to prioritise empathising with and listening to the client. Rosenberg's view was that empathy was a skill that should not be confined to professional therapists, but also practised by everyone in their daily lives.

A cornerstone of Rosenberg's thinking is the idea of 'receiving empathically', which he sums up like this: 'What is essential is our ability to be present to what's really going on within – to the unique feelings and needs a person is experiencing in that very moment.'[20] This is what radical listening is all about. The first element, 'presence', involves emptying your faculties and listening to the other person with your whole being, letting go of preconceived ideas and judgements about them. He quotes the French philosopher Simone Weil to emphasise how challenging this can be: 'The capacity to give one's attention to a sufferer is a very rare and difficult thing; it is almost a miracle; it is a miracle.' A second element is to consciously focus on identifying the other person's feelings, and a third is to make a concerted effort to understand their needs. According to Rosenberg, the primary cause of communication breakdown is a failure to comprehend the other person's needs, and their failure to comprehend our own. 'It has been my experience, over and over again,' he says, 'that from the moment people begin talking about what they need rather than what's wrong with one another, the possibility of finding ways to meet everyone's needs is greatly increased.'[21]

To illustrate exactly what he means, Rosenberg tells a story about a visit he once made to a Palestinian refugee camp to teach a workshop on Non-Violent Communication. On the way in he had noticed several empty tear gas canisters that had been shot into the camp by the Israeli Army the previous night, with the words 'Made in USA' clearly written on them. As he began speaking, his translator said, 'They're whispering that you are American!' Just then a man leapt to his feet and hollered, 'Murderer!' Soon the whole group were chanting, 'Assassin!', 'Child-killer!' 'Murderer!' Rosenberg describes what happened next:

I addressed the man who had called me a murderer.

MR: Are you angry because you would like my government to use its resources differently?

MAN: Damn right I'm angry! You think we need tear gas! We need housing! We need to have our own country!

MR: So you're furious and would appreciate some support in improving your living conditions and gaining political independence?

MAN: Do you know what it's like to live here for twenty-seven years the way I have with my family – children and all? Have you got the faintest idea what that's been like for us?

Our dialogue continued, with him expressing his pain for nearly twenty more minutes, and me listening for the feeling and need behind each statement. I didn't agree or disagree. Once the gentleman felt understood, he was able to hear me explain my purpose for being at the camp. An hour later, the same man who had called me a murderer was inviting me to his home for a Ramadan dinner.[22]

Barack Obama tells a similar story about identifying feelings and needs, translated to a more everyday situation than a refugee camp. Obama grew up in Hawaii and spent his high school years smoking pot, drinking too much booze at parties, and unleashing his rebellious streak on his grandfather, with whom he lived. He rejected the petty household rules imposed on him – such as having to fill up the petrol in the car after he borrowed it – and took joy in using his talent for rhetoric to crush his grandfather in argument. But during his final year in high school, Obama's attitude began to change. 'It was in my relationship with my grandfather,' he recalls, 'that I first internalised the full meaning of empathy.' He made an effort to discover and consider his grandfather's point of view; that he had led a life of struggles and disappointments, and wanted to feel respected and appreciated in his own home. 'I realised that abiding by his rules would cost me little, but to him it would mean a lot. I recognised that sometimes he really did have a point, and that in insisting on getting my own way all the time, without regard to his feelings or needs, I was in some way diminishing myself.' The result was both greater harmony at home and a stronger personal bond with his grandfather.[23]

A challenging aspect of Rosenberg's method is not only that we should listen deeply to others, but that we should show our understanding of them by paraphrasing what they have just said, reflecting their message back to them in the form of questions that use neutral (non-evaluative) language. Rosenberg does this above when he asks the Palestinian man, 'So you're furious and would appreciate some support in improving your living conditions and gaining political independence?' Or imagine your partner complains that you haven't been spending enough time looking after the children lately. Instead of immediately leaping to your own defence, you might say, 'I'm sensing that you're upset with me about how we divide the childcare – am I hearing you right?', or 'Are you reacting to how many evenings I stayed late at the office working last week?' Rosenberg draws on compelling statistics to make his case: 'Studies in labour-management negotiations demonstrate that the time to reach conflict resolution is cut in half when each negotiator agrees, before responding, to accurately repeat what the last speaker said.'[24]

I have done formal training in Non-Violent Communication and it has opened my eyes to the importance of focusing intently on other people's feelings and needs, as well as my own. But I have to be honest and say that I personally find that the paraphrasing technique verges on being too mechanical. When I have tried it during difficult and confronting conversations with my partner and other adults, I feel self-conscious and somewhat artificial. Perhaps I just lack practice (indeed, my trainer told me it can take six months to start applying NVC in a natural, unaffected way). Where I find it easier to do – and where I've noticed startling results – is with my four-year-old children. Many times when my son or daughter has thrown a tantrum or burst into tears, I've helped them name their feelings and needs, saying something like, 'Are you feeling frustrated because I can't play with you right now?' or 'Are you feeling angry with me because I've turned off the computer before you finished watching the video?' And then a near miracle can occur: they stop crying, they nod their heads, they tell me how they are feeling through their sniffles and sobs, I get a chance to explain my viewpoint, and everything calms down. It seems that on some fundamental level, they just want to be listened to and understood (and don't we all?). This kind of empathic listening strategy now appears in many parenting manuals, such as the bestselling *How To Talk So Kids Will Listen And Listen So Kids Will Talk*, which explicitly advises parents to put themselves in their children's shoes, and acknowledge and help articulate their feelings.[25]

A further problem of radical listening is that if you really open yourself with presence to other people's feelings and needs, then you might become overwhelmed by the experience, resulting in emotional distress and inaction. For example, you hear someone's story about their child's death, and you find it incredibly upsetting, and almost feel you can't bear their pain. Psychologists sometimes calls this 'empathic overarousal', which you can think of as leaping *too far* into someone else's imagination. It has been observed especially amongst those working in emotionally extreme and traumatic situations, such as nurses caring for terminally ill children, humanitarian aid workers, and therapists whose clients have suffered sexual abuse.[26] One therapist I spoke with described how it eventually led him to leave the profession:

> In order to be a half-decent psychotherapist, I had to be able to accurately imagine the life and feelings of the person in front of me. When I was actually doing the work, I was absorbed and got a sense of satisfaction from it. When people told me their stories of trauma and pain, I could hold it, contain it and help them learn to manage their depression. The problem was I dreaded my job. On Sundays I dreaded the coming week, and didn't sleep well on work nights. I picked up their trauma from them, it was almost like I was holding their depression. The feelings of dread began to

dominate the feelings of satisfaction. I grappled with it for about three years after it reached a tipping point. Eventually I burned out and gave up my practice.[27]

I am not aware of any systematic studies revealing exactly how many people suffer from this kind of empathic overload, or how often it prevents them from taking action on the behalf of others. But given that empathy is 'normally distributed' (in the sense of the familiar bell curve) amongst the population, a fair estimate is that it affects around only 4 to 5 per cent of people on a regular basis, and perhaps a larger proportion more occasionally.[28]

Is there anything you can do about it? A common approach is to develop self-defence mechanisms to shield yourself from the emotional intensity of other people's suffering. Something I've noticed amongst international aid workers is that they often have a very dark sense of humour, which helps create a protective mental wall to deal with the distress they confront on a daily basis. Psychotherapists frequently limit the number of highly traumatised clients they take on, and make sure they have someone to talk to themselves about challenging cases (it's called 'supervision'). One useful strategy is to develop a self-awareness of where your own boundaries lie, so you can step away from conversations and situations that are pushing you over the empathic edge. As the psychotherapist Philippa Perry explained to me, 'In order not to burn out from empathic overload, you have to set your boundary before reaching your limit; in other words, fit your own oxygen mask before helping anyone else with theirs.' When taking long calls at a suicide centre, she made sure to have a break or debrief with colleagues after each call, ensuring she had plenty of oxygen before trying to empathise with the next caller.[29]

Empathic overarousal is a serious problem, but we should remember that it affects only a minority of people. The larger social challenge is that a far greater proportion of us suffer from an empathy deficit rather than a debilitating empathy surplus.

Take off your mask

I'm all for empathic listening. But there is a danger of turning listening into a cult. Open a typical communications skills book (especially one from the business shelves) and it will repeatedly emphasise listening but say almost nothing about the opposite, which is taking off your mask and sharing part of yourself with the other person. Too often we act like the festival-goers at the annual Carnival in Venice, concealing our identities behind a mask. We hold back our emotions, hide our fears, and keep our anxieties buried within us. But empathic relationships cannot easily develop unless we reveal ourselves and seek connection. Empathy is built upon mutual exchange: if we are open with others, they are much more likely to be open with us.

So we need to think of conversation as a two-way dialogue to create mutual understanding. As Theodore Zeldin suggests, at its heart, conversation is about reciprocity:

> What is a conversation? It is much more than talk, which can be mere chatting about nothing in particular, or communication, which need be no more than transmission of information to a passive audience. Conversation is shared, reciprocal nourishment that enables humans to create and exchange trust, wisdom, courage and friendship. Whenever in the past humans have wanted to change the way they lived or thought, they have changed the subject and the methods of their conversation. Conversation is assuming a crucial role in both personal and professional life, and is becoming a currency as important as money, which enriches both parties with what money cannot buy.[30]

Highly empathic people understand that if we fail to take off our masks, and end up constantly censoring ourselves, the result can be that conversation becomes stultified, repetitive and lacking authenticity. We face the danger of becoming like the male characters in Victorian novels – all stiff upper lip and emotional reticence. We should welcome the gift of the Freudian revolution, which has expanded the social space for people to talk more openly about the issues that really matter to them, from sexual insecurity to feelings of loneliness and pain.

At its core, removing your mask is about embracing vulnerability. The problem is that we live in a culture where making yourself vulnerable – exposing your uncertainties, taking emotional risks – is considered a failing, and something that most of us would rather avoid. Emotions researcher Brené Brown turns this attitude on its head, arguing that vulnerability is actually good for us:

> We're brought up believing and being taught and seeing it modelled in our parents, that vulnerability is weakness, and that going out into the world without armour is basically asking for the hurt that you get. But to me, vulnerability is not weakness – it's the greatest measure of our courage.[31]

Her studies reveal the positive outcomes that emerge from stepping into the arena of vulnerability. It is precisely when we expose our vulnerability, perhaps in a relationship or at work, that 'we have experiences that bring purpose and meaning to our lives'. Doing something risky – like asking for help, sharing an unpopular opinion, falling in love, admitting to being unconfident or afraid – may make us feel vulnerable, but it can also result in deeper relationships, creative breakthroughs, heightened joy, release of anxiety, and greater empathic connection.[32]

I saw the power of vulnerability in action when I interviewed Brené Brown in London, on stage in front of a crowd of five hundred people. The first thing she did after I introduced her was to turn towards the packed hall and say, 'I don't know why but . . . I'm feeling really nervous!' Few public figures would risk revealing so much of their uncertainty, but the effect was to make the audience feel an immediate empathy and warmth for her (and I am sure what she said was spontaneous, not planned).

Later in our discussion, I asked Brown how far we should go when revealing our inner selves. What limits should we set on taking off our masks? On the one hand, she told me, we should not think that vulnerability is about 'letting it all hang out' – we ought to avoid 'over-sharing' and simply dumping all our emotions on others. On the other hand, our ambition should be to experience a 'vulnerability hangover'. If you really take that big step and make yourself vulnerable in conversation with someone, then it is pretty likely that the next morning you will wake up thinking, 'Oh my God! Why did I share that? What was I thinking?' But if you don't feel any vulnerability hangover, then maybe you did not go far enough. When was the last time you woke up with one?

While many people feel they can be vulnerable with their partner or close friends, one place they often consider it taboo is in the workplace. When I discuss this issue in courses I run at The School of Life, typically around half the people in the room admit that they are reluctant to reveal their inner feelings and fears at the office. Can you really say in a meeting that you don't have the self-confidence to run the project? Can you let on to your boss that the reason you are falling behind with your report is that you've just been ditched by your girlfriend and are emotionally fragile? The answer may well be 'no chance', especially if you happen to work in a macho environment. You might worry that people will think you are weak, or incompetent, or lack the mettle to be a team leader. Maybe you are anxious that taking off your mask could risk your chances for promotion.

There are some good reasons to have such concerns. Many workplaces are empathic deserts. The psychologist Oliver James argues that the business world in particular has an unusually high proportion of people who exhibit a 'dark triad' of disturbing personality traits: they can be Machiavellian, narcissistic, and even psychopathic. Those with psychopathic tendencies, whom he describes as 'highly impulsive thrill-seekers who lack empathy for others,' are 'four times commoner among senior executives than in the ordinary workforce'.[33] If your desk happens to be next to someone with the emotional sensitivity of Gordon Gekko (the ruthless corporate raider from the film *Wall Street* who quipped 'lunch is for wimps'), then you may be more than a little reluctant to express even a shred of vulnerability.

Brown's response is that we need to forge work cultures where vulnerability, and the empathy that it helps to generate, are not just accepted but positively admired. As she explained to me:

> When vulnerability is not tolerated in the workplace, we can forget about innovation, creativity, and engagement. Those are all functions of vulnerability. You will never be able to convince me that being vulnerable and human, and getting good work done, are mutually exclusive. I just don't buy that argument. It's a false dichotomy.

She drives her point home with examples of top entrepreneurs who say that the greatest barrier to path-breaking new business ideas is that those who have them fear being ridiculed, laughed at, and belittled by colleagues, because truly innovative ideas tend to sound crazy.[34] So vulnerability and creativity go hand in hand. Marshall Rosenberg also makes the case for vulnerability at work, arguing that those who risk it often get positive responses, since a surprising number of people can be moved by emotional openness and honesty.[35] Moreover, if you admit to uncertainty, it can give others the permission to do so too – and maybe you will discover that your hard-nosed manager is just as fragile and lacking in confidence as you are.

Such views are part of a new movement in business thinking maintaining that emotional intelligence, openness and sensitivity are keys to success in today's highly interconnected and rapidly changing global economy. We need to conceive of organisations not as machines, but as networks of human relationships. It is a mistake to believe that demonstrating traits such as empathy or vulnerability will lead to you being treated as a doormat by unfeeling and backstabbing co-workers; rather, they will help you survive and flourish.[36] Bill Drayton, the world's most renowned social entrepreneur and founder of the Ashoka foundation, argues that empathy is an absolute prerequisite for good teamwork and organisational leadership:

> Anyone who does not master the complex social skill of guiding his or her behaviour through applied empathy will be marginalised. If their team is to succeed, they must master teamwork, which in turn rests on applied empathy . . . If you aren't given the tools of applied empathy as a young child, we shouldn't be blaming you – we should be blaming us. We have to have a revolution so that all young people grasp empathy and practise it. This is the most fundamental revolution that we have to get through.[37]

We can make it easier to reveal our vulnerability, whether at work or elsewhere, if we position ourselves within a 'community of empathy'. Taking off our masks often induces feelings of shame – that we are small and weak, that we are not resilient, that we are not good enough. But as Brené Brown points out, 'The antidote to shame is empathy . . . if we can share our story with someone who responds with empathy and understanding, shame can't survive.'[38] The message here is that we should look to people who will lend us an empathic ear, and listen to our anxieties and uncertainties. In other words, we can best expand our own empathy if we surround ourselves with it. If you drew a map of your social support network, how many people could really offer you the empathy you need? It may be time to seek them out.

Concern for the other

It is quite possible to show a willingness to remove your mask, or to be an excellent listener, but still take a self-centred and utilitarian approach to conversation by putting your personal interests before anybody else's. You might view communication as a way of getting what you want, meeting your own emotional needs, or controlling and manipulating people. That is why highly empathic people bring an attitude of concern for the other into their conversations, and strive to focus on the other person's interests and wellbeing, not just their own.

The importance of this trait becomes clear in the debate over so-called 'empathy marketing'. During the past decade, empathy has become a popular concept in the advertising and marketing industries, where it tends to be seen in purely instrumental terms. In his corporate bestseller *Persuasion: The Art of Influencing People*, James Borg describes empathising – especially the art of accurately reading people's emotions in face-to-face conversation – as a key sales skill to give you 'a competitive edge that can really set you apart and help you get what you want'. 'When you look at the behaviours and mindsets of the most successful people around,' writes Borg, 'it's apparent that they have a great understanding of the role of empathy.'[39] Numerous marketing websites offer tips on how to use empathic communication strategies to lure in customers, such as asking people about their families to help make a personal connection, ensuring that you look people in the eye when talking to them, and becoming observant of their body language and tone of voice as a way of tuning into their state of mind. One marketing consultant observes, 'Obvious though empathic communication techniques may be, my clients routinely neglect to use them . . . and leave billions of dollars on the table as a result.'[40] There are now firms specialising in empathy marketing, training telesales workers to make people feel as if they are really being listened to.[41]

An insightful commentator on this growing role for empathy in business is the political scientist Gary Olson. He argues that empathy marketing – or what he also calls 'neuromarketing' – is often described in benevolent terms as a way for businesses to respond to consumers' needs and desires, by trying to develop a sophisticated understanding of how they think and feel. But in reality, says Olson, it is little more than a clever strategy to boost sales and profits: 'In short, putting oneself in another's shoes is a technique for selling them another pair.'[42] Under this interpretation, empathy is having its moral content sucked out of it because the marketing industry displays little genuine concern for consumers' welfare.

Is empathy marketing as pernicious as Olson claims? Are businesses using empathic communications techniques to exploit their customers rather than to be sensitive to their interests? Looking back over the rise of mass consumerism, he may well be right. Although the concept of empathy is a new one in business circles, it has been used by marketing experts – in all but name – for nearly a century. The first great master of empathy marketing was no less than Sigmund Freud's nephew, Edward Bernays, who founded the public relations industry in the United States in the 1920s. Bernays had fully absorbed his uncle's discoveries in psychoanalysis, but gave them a capitalist twist: he realised that the most effective way to sell a product was not to offer consumers a rational list of reasons why it was so good, but to delve deeper by subtly tapping into and engaging with their unconscious desires and emotions. In other words, to empathise with them.

The effectiveness of his approach was brilliantly demonstrated in New York City in 1929, when Bernays was hired by the American Tobacco Company to break the taboo against women smoking, so that the firm could open up a huge new market. Thinking tactically, Bernays persuaded a small group of debutantes to light up Lucky Strike cigarettes in full public view during the city's annual Easter Parade. Meanwhile, he claimed to the press that the young women were suffragettes puffing on 'torches of freedom' in a symbolic call for equal rights for women. His strategy was a spectacular success: women across the country took up smoking. As Adam Curtis explains in his documentary series *The Century of the Self*:

> What Bernays had created was the idea that if a woman smoked, it made her more powerful and independent – an idea that still persists today. It made him realise that it was possible to persuade people to behave irrationally, if you linked products to their emotional desires and feelings. The idea that smoking actually made women freer was completely irrational, but it made them feel more independent.[43]

This is what empathy marketing is all about – stepping into people's shoes, understanding their mindset, and then using the insights to sell them your product. Olson points out that it has been a prevalent technique in the tobacco industry ever since the era of Edward Bernays. In 1994 Philip Morris ran what it internally referred to as an 'empathy campaign' for its Benson & Hedges brand in the face of growing opposition to smoking in public spaces. Their marketing plan makes explicit reference to 'empathy positioning' and conveying the idea that 'Benson & Hedges understands the societal pressures and constraints upon smokers in the 1990s (Empathy)'. The campaign ads showed images of people taking crazy risks to enjoy a cigarette. In one, a group of smokers are puffing away sky high on an aeroplane wing, accompanied by the caption, 'Have you noticed all your smoking flights have been cancelled?' The tag line reads, 'The Length You Go To For Pleasure'.[44]

It is not only tobacco companies that understand the power of empathy. As my children grow up, I notice just how much the advertising industry uses empathy to entice them to buy products that are not necessarily good for them – and often positively harmful. An obvious example is fast food adverts, which are replete with puppets, cartoons and giggling children to convince them that eating burgers and fries is fun and healthy rather than a one-way street to obesity and heart disease. The advertisers know exactly how to excite my children's minds and make their mouths water with desire. The McDonald's Corporation has been targeting children in its advertising campaigns since the 1950s – how many children today would fail to recognise the friendly clown face of Ronald McDonald? Founder Ray Kroc explained the logic: 'A child who loves our TV commercials and brings her grandparents to a McDonald's, gives us two more customers.'[45]

The current emphasis in marketing on using empathic communication techniques to step into the shoes of customers and clients would seem, therefore, to be a continuation of this long, instrumental tradition of putting empathy to work for the benefit of the balance sheet. Yet this conclusion is too simplistic. We need to ask a question: 'Where does the corporate desire to empathise come from?' The evidence reveals a spectrum of motivations. At the low-empathy end of the spectrum are companies that try to understand people's minds primarily for their own financial benefit rather than due to any genuine concern for their customers' welfare. In other words, they can resemble psychopaths who are skilled at cognitive empathy but seem to be missing a capacity for affective empathy.[46] Here you will find a cluster of firms selling products like cigarettes, sugary sweets and junk food, as well as betting shops and casinos.

At the high-empathy end of the spectrum, however, are businesses that use empathic methods with the intention of improving the quality of people's lives by trying to understand and meet their needs rather than manipulate their desires. These are the kinds of companies that are motivated by more than just the financial bottom line. When Patricia Moore was designing kitchen utensils, and strapped her hands with splints to simulate what it was like for someone with arthritic hands to use a potato peeler, her primary objective was not to maximize profits for her consultancy. Rather, she had an intrinsic desire to make a product that older people would find valuable in daily life.[47] Similarly, when I was proudly pushing my newborn twins around in their double buggy, it became obvious that it had been designed to meet the needs of parents like me: it was easy to turn the seats around so they could face me, it was built to traverse rugged terrain, and it had plenty of space to store nappies and shopping underneath. The company had probably spent a small fortune on focus groups to find out what features new parents were really after – and I'm personally glad they made this effort to empathise with their customers.

Relatively few firms can honestly claim to be at the high-empathy end of the spectrum. Most use empathic communication techniques to keep their profit margins healthy and shareholders happy, rather than to boost consumer wellbeing and welfare. Empathy is reduced to being a tool to help companies succeed in a narrow monetary sense. In such cases the term 'empathy marketing' is something of a misnomer – it's not much more than plain old 'marketing'.

Empathy marketing serves as a warning for how we approach the craft of conversation in our own lives. We need to remain vigilant of our intentions when communicating with others. If we let self-interest get the better of us, and conversation becomes a means for dominating, manipulating and getting our own way, then we are betraying the empathic ideal. On the other hand, if our conversations are led by concern for others, then our empathising will bear the mark of integrity.

Creative spirit

At its best, conversation is a form of adventure. Like the idea of Socratic dialogue, if you bring two people together with different viewpoints and experiences, the encounter between them can create something unexpected and new. This is just what happened in the early 1950s when Francis Crick and

James Watson immersed themselves in endless discussions about genetics from their different disciplinary perspectives – a conversation that resulted in the discovery of the structure of DNA. As Theodore Zeldin writes:

> Conversation is a meeting of minds with different memories and habits. When minds meet, they don't just exchange facts: they transform them, reshape them, draw different implications from them, engage in new trains of thought. Conversation doesn't just reshuffle the cards: it creates new cards . . . A satisfying conversation is one which makes you say what you have never said before.[48]

A fifth trait of highly empathic people is that they approach conversation in this creative spirit. They believe that by delving into the worldview of another person, and sharing their own with them, they might emerge slightly altered by the experience, and have empathic insights that offer fresh thoughts and perspectives. For this to happen in our own lives, we need to break the pattern of dialogue that dwells on the superficial and skates over the surface of our most important concerns and priorities. There are great benefits of doing so. A study at the University of Arizona revealed that people with high levels of life satisfaction or 'happiness' have twice as many substantive conversations (e.g. about love, religion, politics) and engage in only one-third as much small talk (e.g. gossip, talking about the weather) than those with low life satisfaction.[49] The research suggests that conversation, like empathy, is good for us.

How should we go about having more of these creative and substantive conversations? One reason that conversational life can lack depth and excitement is that we easily fall into using formulaic questions to open a dialogue – How are you? What was the weather like? What do you do? How was your weekend? Although such questions can be important social lubricants, in themselves they generally fail to spark an engaging and enriching empathic exchange. We answer 'fine' or 'OK' then move on down the corridor.

The way a conversation begins can be a major determinant of where it goes. So it is worth experimenting with adventurous openings. Instead of greeting a workmate with 'How are things?', try taking your conversation in a different direction with something mildly unusual like, 'What have you been thinking about this morning?' or 'What was the most surprising thing that happened to you over the weekend?' You need to come up with the kinds of questions that suit your own personality. The point is to break conventions so your conversations become energising, memorable and vehicles for empathic discovery. (I recommend steering clear of clichés like, 'If you could be any animal, what would you be?') By the way, if you are bold with your questions, people won't think you are mad – just a little eccentric. And they might even thank you for it.

Sheer courage

There is a final conversational habit that is essential for making the empathic leap into other minds, and that serves as a common denominator of those I have already discussed: sheer courage. We need courage to experiment with creative openings, to put others' concern before our own, to take off our masks, to listen sensitively to people's feelings and needs, and to exercise curiosity about strangers. Moreover, courage enables us to have those really difficult conversations that we would much rather avoid, but which may offer the greatest scope for cementing empathic attachments. What does a courageous conversation look like? Jo Berry knows.

In 1984, when Jo was twenty-seven, her father, Conservative MP Sir Anthony Berry, was killed by an IRA bomb at the Party Conference in Brighton. In 1999, one of the IRA members who had been convicted for the bombing, Pat Magee, was released from prison under the terms of the Good Friday Agreement. Jo's immediate response was a desire to meet him. She felt that attempting to create a relationship with the man who had killed her father was what she needed to overcome her anguish and anger. 'I wanted to meet Pat to put a face to the enemy, and see him as a real human being,' she said. Pat agreed to talk with her, and since their first encounter they have met over fifty times, gradually – and often painstakingly – developing an understanding of one another's perspectives on the bombing. 'For me the question is whether I can let go of my need to blame, and open my heart enough to hear Pat's story and understand his motivations,' explains Jo, 'and the truth is that sometimes I can and sometimes I can't.' Jo is often asked whether she forgives Pat, and her response is that forgiveness is not the right word. What really matters, she says, is empathy:

> I don't talk about 'forgiveness'. To say 'I forgive you' is almost condescending – it locks you into an 'us and them' scenario keeping me right and you wrong. That attitude won't change anything. But I can experience empathy. Sometimes when I've met with Pat, I've had such a clear understanding of his life that there's nothing to forgive. I've realised that no matter what side of the conflict you're on, had we all lived each other's lives, we could all have done what the other did. In other words, if I had come from a Republican background, I could easily have made the same choices Pat made.[50]

Jo's courage to empathise with the enemy has had a major impact on her life. She has forged an unlikely and remarkable friendship, found a way to deal with her despair about her father's death, and has been moved to start an organisation called Building Bridges for Peace, which aims to use dialogue and non-violence to promote peaceful solutions to violent conflicts.

Her story shows that not only can empathy emerge in the most extreme contexts, but it has the power to transform individual lives and contribute to social change. It also raises a question. If Jo Berry can find the courage to talk to Pat Magee, couldn't we each discover the courage to embark on those difficult conversations that we have been putting off for months or even years? We might issue ourselves a challenge: over the next twenty-four hours, what action could we take to begin one of these conversations? Perhaps you could pick up the phone and speak to your daughter about the issue that has been keeping you apart. Or maybe write a snail-mail letter to someone you've hurt or betrayed. The choice – and the opportunity – is yours.

Jo Berry *(right)* standing next to Pat Magee, the man who killed her father.

Empathy with yourself?

Having now explored the six elements of the craft of conversation – curiosity about strangers, radical listening, removing your mask, concern for the other, a creative spirit, and sheer courage – it becomes possible to appreciate just how powerful the simple act of talking to another human being can be for making the empathic leap into their mind. To harness the full potential of conversation, however, we must always be wary of reducing it to a set of techniques. Bringing each element to life involves rethinking your philosophy of conversation rather than following a check list that tells you what to say, and exactly how and when to say it. Only with an attitude of freedom and spontaneity will empathic conversation fully flower.

But could there be a seventh element in the craft of conversation? Over the past two decades a growing number of thinkers have suggested that extending empathy towards other people, particularly in conversations, requires a degree of 'self-empathy'.[51] If we cannot empathise with ourselves, they believe, we will lack the psychological foundations necessary to connect with others. Advocates of self-empathy typically describe it as becoming aware of our own feelings and needs, and not constantly beating ourselves up and judging ourselves too harshly (e.g. not blaming ourselves, feeling guilty, or being consumed by a sense of failure). In some fundamental way, self-empathy is about being good to yourself and liking who you are.

Despite its increasing popularity, I am sceptical about the notion of self-empathy. One reason is that it strikes me as conceptually flawed. The central meaning of empathy, for more than a century, has been about breaking out of the boundaries of the self, and comprehending the feelings and perspectives of *other people*. It is about looking through *their* eyes rather than staring into your inner self – that is, empathy concerns outrospection rather than introspection. A second reason is that it makes the meaning of empathy too broad and indistinct. Once empathy becomes associated with the whole gamut of ways in which we think about our own self-worth and internal emotional landscape, there is a danger that it loses its analytical bite and potential as a clear guiding concept for individual and social transformation. Just as I believe the word empathy should not be simply equated with acts of kindness and everyday generosity, so too I think it should not be watered down to cover the various aspects of what has been described as 'self-empathy'.

But this is not to say that how we feel about ourselves is unimportant for our ability to bond empathically with others. It is just that we need another word. What are the contenders? One is 'self-compassion', a term that, like 'self-empathy', has emerged since the 1990s as a product of our individualist culture, but that may have firmer conceptual foundations. Drawing on Buddhist notions of compassion, psychologist Kristin Neff defines self-compassion as having three components: 'self-kindness – being kind and understanding toward oneself in instances of pain or failure rather than being harshly self-critical; common humanity – perceiving one's experiences as part of the larger human experience rather than seeing them as separating and isolating; and mindfulness – holding painful thoughts and feelings in balanced awareness rather than over-identifying with them.'[52] As with self-empathy, however, I find self-compassion a somewhat confusing idea, because the linguistic origin of 'compassion' is to share in the suffering of another person. The second component of Neff's definition touches on other people's suffering, but not the first or third.

My own preference is to revive the ancient Greek term *philautia* or 'self-love'. The Greeks recognised a negative version of self-love, which was about being self-interested and narcissistic, and only concerned with the pursuit of your own wealth, power and glory. But there was also a more positive and healthy version of *philautia*, which was the idea that if you like yourself and feel secure in yourself, then you will have a deep well of inner emotional strength and self-knowledge to draw upon to care about others. Aristotle was especially aware of the importance of this benevolent form of self-love, when he wrote, 'All friendly feelings for others are an extension of man's feelings for himself.'[53]

If Aristotle were alive today, I think he would have been an enthusiastic advocate of *philautia* as a necessary basis for empathic understanding, believing that people who are not at ease with themselves or who harbour a degree of self-loathing will struggle to relate to the feelings, needs, and worldviews of others. If you want to step into someone else's skin, you need to feel comfortable in your own.

With a helpful dose of self-love, most of us can become fine practitioners of the craft of conversation, and penetrate the great darkness of hidden thoughts that surrounds us.

HABIT 5

TRAVEL IN YOUR ARMCHAIR

Can you change the world from your living room?

'It was through books that I first realised there were other worlds beyond my own; first imagined what it might be like to be another person,' wrote the novelist Julian Barnes.[1] It is an enticing thought that reading fiction might help us escape the straitjacket of our egos and personal experiences, and expand our empathic horizons. Many modern literary theorists are, however, decidedly sniffy about the notion. 'They see the idea as too middlebrow, too therapeutic, too kitsch, too sentimental, too Oprah,' according to psychologist Steven Pinker.[2] Reading even the most moving story, say the critics, may have almost no impact on our actual behaviour, and possibly leave us more prejudiced than when we began. Yet there is a growing body of evidence confirming that literature, photography, film and other art forms do indeed have the ability to take us on imaginative journeys into lives that are profoundly unlike our own, and also to inspire empathic acts on the behalf of others once we have put down the novel or left the cinema.

Highly empathic people recognise that while words and pictures offer only second-hand experience rather than the real thing, they deserve to be taken seriously, and not dismissed as little more than 'empathy lite'. Why? Because art has a long and distinguished history, going back centuries, of kicking our empathic selves into action, be it for the struggle against child labour or the anti-war movement. We need to explore how we can become discerning in our consumption of books and artworks, so that we are not simply entertained, but also empathically engaged.

I think of this as 'armchair empathy', a form of travel that you can do in your own living room. But as you recline in your rocker, there is a good chance that as well as having books by your side or a DVD remote control in your hand, you are probably also within easy reach of a laptop or smart phone. Social networks, video games, chat rooms and other forms of online culture have opened up new possibilities for the pursuit of armchair empathy, enabling us to connect with millions of people around the planet. The arrival of the digital age raises important questions for the future of empathy. Can networks such as Facebook help promote meaningful human relationships, or are they fuelling superficial interactions? Are we developing 'e-personalities' that amplify the narcissistic side of our natures more than our *homo empathicus*? And what might the ideal 'empathy app' look like?

As we will discover, the potential of the internet has been exaggerated and it may in fact pose one of the greatest threats to a global empathy revolution. First, though, let's travel from the digital age back to the Iron Age, and take our seats in the world of ancient Greek theatre.

Theatre and film: war through enemy eyes

In the spring of 472 BC the people of Athens queued up to see the latest play written by Aeschylus, the founder of Greek tragedy. *The Persians* was an unusual production, and not only because it was based on an historical event rather than the usual legends of the gods. What must have really shocked the audience was that it was told through the eyes of their sworn enemy, the Persians, who only eight years earlier had fought the Athenians at the Battle of Salamis.

It recounts the story of the expeditionary forces sent by the Persian monarch Xerxes, and how the invaders were utterly crushed by their Greek rivals. When a messenger brings news of the defeat of their army and navy at Salamis, the Persian council of elders cry out: 'O grief and grief again! Weep every heart that hears / This cruel, unlooked-for pain.' Instead of glorifying the Athenians, Aeschylus focuses attention on the wives of lost Persian soldiers, who 'each with tender tears in vain, weeps out her lonely life'. The audience is drawn in to feel the personal sorrows of their military rivals and to see the battle from the perspective of the vanquished barbarians.

Although some Athenians watching the unfolding drama may have been gloating over their victory with uncharitable *Schadenfreude*, Aeschylus was asking them to undertake the radical act of empathising with the defeated enemy just at their moment of triumph. Even more striking is the fact that the playwright had himself fought the Persians at the earlier Battle of Marathon, where his own brother had been killed. Perhaps when composing the play, he was remembering that while 191 Athenians died in the conflict, 6,400 Persians had been killed. 'It won't have escaped him,' writes the classics scholar Peter Smith, 'that many Persian women had been widowed that day, that many more Persian mothers than Greek ones had lost their sons.' Their imagined cries may have been haunting Aeschylus ever since.[3]

Tragedies such as *The Persians* were performed at the annual festival of Dionysus, the god of transformation. Indeed, the Greeks believed that drama could have a transformative effect on the audience. Unlike the social isolation of watching a DVD at home today, Greek theatre was a deeply communal activity, where the experience of weeping together in response to the characters' personal suffering and moral dilemmas helped to strengthen the bonds of citizenship. Aristotle observed that tragedy also educated the emotions: it enabled people to see their own troubles in wider perspective, and encouraged those who were self-centred to feel compassion for others. As Karen Armstrong suggests, when the audience shed tears for the Persians or were moved by the grief of Heracles after he kills his wife and children in a fit of divine madness, they

> had achieved a Dionysian *ekstasis*, a 'stepping out' of ingrained preconceptions in an empathy which, before seeing the play, they would probably have deemed impossible . . . Tragic drama reminds us of the role that art can play in expanding our sympathies. Plays, films and novels all enable us to enter imaginatively into other lives and make an empathic identification with people whose experiences are entirely different from our own.[4]

Theatre was a genuinely popular art form in Ancient Greece: even prisoners were temporarily released from gaol so they could watch the drama competitions during the festival of Dionysus. Now we are much more likely to sit down in front of a film than to see a play. But how often do our cinematic experiences result in empathic *ekstasis*, a stepping out of ourselves? The answer depends on our personal tastes. You could easily spend your days watching action films, fantasy adventures or comedies that rarely catapult you into the perspectives of other people. Yet there are a surprisingly large number of feature films whose power derives from the director's effort to create an empathic immersion that rivals Greek tragedy.

An especially effective genre, whose origins go back to plays like *The Persians*, is war movies in which the story is told from the viewpoint of enemy soldiers. An example appears in a pair of films directed by Clint Eastwood, released in 2006, about the Battle for Iwo Jima in the Second World War. One film, *Flags of Our Fathers*, is a fairly standard portrayal of the sorrows of war, depicting the battle through the eyes of US Marines. More unusually, *Letters from Iwo Jima* reveals the very same bloody encounter from the perspective of Japanese soldiers – and is entirely in Japanese. By showing the 'enemy' standpoint, especially the suffering and humiliation of their defeat, the film questions simplistic notions of nationalism, patriotism and triumphalism, and breaks down the barriers between 'us' and 'them'. As Eastwood remarked of the film, 'What it boils down to is when mothers are losing their sons, whether Japanese or American – whatever nationality – their reaction always has the same pathos.'[5] Aeschylus would have surely agreed.

If you are looking for an unforgettable experience of Dionysian *ekstasis*, the film to watch from this genre is the 1930 version of *All Quiet on the Western Front*. Based on the novel by Erich Maria Remarque, it tells the story of a German foot soldier, Paul Bäumer, who enlists in the fervour of schoolboy patriotism to fight against the French in the First World War. It is astonishing that an anti-war movie from the perspective of a German soldier was produced in Hollywood only a dozen years after the armistice. An even greater achievement is that it contains what may be the most powerful empathic scene in cinema history – one that Studs Terkel thought 'tells us all we need to know of the absurdity of war'.[6]

Paul is surrounded by gunfire and jumps into a trench for cover. An instant later, a French soldier drops into the trench with him. Without a moment of thought, Paul draws his dagger and stabs him in the chest. The soldier is mortally wounded, but still breathing. Paul washes the blood off his hands and the soldier writhes before him, slowly dying. The gunfire continues and Paul, forced to take shelter in the trench overnight, cannot escape the soldier's presence. At first he is irritated by the Frenchman's wheezing final breaths, yet with the passing hours he is overcome by remorse. 'I want to help you,' Paul pleads, offering his enemy a little water. But it is too late, the soldier is dead. Paul responds with an anguished soliloquy:

> I didn't want to kill you. I tried to keep you alive. If you jumped in here again, I wouldn't do it. You see, when you jumped in here, you were my enemy – and I was afraid of you. But you're just a man like me, and I killed you. Forgive me, comrade. Say that for me. Say you forgive me! . . . Oh, no, you're dead! Only you're better off than I am – you're through – they can't do any more to you now . . . Oh, God! why did they do this to us? We only wanted to live, you and I. Why should they send us out to fight each other? If they threw away these rifles and these uniforms, you could be my brother.

Paul in the trench, comforting the French soldier he has just stabbed. From *All Quiet on the Western Front* (1930).

It is a classic instance of humanising the 'other': Paul has come to see his adversary as a fellow human being who has also been used as a pawn by the generals and politicians. But there is a final moment of empathic recognition still to come. Paul reaches inside the soldier's coat pocket and draws out his identification papers. He has a name, Gérard Duval, and there is a photo of his wife and daughter. Paul now understands that he has killed not only a brother in arms, but a unique individual, with a family, with emotions, with a home to go back to, just like him. 'I'll write to your wife,' he tells the dead man. 'I'll write to her. I promise she'll not want for anything. And I'll help her, and your parents, too. Only forgive me. Forgive me. Forgive me . . .' He weeps, his head at the feet of the frozen body of Gérard Duval.

All Quiet on the Western Front won the Academy Award for Best Picture in 1930 and was an international blockbuster seen by millions of people around the world. Its empathic, anti-war message had an electrifying effect that went far beyond the movie houses. 'Having seen *All Quiet on the Western Front* I became a pacifist,' remembers the film historian Andrew Kelly. So too did tens of thousands of others. Even the actor who played Paul, Lew Ayres, was converted into a conscientious objector as a result of his role, and refused to fight in the Second World War. Reflecting on the enormous influence of the film, Ayres thought that it 'showed the Germans as having the same values as you and I have . . . just people caught up in this thing that's bigger than all of us . . . *All Quiet on the Western Front* became one of the first voices of universality . . . [it said] that unity was possible within the world'.[7]

At the time of its release, the film was deemed so powerful and incendiary that many governments went out of their way to stop people watching it, believing that it encouraged anti-nationalist and anti-war sentiment. *All Quiet* was banned in Austria, Italy, New Zealand, the Soviet Union and China, and heavily censored in Australia, France, and other countries. It was especially controversial in Germany. A Nazi newspaper described it as 'a

Jewish lie' and 'a hate film slandering the German soldier'. On the film's opening night in Berlin, Nazi activists released white mice and stink bombs in the cinema, causing a riot, and Joseph Goebbels led a street demonstration outside. Six days after the premiere, it was banned nationwide.[8] When Hitler came to power in 1933, Remarque fled Germany to Switzerland to avoid persecution. His sister was not so lucky: ten years later, in revenge for her brother's escape, she was put on trial in a People's Court and beheaded.

There is little doubt that films can ignite the *homo empathicus* that dwells within us. We can journey into the lives of persecuted minorities through films such as *Schindler's List*, or the Australian drama *Rabbit-Proof Fence*, based on a true story about two mixed-race Aboriginal girls – part of the so-called 'Stolen Generations' – attempting to escape forced internment in a re-education camp in the 1930s run by white government authorities. An alternative is *The Elephant Man*, which concerns the Victorian social outcast John Merrick who was disfigured by a terrible disease; you will never forget him crying out, 'I am not an animal – I am a human being!' Other films transport us into distant cultures, like the dilemmas of being a young boy growing up on the streets of Kabul (*The Kite Runner*), or convey the experiences of those confronting life's challenges, such as being deaf (*Children of a Lesser God*) or destitute (*The Grapes of Wrath*). Some directors strive to convey the visceral feeling of being another person: skilful camera work in Julian Schnabel's *The Diving Bell and the Butterfly* creates an almost unbearable sense of being trapped inside the body of a man who is completely paralysed, except for the ability to blink his left eyelid.

The empathic impact of a film can be undermined, however, when there is an overload of cinematic wizardry that gets in the way. A recent example is James Cameron's sci-fi extravaganza *Avatar*, which the political scientist Gary Olson describes as 'a dangerously empathic film of the first order' ('dangerous', for him, is a positive attribute, meaning 'politically radical').[9]

Cameron wants us to empathise with the cyan-skinned, ten-foot tall, nature-loving Na'vi people, whose planet is being destroyed by human beings and their anonymous corporations – an obvious metaphor for our current degradation of the environment and the habitats of indigenous peoples. The main character, Marine Jake Sully, literally occupies the body of a Na'vi and, by walking in their shoes, is converted to their way of life and to fight for their cause. The problem is that this empathic messaging is buried under an assault of special effects and hi-tech gadgetry, such as spectacular flying battles between giant alien dragons and menacing spacecraft with blazing gunfire. In contrast, a movie such as *All Quiet on the Western Front* has a sparse, theatre-like quality that brings out the personal, empathic moments with an emotional power that *Avatar* lacks.[10]

I am not saying that we should dismiss films that fail to set our empathic brains alight, or that do not even attempt to do so. Rather, my point is that cinema offers opportunities for stepping into the shoes of people whose lives we may never have a chance to understand through direct experience or conversation. We can all develop the habit of valuing films not just for their ability to entertain us, but for their capacity to stimulate us to think and act with greater empathic sensitivity. So here is an idea: set up your own Empathy Film Club. Gather some friends and jointly draw up a list of films on empathic themes that interest you all – maybe the struggles of ageing or life in prison. After watching and discussing them, you can then share them online.

Photography: the political power of empathic images

Since the Middle Ages, Christian paintings of the crucifixion have been used to communicate the physical reality of Jesus's suffering on the cross. Early works were quite genteel, but by the sixteenth century they had become far more gory, depicting nails piercing flesh, gaping wounds and seeping blood, so the viewer could both see what Christ endured and also feel something of his bodily agony. In Matthias Grünewald's 1515 Isenheim Altarpiece, for example, Christ's torturously extended arms and upturned fingers give the impression that he has been stretched out on an inquisitor's rack before being nailed to the cross. Just looking at a reproduction makes my fingers twitch and hands sweat (and gives me a few goosebumps too, despite my lack of Christian belief). This kind of empathic contagion effect is entirely intentional, suggests art historian Jill Bennett:

> The images developed from the late medieval period with the express function of inspiring devotion were not simply the 'Bible of the unlettered' in the sense of translating words into images. Rather, they conveyed the essence of Christ's sacrifice, the meaning of suffering, by promoting and facilitating an empathic imitation of Christ.[11]

The empathic effect of paintings – both religious and secular – has been confirmed by research in the new scientific field of neuroaesthetics. A study of works by Michelangelo and Goya argues that the mirror neurons in our brains enable us to have 'automatic empathic responses', in which we directly experience the emotional content of the images through a process known as 'embodied simulation'.[12] Yet to what extent can looking at a picture not just stimulate our neural networks but actually result in changes in individual and social behaviour? Answers can be found in photography, which by the early twentieth century had replaced painting as the dominant medium for the still image. To understand the potential force of photos to erode our empathy deficits, we need to travel back to the early days of social documentary photography and the ground-breaking work of Lewis Hine.

Child labour was rife in the United States at the beginning of the last century: around one in every six children aged under fifteen was employed in industry or agriculture.[13] In 1904, the National Child Labor Committee, a major charitable foundation, was founded to fight for new laws to ban the use of under-age workers. As part of their strategy, between 1908 and 1924 they employed Lewis Hine – a former school teacher in New York City – to document cases of child labour around the country. It was a challenging assignment: the last thing factory owners wanted was a photographer snooping around and gathering evidence of barefoot children slaving away on poverty wages. But Hine managed to talk his way in, often pretending to be a machinery salesman or fire inspector, taking incriminating photos as he walked the factory floors. Over the years, his subjects included six-year-olds who repaired the threads on giant spinning machines in textile mills, young boys gritted in black dust from working in coal mines, little girls who shucked oysters in canneries at three in the morning, and thousands of their fellow child labourers at work in cotton fields, sweatshops, and glass factories.

Lewis Hine's photo of a 'little spinner' in the Mollohan Cotton Mill, Newberry, South Carolina, 1908. What was she thinking?

Hine's shocking images were seen by people nationwide in newspapers and magazines, and in a stream of publications issued by the National Child Labor Committee. They were undeniable evidence that exploitative child labour was a reality – not just a figment of the imagination of Progressive reformers. The photos created a mass public outcry. One newspaper reporter, who saw an exhibition of Hine's work in Birmingham, Alabama, wrote:

> There has been no more convincing proof of the necessity of child labour laws . . . than these pictures showing the suffering, the degradation, the immoral influence, the utter lack of anything that is wholesome in the lives of these poor little wage earners. They speak far more eloquently than any [written] work – and depict a state of affairs which is terrible in its reality – terrible to encounter, terrible to admit that such things exist in civilized communities.[14]

According to cultural historian Alan Trachtenberg, what made Hine's images so compelling was that they went beyond cold statistics and awakened the viewer's 'imaginative empathy with the pictured others', and created an 'empathetic response to the inner humanity of the subjects'.[15] The images profoundly affected people on an individual level, but also shifted public policy. They 'were so devastating', writes historian Russell Freedman, that 'they convinced people that the United States needed laws against child labour'. In 1912 they helped bring about the establishment of the United States Children's Bureau, a federal government agency charged with preventing child labour. Partly as a result of Hine's photos, the number of child workers in the US was halved between 1910 and 1920.[16]

Since Hine's era, social documentary photography has passed through several defining stages that have reshaped its empathic impact. During the Great Depression in the 1930s, Dorothea Lange and Walker Evans produced images enabling millions of Americans to understand what it might be like to experience rural poverty – the worn and desperate look of a migrant mother with her hungry children, the tragic gaze of an Alabama tenant farmer. In the 1960s, photographs of the Vietnam War revealed the power of images of violence to create political change. Nick Ut's photo of a naked, napalmed girl was amongst those that helped mobilise opposition to the war in the United States – and simultaneously convinced military and government officials that they needed to maintain far tighter control over the images that reached the public eye. Such photographs often derived their force not just by generating empathy for the victims, but by provoking feelings of horror, anger, moral repugnance and guilt in the viewer.[17] This was similarly the case with the images of famine in developing countries that began to emerge in the late 1960s, such as Don McCullin's renowned picture of a starving albino boy in Biafra.

By the mid-1970s photography critics were starting to question whether images of poverty and violence still had the power to produce significant social and empathic impact. Leading the charge was Susan Sontag, who argued in her influential essay On Photography that people had now seen so many images of suffering and destitution in newspapers, magazines and on television, that they no longer had much effect. 'The shock of the photographed atrocities wears off with repeated viewings,' she wrote, and 'in these last decades "concerned" photography has done at least as much to deaden conscience as to arouse it'.[18] Since then, Sontag's many postmodern followers have reinforced her message that we have seriously overdosed on images of misery, social injustice and human rights abuses. Looking at a newspaper photo of refugees scrambling for rations or a child soldier staring down the camera lens might still sometimes shock us or induce feelings of pity, but typically does little to generate sustained empathic action. We are, they suggest, victims of emotional fatigue.[19]

Yet are we really so immune? Thousands of organisations working on social justice issues clearly do not agree, since they continue to use photographs to alert the public to human suffering and to gain support for their causes. Just look at the charity appeals that come through your letter box: an image of a girl with a missing arm that was blown off by a land mine, or a family next to their home that was reduced to rubble by an earthquake. Humanitarian organisations know from their research that while some people will throw the pamphlets straight in the bin, others will be moved to donate or take other forms of action.

Over the last decade there has been a noticeable shift in the kinds of photographs that are used for such public appeals, which is revealing of the growing importance of empathy in cultural life. In the past, an international development charity might show a harrowing photo of a starving child standing forlorn in a parched landscape. These images were used to convey helplessness, suffering and the violation of childhood innocence, and their main effect was to invoke sympathy and guilt in the viewer. While these kinds of photographs remain common, we are increasingly likely to see images that portray the subjects with dignity and a sense of empowerment, such as a group of women farmers in Africa carrying hoes on their shoulders or children playing together near a new water well. The latter photos are much more about empathy than sympathy: they reveal our common humanity with the subjects, and convey that they deserve our respect rather than our pity.

Even stronger evidence of the power of empathic photography emerges from what we *don't* see, or more accurately, what we are not permitted to see. In the recent wars in Iraq and Afghanistan, for instance, thousands of soldiers and civilians have been killed, but how often have we seen images of their maimed and charred bodies? Hardly ever. Western governments regularly censor the pictures, so we are not exposed to the shattered skull of one of 'our' soldiers, or the bullet-ridden corpse of a child who happened to get in the way of a raid, even after the evening watershed (although we are allowed to look at mutilated bodies in late-night crime thrillers). The Bush Administration went so far as to prohibit media images of the flag-draped coffins of US military personnel killed in action in Iraq. As political scientist Gary Olson contends, governments try to shield us from photographs of the violent realities of war because they worry that our empathic responses could jeopardise support for military intervention: 'the tremendous amount of deception and fraud expended by US elites on behalf of dampening or denying opportunities for empathic engagement are based on a real fear of the public's nascent sense of empathy.'[20] This fear of empathic images is revealing of their potentially subversive power.

How does this all relate to developing our empathic selves? If we listened solely to critics like Susan Sontag, we might place little hope in photography as a way of stepping into other people's lives. But we need to recognise that it continues to be a potent means of helping us understand the pain and suffering of strangers. 'Why are photographs so good at making us see cruelty?' asks the cultural thinker Susie Linfield. 'Partly, I think, because photographs bring home to us the reality of physical suffering with a literalness and irrefutability that neither literature nor painting can claim . . . Photographs excel, more than any other form of either art or journalism, in offering an immediate, viscerally emotional connection to the world.'[21] Lewis Hine knew this well, and his legacy lives on in the great social documentary and political photographers of our own era, such as James Nachtwey, Sebastião Salgado, Gilles Peress and David Goldblatt.

Photography also works because it feeds our visual intelligence. We learn not just through reading words or analysing statistics, but by having images branded onto our minds and memories. If you want to understand life under Apartheid in South Africa, you should certainly read Nelson Mandela's autobiography. But it can be just as illuminating to spend time at an exhibition of David Goldblatt's photos from the 1970s and 1980s of Afrikaner farmers and black bus commuters. Equally, anyone hoping to grasp the humanitarian consequences of wealth inequality and debt bondage in Brazil should turn to Sebastião Salgado's unforgettable images of workers at the Serra Pelada gold mine. Photography, like film, remains a potent medium for our empathic education.

Literature: can we learn empathy from novels?

For nearly three hundred years literary critics and writers have debated whether reading fiction has the power to expand our empathy and deepen our morality. In the eighteenth century, there was a great distrust of literature. It was commonly argued that the growing corpus of romantic novels – especially those coming from France – would corrupt the young and pervert their imaginations, stirring up passions that might result in illicit sexual activity. During the Victorian period, however, it was increasingly believed that fiction, particularly 'social problem' novels, could have a positive influence on individual morality and civic life. Spending an evening absorbed in Charles Dickens' *Oliver Twist* or *Hard Times* alerted the comfortable middle-class reader to grinding urban poverty and the growing gulf between rich and poor in industrial England.[22] Amongst the most vocal nineteenth-century advocates of the power of literature was the novelist George Eliot (Mary Anne Evans). She was convinced that reading could develop 'sympathy', or what we would now call empathy:

> The greatest benefit we owe to the artist, whether painter, poet or novelist, is the extension of our sympathies. Appeals founded on generalizations and statistics require a sympathy ready-made, a

moral sentiment already in activity; but a picture of human life such as a great artist can give, surprises even the trivial and the selfish into that attention to what is apart from themselves, which may be called the raw material of moral sentiment. When Scott takes us into Luckie Mucklebackit's cottage, or tells the story of 'The Two Drovers,' – when Wordsworth sings to us the reverie of 'Poor Susan,' – when Kingsley shows us Alton Locke gazing yearningly over the gate which leads from the highway into the first wood he ever saw, – when Hornung paints a group of chimney-sweepers, – more is done towards linking the higher classes with the lower, towards obliterating the vulgarity of exclusiveness, than by hundreds of sermons and philosophical dissertations. Art is the nearest thing to life; it is a mode of amplifying experience and extending our contact with our fellow-men beyond the bounds of our personal lot.[23]

In recent years there has been a revival of this Victorian faith in literature as a vehicle for empathic transformation. The philosopher Martha Nussbaum recommends the reading of realist novels, which dwell on the experiences of everyday life rather than being excessively romantic or stylised. The realist fiction of writers such as Dickens and Eliot promotes 'empathetic imagining', which is an essential ingredient for strengthening the place of ethics in public life and countering our culture of self-interest. When we immerse ourselves in the struggles and suffering of the characters on the page, says Nussbaum, 'experiencing what happens to them as if from their point of view', the result can be that we come to 'concern ourselves with the good of other people whose lives are distant from our own'. Psychologist Steven Pinker takes a similar position, arguing that 'reading is a technology for perspective-taking' and that realist fiction 'may expand readers' circle of empathy by seducing them into thinking and feeling like people very different from themselves'. Likewise Keith Oatley, a cognitive psychologist and novelist, draws on a new wave of neuroscientific research providing evidence that 'the process of entering imagined worlds of fiction builds empathy and improves your ability to take another person's point of view'.[24]

So should all prospective empathic revolutionaries be putting themselves on a strict diet of realist fiction, priming their inner *homo empathicus* with novels by John Steinbeck, Zadie Smith and other heavyweights from the genre? Not so fast, warns the literary scholar Suzanne Keen, the leading contemporary sceptic of the empathic power of literature. In her view, advocates like Nussbaum and Pinker are victims of wishful thinking because the evidence that identifying with a character's feelings results in altruistic or pro-social behaviour is 'inconclusive at best and nearly always exaggerated in favour of the beneficial effects of reading'. In other words, you might feel a deep affinity with Dorothea in Eliot's *Middlemarch*, but reading about her is unlikely to change how you treat other people. Keen lays out a series of further charges. It is not clear whether reading novels makes people more empathic or whether the causal relationship runs the other way around, with those who read fiction being more likely to be empathic in the first place. A clever novelist, she suggests, might make us empathise with a protagonist whose views are morally repugnant, so we come to share their prejudices and biases. Furthermore, reading is so imbued with subjectivity, where we each respond in different ways to fictional worlds, that it is difficult to draw any definite conclusions about the kinds of narrative techniques – such as first-person narration – that are most likely to inspire empathy.[25]

I think Keen overstates her case. While I agree that empathically feeling the pains of a character in a novel may well have little discernible impact on our worldly actions, there is abundant evidence that fiction can have life-changing effects on readers, as we know from the myriads who turned against slavery after finishing *Uncle Tom's Cabin*, who campaigned against the workhouse system thanks to *Oliver Twist*, or who became pacifists after reading *All Quiet on the Western Front*.[26] Readers of early feminist novels such as Doris Lessing's *The Golden Notebook*, published in 1962, were swept up in a new understanding of women, which contributed to the budding women's liberation movement. Whole generations have had their minds altered by books such as *To Kill a Mocking Bird*, with its message that 'You never really understand another person until you consider things from his point of view – until you climb inside of his skin and walk around in it.'

Moreover, if you consider your personal experience, it is quite likely you can pinpoint novels that have expanded your own circle of empathy. What immediately comes to mind for me is a scene from Zadie Smith's *White Teeth*. A waiter in an Indian restaurant, barely noticed by the customers as he takes their orders, dreams of recovering his dignity by hanging a placard around his neck that declares to the world: 'I am not a waiter. I have been a student, a scientist, a soldier, my wife is called Alsana, we live in East London but we would like to move North. I am a Muslim but Allah has forsaken me or I have forsaken Allah, I'm not sure. I have a friend – Archie – and others. I am forty-nine but women still turn in the street. Sometimes.' Today, whenever I am in a restaurant, I wonder what each waiter or waitress would choose to write on their own biographical placard. That simple act of empathic imagining opens me to their individuality and subtly shifts my interactions with them.

Another novel that has become one of my empathic favourites is Christopher Wakling's *What I Did*, which is narrated by a six-year-old boy. The story opens with the boy sitting on the stairs at home, shoes in his hands, while his father shouts at him for taking so long to come down, since they are on their way out to the park. What we discover, by being immersed inside the boy's head, is that he is taking his time not to annoy his father, but because he is in the process of conducting an intricate scientific experiment about how friction operates to prevent his backside from sliding down the stairs. It made me laugh, but it also gave me an insight into my own four-year-old son. I suddenly understood that many of his infuriating habits – such as pouring his drinks from one glass into another and back again, often making a huge mess – could well be similar experiments that I should probably encourage rather than quash. The novel helped me recognise that I was not making enough effort to discover what was going on in his mind. I later interviewed Wakling, who is also a teacher of creative writing, and asked him whether he thought a novel could work if the author fails to make the reader empathise with the main characters:

> No. I don't think the reader has to like the main characters (though book-groups up and down the land are testimony to the fact that it helps if they do), but in order to believe in a fictional protagonist readers certainly have to understand where that character is coming from. What does the character want? Where did they begin? Where are they trying to go? These questions establish motive and are useful for the plot. But the bigger question – how does the character see the world? – has the power, if answered convincingly by a novelist, to immerse the reader in a new consciousness. Do that well and readers will care about the world of the novel beyond the last page.[27]

Empathy is at the heart of storytelling itself. Whether it is through high-brow literature or popular fiction, a fine novelist is an empathic magus who can enable us, if only temporarily, to shed our own skin and step into another way of looking at the world. It is worth thinking hard about which authors and what kinds of writing are most likely to expand your sensitivity to other people's lives. You could try out novels from the realist canon (though avoid those that are too didactic), but it might be more interesting to seek advice from a 'bibliotherapist'. Bibliotherapy, which has been pioneered at The School of Life in London since 2008 by writer-artist Ella Berthoud and novelist Susan Elderkin, is an unusual form of literary therapy. You talk to an expert advisor about both your reading habits and your dilemmas in life, and are then offered a bespoke reading 'prescription' based on your tastes and circumstances.[28] If you are a sci-fi buff seeking to expand your empathy, the bibliotherapists might suggest Ursula Le Guin's feminist sci-fi classic *The Left Hand of Darkness*. About to travel to India? They may advise you take Rohinton Mistry's *A Fine Balance*. Want to drill down deep into human nature and the limits of empathy? There is probably nothing better than Cormac McCarthy's *The Road*.

One day I hope all public libraries will offer a professional bibliotherapy service to help us choose wisely amongst the hundreds of thousands of books that are published each year. More immediately, you can post lists of your favourite empathy novels on the world's first digital Empathy Library, which you will find on the website for this book (www.romankrznaric.com/empathyrevolution), together with the non-fiction books, films, photographs and other artworks that do most to transport you into the shoes of strangers. By doing so, you will be playing a part in creating a global resource for the future of human relationships. My own suggestions for the library appear at the end this book and on the website.

Online culture: from digital revolution to empathy revolution?

The digital revolution is ushering in a new era for the pursuit of armchair empathy. Unlike books, movies or photographs, digital networks offer the prospect of instant connection with millions of people worldwide. The internet now has a genuinely global reach of 2.7 billion users. Even factory workers in Shanghai and smallholder farmers in Malawi are wired into digital communities through their phones (there are more phones in sub-Saharan Africa than in Europe).[29] Moreover, social media allows for two-way interactions, unlike the one-way communication of a film or a novel. With just a couple of clicks we could be talking to someone from almost any nation on the planet – and looking into their eyes – while still sitting in our homes and stroking the cat. According to social scientist Jeremy Rifkin, online culture may be leading us towards a truly empathic civilisation. 'New developments in internet connections,' he argues, make it 'possible to imagine a paradigmatic shift in human thought and a tipping point in global consciousness in less than a generation . . . the potential to experience empathic sensibility and to take it to a global level is now within reach'.[30]

How might we harness digital technologies to forge an age of empathy in the twenty-first century? I decided to tackle this question by setting out on a quest to discover the ultimate empathy app – one that would enable vast numbers of people to step into others' shoes and create strong emotional bonds with them. But my search has not been nearly as successful as I had imagined it would be. It turns out that existing online platforms provide limited scope for creating an empathy revolution. Instead, the digital technologies and applications currently on offer could be taking us back to an empathic dark age through their corrosive effects on the human personality.

My own hopes for empathy in online culture begin in my kitchen. Every Sunday morning my children wake up in Oxford and come down to have breakfast with their grandparents in Sydney. How so? Courtesy of Skype, Grandma and Grandpa appear on a laptop next to the jam and toast. The conversations were stilted at first – in part because my children were still learning to talk, and my father was learning not to talk over them – but gradually the technology has become less intrusive and their regular chats have been building bonds of love and empathy across the oceans that divide us all. Skype and other tools have been opening up such empathic conversations far beyond my kitchen. I have met school teachers in England who have digitally twinned their class with another in Kenya, so the pupils can speak to each other online and learn about their very different lives. I have come across organisations trying to create online conversations between coffee drinkers in rich countries and the people who grow the beans in poor ones.[31]

Early in my quest for the world's greatest empathy app, I became especially curious when I heard about Chatroulette, a chat website created by a Russian teenager in 2009, which now has around 1.5 million users worldwide. When you log in you are randomly connected with another person to have a live webcam conversation with them. If you would rather speak with someone else, simply click 'next', and you will be transported into another living room, anywhere from Murmansk to Minnesota. I quickly found out that there is not a lot of empathy on Chatroulette. People hit 'next' every two seconds on average, so there is little chance for deep dialogue. More significantly, as the technology researcher Sherry Turkle discovered, you are frequently presented with people masturbating, being rude to you, or just plain uninterested. 'Chatroulette takes things to an extreme: faces and bodies become objects,' observes Turkle, and there appears to be little desire or incentive to seek out our common humanity.[32] In principle a site like Chatroulette could be a massive empathy generator, since the technology lends itself to creating face-to-face conversations between strangers. With a different name – something like Empathy Connect – and a pop-up Menu of Conversation, it could attract people in search of cross-cultural understanding.

I felt a little more hopeful when I found Ambient, an app to 'connect with people around you who spark your interest, make your day or even change the course of your life'. You begin by creating a personal profile listing your favourite music, books and other passions, then as you walk the streets your phone will tell you if you are in the vicinity of another Ambient user who shares similar interests. The screen also lists the friends, if any, you have in common. You are then able to send a message to the person, for instance inviting them to meet for a coffee. The difficulty is that Ambient, like most interpersonal apps, is designed to connect you with people who share your interests and friends, whereas the most stimulating empathic encounters often grow from meeting people who are wildly different from you.

What about video games? I thought this was sure to be a barren realm, since so many games feature guns and violence. In *Grand Theft Auto: Vice City*, for example, players gain points by soliciting and killing prostitutes. Such games are hardly a training ground for the empathy revolution: in effect, players are groomed to be virtual psychopaths in a Hobbesian world.[33] But I have learned that there is an emerging community of people who are playing a growing number of empathy-based games, which are known in the industry as 'other people simulators'. One I have recently tried in a prototype version is *That Dragon, Cancer*, in which you take on the role of a man coping with his four-year-old son having been diagnosed with terminal cancer. Unlike most games, you are not granted any special powers, and instead have to deal with the emotional traumas of death and dying. Playing it is a compelling and emotionally wrenching experience.[34] I can also recommend a game called *PeaceMaker*, where you inhabit the role of either the Israeli Prime Minister or the Palestinian President and attempt to create a 'two-state solution' during a period of violent conflict. The creators describe it as a 'video game to promote peace' and stress that 'the primary conflict management issues that we address revolve around creating empathy and a deeper understanding of multiple perspectives'.[35] The game encourages cognitive empathy since it turns out that success depends on fostering cooperation by considering the viewpoints of a range of stakeholders including extremist and moderate political groups. It also stimulates affective empathy by using real photos and video footage of

A screen shot from the game PeaceMaker.

the conflict's impact on individual lives, such as a Palestinian mother weeping over dead relatives.

Let's be realistic. Games like *PeaceMaker* are still a minority sport. And in any case, the link between playing an empathy video game and then taking empathic action in the real world has not yet been subject to serious research. At the same time, most software developers have expressed little interest in creating platforms that are specifically designed to foster empathic connection, so we are left with the likes of Chatroulette instead. But surely, you might think, Facebook, Twitter and other popular social networks are enabling millions of people to be in constant touch with each other, and to share their thoughts and feelings about everything from their relationship troubles to their political ideologies and religious views. Isn't this vast web of digital connections and conversations giving a serious boost to the global empathy quotient?

This is, unfortunately, a utopian dream. Social media, and digital technologies more broadly, pose as many threats to empathy as they offer opportunities. A useful way to explore this – and the implications for each of our lives – is to take some advice from philosopher and virtual reality pioneer Jaron

Lanier, who believes that 'the most important question to ask about any technology is how it changes people'.[36] We need to investigate what the online world is doing to our minds and characters.

Lanier's pessimistic view is that the forms of social media and digital connectivity that dominate today are eroding human uniqueness and individuality. He points out that the first wave of web culture in the 1990s displayed a 'proud extroversion' that was visible in the quirky websites people designed for themselves. Following this early flowering, 'an endless series of gambits backed by gigantic investments encouraged young people entering the online world for the first time to create standardized presences on sites like Facebook'. Internet users have been increasingly fitting themselves into pre-existing personality boxes that define who they are, and have been reduced to 'multiple-choice identities'.[37] The result, declares novelist Zadie Smith, is that 'whatever is unusual about a person gets flattened out'. She reminds us that

> Facebook, our new beloved interface with reality, was designed by a
> Harvard sophomore with a Harvard sophomore's preoccupations.
> What is your relationship status? (Choose one. There can be only
> one answer. People need to know.) Do you have a 'life'? (Prove it.
> Post pictures.) Do you like the right sort of things? (Make a list.
> Things to like will include: movies, music, books and television,
> but not architecture, ideas, or plants.)

Such categories may make it easier to discover commonalities with other people and 'connect', but they also impoverish the complexity of human character. Moreover, there is the question of the quality of the connection. Most social media, claims Smith, 'encourages people to make weak, superficial connections with each other . . . Zuckerberg thinks the exchange of personal trivia is what "friendship" *is*'.[38] The pride people often take in having amassed thousands of 'friends' on Facebook or 'followers' on

Twitter is testament to the belief that it is the quantity rather than the quality of our relationships that is important. None of this is helped by the accumulating evidence that high-velocity digital culture is making our attention spans shorter and shallower. As we flit incessantly between windows and programmes, we are getting used to being in a state known as 'continuous partial attention', where our ability to fully concentrate for a prolonged period on a single task – such as reading an article or having a conversation – is diminished.[39]

The trouble is that empathy thrives best in relationships that have depth, and when we can immerse ourselves in other people's unique view of the world rather than a prefabricated online profile. Social networks might bring us into contact with global communities we feel part of (everyone who shares your love of origami, or Abba, or rainforest conservation), and alert us to important events in the lives of strangers (a news report on a tsunami in Japan, or a revolt on the streets of Damascus), but in and of themselves these networks are not usually designed to facilitate making the imaginative leap into other minds. They are about the efficient exchange of information rather than the less easily packaged exchange of intimacy. Can we really convey our most fundamental thoughts and feelings in a text or tweet and using emoticons? I fear not :-(. For anyone but a haiku poet, who we are, and what we care about in life, is difficult to express in one hundred and forty characters.

The Stanford psychiatrist Elias Aboujaoude argues that the problem is not so much that digital culture 'flattens' our personality but that it splits us in two. We gradually develop an 'e-personality' or 'e-identity' that is distinct from our offline personality: 'for every real being with an Internet hookup, there exists now a virtual version living side by side.'[40] What is more, our virtual selves are starting to dominate our lives. Being online is fast becoming our default state, with a growing proportion of people spending over half their waking hours wired into digital technology: the typical US teenager clocks up nearly eight hours each day online, updating their Facebook status, consuming media and texting their friends.[41]

There are some very real advantages to having a separate e-personality, according to Aboujaoude. Some people, he notes, find it easier to be emotionally open through their online self. It may also be a way to express your identity without fear of prejudice: if you are a gay teenager living in rural Texas, you might find an empathic community of interest online, whereas revealing your sexual orientation offline might lead to ostracism in your home town. But the dangers of the e-personality are all too apparent. One he highlights is the tendency to behave in a deceptive and self-aggrandising way. Whether it is through an online dating profile or a fully-fledged avatar on Second Life, we can find it hard to resist 'pretending to be thinner, more popular, and more successful than we really are'. There is always that temptation to tell a few lies on dating sites about our job, salary or education – and to airbrush our photograph as well.

Another danger is that the possibility of anonymity and invisibility creates an 'online disinhibition effect' where people feel licensed to engage in antisocial behaviour. I regularly receive extraordinarily rude and cruel comments on my online newspaper articles and video talks that people would almost certainly never be willing to say to my face. Cyberbullying, too, has become a serious problem amongst schoolchildren. Aboujaoude makes clear that 'the normal brake system, which under usual circumstances keeps thoughts and behaviours in check, constantly malfunctions on the information superhighway'.[42]

The most fundamental problem, however, is that our e-personality can drift towards narcissism, which then comes to infect our offline personality too. The most obvious manifestation of digital self-absorption is 'egosurfing' (also known as 'narcissurfing' or 'autogoogling'), defined as 'Googling yourself to see where, when, and how often you show up on the Internet' – 47 per cent of US adults admit to having done a vanity search.[43] It also appears in addictions such as constantly checking how many Twitter followers you have, or spending hours revising and fine-tuning your social media profiles, and posting messages designed to gain new 'friends' or more 'likes'. In effect, we are turning ourselves into virtual billboards, advertising and marketing our personalities to online consumers. It may be no surprise to learn of studies revealing that the more Facebook interactions people have with other users, the higher they score on narcissism tests.[44]

Yet clearly not everyone online is egosurfing and checking their 'friend' requests. Others are attempting to tap into the power of social media to create mass empathy and political change, as was seen during the Arab Spring and the Occupy Movement. The wave of global political revolt between 2009 and 2012, from Occupy Wall Street and student protests in Madrid to the mass demonstrations in Tunis and Tehran, would have been impossible without digital technology and social networks. Protesters were using Facebook to form groups, Twitter to disseminate news, and Yfrog, Flickr and YouTube to spread photos and videos. Underpinning the social media, says political analyst Paul Mason, was mobile telephony: 'in the crush of every crowd we see arms holding cellphones in the air, like small flocks of ostriches, snapping scenes of repression or revolt, offering instant and indelible image-capture to a global audience.'[45]

The protest movements were driven by a heady mixture of anger, anti-authoritarianism, political frustration, economic desperation, and the desire for individual freedom and community belonging. As Jeremy Rifkin points out, empathy also played a key role:

Young people took to the streets in protest against the flawed results in the Iranian election. One young woman, a pre-med student named Nadia, was demonstrating and her friend was videoing her and she was gunned down by the troops. Within an hour millions around the world knew her Facebook, her family, her relatives, what she was about. She was now a sister to millions of young people who could identify with her in a very, very deep way. That's global empathy. That's the beginning of an empathic civilization.[46]

The Arab Spring and Occupy Movement revealed that digital technology can help to channel and spread powerful emotions such as empathy and anger. But the revolts also showed that new technologies and social media platforms cannot in themselves sustain the emotional energy and practical action that mass movements require. Social media was a superb tool for the short-term objective of mobilising people to take part in public protests, and to communicate what was happening around the world, but it was less good at providing other essential ingredients of long-term social movement success. No amount of tweeting could help the Occupy Movement clarify their very general political goals, develop their leadership capacity and strategy, or maintain the passion of their supporters over a prolonged period. All these typically require face-to-face meeting and the hard, time-consuming work of collective organising. Moreover, let's not forget that while the web can generate intense empathic responses on a large scale – remember the Kony video? – it then often fails to convert them into widespread action in the real world. We could be sliding towards an era of what has been called 'slacktivism', where people delude themselves into thinking that watching a film clip or clicking an online petition constitutes authentic political activism.[47]

Bringing the analysis back to our own lives, how should we think about our personal relationship to digital technology?

As we become increasingly hooked into the wired world, we need to ask ourselves how it is re-shaping our character and relationships. Is the internet offering us 'thin' hyper-connection at the expense of 'thick' friendships where empathy can thrive? Are we using social media in selfish, self-aggrandising ways that feed our nascent narcissism? We are still at the earliest stages of understanding how this new culture is affecting the human personality. While I would like to be more optimistic, there is mounting evidence that the digital revolution, in its present form, is failing to send us on the path towards an empathic civilisation. Rather, we may be witnessing a revival of the 'Me Decade' of the 1970s. Digital technology, it seems, is amplifying the voice of *homo self-centricus*.

Anybody hoping to expand their empathy – and also preserve what they have got – should take a thoughtful, even cautious, approach to internet culture. The worst mistake we can make is to cultivate our online life without reflecting on how it is affecting our offline identity and the way we relate to other people. As Socrates would have put it, know thy digital self. If you find that the quick-fire repartee of social media is leaving you hungry for more profound friendships, or that you are being lured into egoism or apathy, then it might be time to go on a digital diet and start rationing your hours linked into the global electronic brain.

Despite such warnings, I remain committed to my quest to discover the most effective empathy app. But I have realised that we may have to look beyond what is currently on offer and invent new software that is intentionally designed to expand cognitive and affective empathy. My hope is that readers of this book with the right technical skills will be at the forefront of creating empathy apps that rival Chatroulette and Grand Theft Auto in their popularity, but which aim, instead, to provoke waves of action on the scale of Occupy and the Arab Spring.

In praise of *ekstasis*

Art and literature have been taking human beings on empathic journeys ever since the citizens of ancient Athens wept for the characters on stage during the festival of Dionysus. Theatre, film, fiction, painting and photography have all played a role in generating what the Greeks called *ekstasis*, or ecstasy, where we temporarily step outside of ourselves and are transported into other lives and cultures. At its very best, empathic *ekstasis* resembles the film *Being John Malkovich*, in which people crawl through a tiny door in a New York office block and slide down a tunnel into the mind of the famous actor, where they can literally look at the world through his eyes.

The limits of armchair empathy have been exaggerated. There may be critics who believe that mediums such as photography and the novel can do little to offer us deeply empathic experiences that lead to practical action, and are more likely to leave us emotionally numbed or unmoved. Yet if we remain discerning in our tastes, and opt for the finest empathic works that our cultures have produced – the kind that should be available in a virtual Empathy Library – then we may well be inspired to see the world in new ways and become makers of social change. On the other hand, I fear that we have been overstating the empathic potential of the digital technologies that we can so easily access from our armchairs. We must be vigilant that we do not use them in ways that erode our capacity to make the leap into other minds. We must also be wary of the internet's growing role as a 'meta-medium' through which we encounter photography, film, literature and other art forms, and ensure that it does not dampen our empathic responses to them.

In our ongoing efforts to expand our empathic abilities it may be difficult, or even impossible, to explore some people's lives through approaches such as direct experience or conversation.

How can a man ever experience what it feels like to be pregnant? What chance do you have of meeting a Samoan elder who you can talk to about religion or the meaning of love? So we will always need armchair empathy – to help us imagine all those hidden worlds that lie out of reach in our everyday lives.

HABIT 6
INSPIRE A REVOLUTION

Empathists of the World Unite!

You won't find the words 'Empathy Revolution' printed on many T-shirts. That is because empathy is usually associated with relationships between individuals rather than with radical social and political change. Yet it is time we rescued empathy from the realm of private life and unleashed its potential to transform public life as well. To do this, we need to grasp that empathy can be as much a collective phenomenon as an individual one. When a critical mass of people join together to make the imaginative leap into the lives of others, empathy has the power to alter the contours of history. For each and every one of us, the culmination of our empathic journeys is to help create these waves of collective empathy that can play a part in tackling the great problems of our age, from poverty and inequality to armed violence and environmental collapse.

The idea of collective empathy is especially relevant today because it counterbalances the highly individualistic focus of modern self-help culture, which tends to view the search for happiness or wellbeing as a personal pursuit concerning our own ambitions and desires, rather than one that involves working with others towards common goals. Yet thinkers going back to Aristotle have recognised that we are social animals, and that joy and meaning in life grow, in good part, from being immersed in something larger than ourselves. Human beings thrive on 'we' as much as 'me'. We may have *homo self-centricus* and *homo empathicus* jostling for space within us, but we need to make some room for *homo socioempathicus* too: we are creatures whose empathic selves are fully realised by acting together to create change.

How can we produce a surge of collective empathy that propels us from the self-obsessed Age of Introspection into a new Age of Outrospection? To start, we will find out what collective empathy looks like by exploring the greatest meetings of strangers in British history. We will then draw out lessons for practical action from the three great waves of empathy that have shaped the course of Western history: the invention of humanitarian organisations in eighteenth-century Europe, the extension of rights after the Second World War to new groups such as ethnic minorities, and the expansion of empathy in realms such as education and peace-building since the neuroscientific advances of the 1990s. Finally we will look to the future. Could we be developing a global empathic consciousness that embraces not only all human beings, but also animal and plant life, and even Gaia herself?

Empathy, as you are about to discover, can change not just ourselves, but the world. So let's get the T-shirt, unfurl the banners and launch an Empathy Revolution in the streets.

The greatest meeting of strangers in history

It is common to read accounts of mass empathic collapse – there are plenty of books about the massacres during the Crusades, the violence of colonialism in Latin America, or the genocide of the Holocaust. Far less effort, however, has been put into documenting when empathy has bloomed on a collective scale

– where whole communities have imaginatively stepped into the shoes of strangers, understood something of their suffering, and taken action to alleviate it. One of the most illuminating examples, which helps reveal how we might harness empathy to transform society, concerns the greatest meeting of strangers in British history.

A classic image of life in wartime Britain is a train platform filled with children clutching tiny suitcases and food parcels, being evacuated from the cities to escape the German bombs. There were several waves of evacuation between 1939 and 1944, in which over two million children were relocated from town to country as part of government schemes.[1] Rather than being placed in camps, they were mostly accommodated in private homes, and many stayed with their foster families for several years. The historian A.J.P. Taylor described evacuation as a 'social revolution' because of its huge impact on the creation of new

Evacuees waiting to board a train, 1940

child welfare policies.[2] And it was a revolution in which empathy played a crucial – though often overlooked – role.

The process of evacuation was fraught with practical and emotional difficulties, especially in the initial phase, before the Blitz in 1940. Billeting officers in the receiving towns and villages often could not find enough homes for the new arrivals, with upper-middle-class families being particularly reluctant to take in any children.[3] There were the notorious 'slave markets', where potential foster parents were able to pick and choose amongst the evacuees, stigmatising those who were left behind. Children suffered the trauma of being separated from their parents for long periods, and there were isolated cases of abuse. Foster mothers complained of bed-wetting, swearing and delinquency, and that the government payments were insufficient to cover the costs of their little guests.[4]

It is too easy, though, to dwell on the problems. Given the conditions of wartime austerity, the lack of time for planning, and the sheer novelty and extent of evacuation, it was extraordinarily successful. By and large, children were found accommodation, were well cared for by their host families, went to school and made friends. In the most authoritative study of social services in the war, Richard Titmuss asks us not to forget all those householders and evacuees 'who met each other in a spirit of tolerance and overcame the difficulties of living together'.[5] A 1947 report on evacuation in Oxfordshire suggested that 'this survey should be called the war memorial to the Unknown Foster-mother' since it showed how devoted most of them were to their young charges.[6]

The debates on the quality of care mask a vital aspect of evacuation: for the first time relatively well-off rural householders were exposed to urban poverty. Suddenly, hundreds of thousands of homes in small towns and villages were filled with scrawny children from the slums of London, Liverpool and other cities, who were malnourished, suffering from rickets and lice, and lacking shoes or decent underwear. The nation was shocked by the destitution thrust into its provincial living rooms. According to an editorial in *The Economist* in 1943, the great migration of evacuation 'revealed to the whole people the black spots in its social life'.[7]

Evacuation created the conditions for one of the biggest explosions of mass empathic understanding in British history, by enabling rural people to step into the lives of the urban poor. Although they had not observed the squalor of East End tenements with their own eyes, they were able to hear first-hand accounts from the children and to see the terrible consequences of poverty standing in front of them. The extremes of city deprivation that had until then been hidden from view became etched into the imaginations of the regional population. Foster parents did not always like what they saw: many middle-class people were disgusted by the filthy children soiling their nice settees.[8] Others were moved to tears. But in both cases there was clear acknowledgement that something had to be done. The conscience of the nation had been roused.

A wave of public action followed the revelations of evacuation. Letters were written to *The Times*, organisations such as the National Federation of Women's Institutes and the Women's Voluntary Service lobbied for changes in child health policy, and members of parliament called for reform. Neville Chamberlain, Prime Minister during the first stage of evacuation, wrote in a letter to his wife: 'I never knew that such conditions existed, and I feel ashamed of having been so ignorant of my neighbours. For the rest of my life I mean to try to make amends by helping such people to live cleaner and healthier lives.'[9]

There was an almost immediate response from the government in the form of a far-reaching expansion of child welfare provisions. This was all the more striking because it took place while the country was immersed in fighting a war. The standard of school meals was raised, cheap milk was made available for children and expectant mothers, and vitamins and cod liver oil became part of their rations. Throughout the early 1940s, new legislation was introduced to ensure improved public health, nutrition and education for children, most of which became permanent after the war ended.[10] Within just a few years, decades of inadequate social care rooted in the Poor Laws of the nineteenth century were reversed. It is no wonder that A.J.P. Taylor concluded: 'Evacuation was itself a disguised welfare scheme, and the most dangerous period of the war became paradoxically the most fruitful for social policy . . . The *Luftwaffe* was a powerful missionary for the welfare state.'[11]

The history books often say that the welfare state was born out of the Beveridge Report of 1942, which led to the establishment of the National Health Service by the post-war Labour government. But the most significant social provisions for children emerged from a more unlikely source: the surge in empathy that took place when foster families met evacuees in the households of rural England.

The story of evacuation tells us that empathy is much more than a feel-good emotion that is limited to the realm of individual experience: it can also be a collective force with the power to change society. Just imagine if we could replicate this experiment today. What would happen if hundreds of thousands of Afghani, Iraqi and Syrian children affected by warfare in their own countries were billeted into foster homes across Europe and North America? Or if shanty-town dwellers in Latin America's megacities were suddenly granted beds in the luxury apartments of wealthy citizens who live in the gated communities overlooking their corrugated iron rooftops? Neither of these are even remote possibilities. The reality is that many instances of collective empathy, such as evacuation, arise from a confluence of complex social, political and economic forces that cannot be easily duplicated. There is no evidence that the bureaucrats and politicians who instigated evacuation had any intention of sparking a substantial change in child welfare policy. Rather, this was what the Ancient Romans called *Fortuna*, or chance, shaping people's lives.

So does this mean that each of us should sit back and wait to be swept up in the whirlwind of some similar episode, since it is all out of our personal control? Absolutely not. Throughout history, people have made a conscious effort to bring about collective empathy by organising and joining in social movements to alter the cultural and political landscape. And they have often been enormously successful in their efforts. If we hope to learn from their example, so we can kindle collective empathy in our own era, we need to look at the three waves of empathy that have transformed Western history, beginning with the humanitarian revolution in eighteenth-century Europe.

The First Wave: the rise of humanitarianism in the eighteenth century

Marx said that the fundamental driver of human history was the conflict between classes. Darwin believed it was the evolutionary struggle for survival. Others have claimed that the most important force for change is the clash of civilisations, or struggles for political power, or advances in technological development.[12]

A growing number of thinkers now recognise that there is something missing from these traditional narratives: empathy. History, they believe, has been influenced just as much by empathy as by factors such as class or technology. 'The extraordinary evolution of empathic consciousness,' argues social scientist Jeremy Rifkin, 'is the quintessential underlying story of human history.' Psychologist Steven Pinker suggests that an 'expansion of empathy' has been one of the major causes of the marked decline in violence over the past half a millennium – including judicial torture, slavery, and the persecution of minorities.[13]

I too am convinced that empathy is a vital – although neglected – force for historical change. But I do not share the optimistic, linear vision of writers such as Rifkin and Pinker, who seem to assume that humanity's circle of empathic concern has been steadily extending outwards over the centuries, initially from family and tribe, then to community and nation, and now increasingly to encompass all humankind and the natural world. This approach, imbued with the Enlightenment ideology of continual progress in human affairs, cannot easily explain recurring instances of mass empathic collapse, such as the Holocaust, the Rwandan genocide, and the atrocities in the former Yugoslavia in the 1990s. In contrast, I think of history much more as a series of waves, where different regions, at different times, experience periods of collective empathic flowering, which are always at risk of being followed by periods of horrific breakdown. The empathic gains made by one generation can never be guaranteed to survive into the next.

In modern Western history there have been three major waves of collective empathy, each of which has resulted in a widening of the circle of moral concern. The first wave, which took place in the eighteenth century (and continued into the nineteenth), saw the rise of humanitarian organisations and movements across Europe.

To fully appreciate the impact and achievements of this empathic revolution, it is essential to understand that before 1700, daily life in Europe was saturated with violence to a degree that we can barely comprehend today. Torture was an accepted part of judicial proceedings – hooks, spikes, screws and saws were used to break bones and rip apart human flesh. If you were unlucky enough to be accused of witchcraft or blasphemy, or deserted your military duties, you might be burned alive in the town square, or hanged, drawn and quartered. Cruelty against children was commonplace, and an astonishing number of babies were abandoned by their parents, or subject to infanticide.

Standard judicial practice in the era before the humanitarian revolution in the eighteenth century. Cuthbert Simpson, a Protestant, is being tortured on the rack in the Tower of London during the Catholic reign of Queen Mary in 1558. He was later burned alive for his heretical beliefs.

Slavery was a deeply embedded institution, while people frequently resolved their disputes not with words but through time-honoured traditions of revenge killings and duels to the death.[14]

Yet something unexpected happened during the following hundred years. Many of these brutal practices became outlawed, or at least uncommon, and a wave of humanitarian concern swept across the continent. There was an outbreak of activism, with the foundation of organisations to oppose slavery, to reform prison systems, to tackle child neglect, and to stop judicial cruelty.[15] According to Steven Pinker:

In the modern West and much of the rest of the world, capital and corporal punishment have been effectively eliminated, governments' power to use violence against their subjects has been severely curtailed, slavery has been abolished, and people have lost their thirst for cruelty. All this happened in a narrow slice of history, beginning in the Age of Reason in the 17th century and cresting with the Enlightenment at the end of the 18th.[16]

What explains this fundamental transformation? Was it due to the rise of rationalist ideals such as the equal value of all human beings? Can it be accounted for by the expansion of commerce, which may have encouraged a desire for peace and cooperation in which trade could thrive? There are, of course, many competing explanations, but the one that has captured the attention of scholars in recent years is the emergence of a new culture of empathy. Pinker describes it as 'an emotional change: a habit of identifying with the pleasures and pains of others'.[17] Yet where did this habit come from?

One of its foundations was what is known as the 'reading revolution'. The spread of literacy, and the reading of novels and newspapers, offered the growing middle classes a way of understanding what it might be like to be an orphaned child or a poor farm labourer or a suffering slave, which helped to forge human solidarity across social divides. Historian Lynn Hunt argues that it was the imaginative act of reading that not only motivated many people to found humanitarian organisations, especially in the second half of the eighteenth century, but which underpinned the demand for political rights and equality in the French and American revolutions. Emotionally wrenching novels such as Rousseau's *Julie* or Richardson's *Pamela* encouraged 'sensibility' and sparked people's empathic circuitry on an unprecedented scale. According to Hunt:

> . . . 'imagined' empathy serves as the foundation of human rights. It is imagined, not in the sense of made up, but in the sense that empathy requires a leap of faith, of imagining that someone is like you. Accounts of torture produced this imagined empathy through new views of pain. Novels generated it by inducing new

sensations about the inner self. Each in their way reinforced
the notion of a community based on autonomous, empathetic
individuals who could relate beyond their immediate families,
religious affiliations, or even nations to greater universal values
. . . Without this learning process, 'equality' could have no deep
meaning and in particular no political consequence.[18]

So our modern, legalistic notion of human rights, suggests
Hunt, is built upon an ethics of empathy. It is, however, difficult
to trace the exact causal chain that led from people reading
novels to the subsequent formation of associations campaigning
against slavery, or to the French Declaration of the Rights of Man
in 1789. In fact, the humanitarian revolution of the eighteenth
and nineteenth centuries was fuelled not just by reading, but by
the focused effort of individuals and groups to establish social
movements that could mobilise even those people who did not
spend their evenings with a novel in their hands. And a striking
aspect of many of these movements is that they were based on
empathy: they made an explicit attempt to get people to step into
the shoes of others and understand their suffering.

A significant portion of the new empathy-driven humanitarian
organisations were established by Quakers, a Protestant sect
more formally known as the Society of Friends, which had been
founded by a shoemaker's apprentice, George Fox, in the mid-
seventeenth century. The Quakers were distinguished not just
by their simple dress and credo that every person has a direct,
unmediated relationship with God, but by their belief in equality,
pacifism and the value of social activism. In their three centuries of
existence, says historian Theodore Zeldin, the Society of Friends
'has had more influence on how human beings treat each other
than any government ever had'.[19] Throughout their history, the
Quakers have believed that we should strive to understand the
lives and suffering of others. Back in 1763, the radical American
Quaker John Woolman visited Native Americans in Wyalusing,

Pennsylvania, who had been in conflict with local white settlers. In trying to see the situation from their perspective, he wrote that, 'I was led to meditate on the manifold difficulties of these Indians . . . and a near sympathy with them was raised in me.' Woolman preached the importance of developing 'sympathy' (by which he meant 'empathy') with all human beings, and refused to pay taxes to finance wars against Native Americans, and was a vocal opponent of slavery.[20]

The Quakers were particularly prominent agents of social change in the eighteenth and nineteenth centuries. In 1783, British Quakers founded the world's first organisation to agitate against slavery and the slave trade. The abolitionists, argues their historian Adam Hochschild, 'placed their hope not in sacred texts but in human empathy.' They aimed to give members of the public a vivid, almost visceral sense of what it might be like to be a slave. They printed a shocking poster of the Brookes slave ship, showing how nearly 500 African slaves were packed into the dark, airless hull on their voyage to British sugar plantations in the Caribbean. They supported talks around Britain by former slaves, who described their treatment in graphic detail, such as being hooked on cranes with fifty-six-pound weights hanging from their feet, and then being whipped with sharp ebony bushes. They put torture instruments on public display, including thumbscrews, iron collars and the *speculum oris*, a force-feeding instrument that was used to pry open the mouths of slaves who were attempting to commit suicide by not eating. They also organised the first ever fair trade boycott of slave-produced sugar. The result of the Quakers' determined work was that tens of thousands of people had their minds opened to empathise with the hardships faced by slaves. Their innovative campaigns – alongside other factors such as slave revolts – played a vital role in the abolition of the slave trade in 1807, and later the end of slavery itself.[21]

Quakers were also extremely active in other fields, such as prison reform. Their leading figure was Elizabeth Fry, who in 1813 began visiting British prisons and was appalled at the squalid, inhumane conditions she discovered, especially for women prisoners and children. She revealed all to the public in books such as *Prisons in Scotland and the North of England*, where she recounts how she stayed overnight in some gaols herself – an early case of experiential empathic immersion – and she urged members of the aristocracy to do the same, so they could experience the deplorable conditions first hand. In 1817, Fry helped found the Association for the Reformation of the Female Prisoners in Newgate, which later became the first national organisation for women prisoners. Fry was a firm adherent of the Golden Rule, believing we should strive to 'Do as thou wouldest be done unto', whether it was in relation to prison inmates, homeless people or servants.[22] Apart from their work in prisons, Quakers invented the idea of giving humanitarian aid to civilians during war: in the Franco-Prussian war in the early 1870s, they brought food, clothing and medicine to both sides of the conflict. They were also behind early political campaigning for women's rights, providing four of the five leaders of the feminist movement in nineteenth-century America.[23]

The Quakers' role in the humanitarian revolution is instructive. Collective empathy was at the forefront of their thinking: their organisations endeavoured to shift the empathic imaginations of whole societies, alerting members of the public on both sides of the Atlantic to neglected human suffering, and reminding them of their common humanity with distant strangers such as slaves, prisoners and the casualties of war. Their example also shows that empathy is at its most powerful when it is embedded as part of a community ethos. Quakers today continue to advocate stepping into other people's shoes, just like John Woolman and Elizabeth Fry: the word 'empathy' has a prominent place in the mission statements of many Quaker organisations. There may be no other group in modern society so committed to the ideal of a revolution of human relationships.

There is a message of hope in the Quakers' empathic activism. They were constantly faced by barriers and campaigning against the odds. In the struggle against slavery, they engaged in the seemingly impossible task of mobilising public opinion for strangers of a different race on the other side of the planet, at a time when most people believed that slavery was morally justified or an economic necessity. The success of their movement confirms that collective empathy can take history in new directions. When we contemplate addressing contemporary crises such as global inequality or climate change, we should remember the Quakers' faith in the spirit of empathy.

The Second Wave: the expansion of rights after the Second World War

The first wave of collective empathy in Western history produced remarkable achievements. But let us not get complacent. Two world wars in the twentieth century seemed to put the gains of the humanitarian revolution into reverse, tragically demonstrating that the capacity for cruelty and barbarism remains part of our natures. In the decades following the Second World War, however, a second wave of collective empathy emerged, which expanded rights to new social groups, and pushed the boundaries of ethical concern beyond the limits of national frontiers. According to Jeremy Rifkin:

> In the aftermath of the Holocaust in World War II, humanity said 'never again'. We extended empathy to large numbers of our fellow human beings previously considered to be less than human – including women, homosexuals, the disabled, people of colour, and ethnic and religious minorities – and encoded our sensitivity in the form of social rights and policies, human rights laws, and now even statutes to protect animals. We are in the long end game of including 'the other,' 'the alien,' 'the unrecognised.'[24]

The end game is indeed long, and full of backtracking, broken promises and partial victories. Women are still discriminated against in the workplace and subjected to domestic violence, gay marriage remains banned in most countries, and the rights of indigenous people continue to be violated with impunity around the world. Yet the advances have been very real, and could not have happened without a concerted effort to forge empathy on a mass scale.

The civil rights movement in the United States in the 1950s and 1960s provides a compelling example of the political impact of empathy. Martin Luther King explicitly drew on empathic thinking when making the case for racial equality. In his famous 1963 *Letter from Birmingham Jail* – one of the most influential documents of the civil rights struggle – he refers directly to the empathic ideas of the philosopher Martin Buber, especially Buber's distinction between an 'I–thou' and an 'I–It' relationship. Segregation laws, wrote King, take the latter form, where people are treated as inferior and inhumanely relegated to the status of objects or 'things'. Others apart from Martin Luther King brought empathy to bear on the civil rights movement. Recall how John Howard Griffin conducted an empathic immersion to communicate to white Americans what it might be like to be an African-American living in the racist Deep South, and writers such as James Baldwin revealed the injustices of segregation and discrimination through African-American eyes. Together with non-violent protests, legal action, and other strategies, empathy played a fundamental role in bridging the divide of race, and in getting equal rights legislation onto the statute books.

The post-war period also saw the rise of a new generation of humanitarian organisations working to spread empathic concern from within national borders to include people living in the developing world. Oxfam, initially founded in Britain in 1942 to send food aid to Greeks who were starving under occupation by the Axis powers, soon extended its famine relief work to

Africa, Asia and Latin America. Amnesty International – which, like Oxfam, had Quakers amongst its founders – took a similarly internationalist perspective. These and other international humanitarian agencies such as Médecins Sans Frontières have based their campaigns both on direct appeals to ideals like human rights, and on helping us make an empathic connection with those suffering from economic deprivation and political violence. The use of photography, film and oral testimony have all been part of this effort to ignite our latent *homo socioempathicus*.

While the first wave of collective empathy was largely based on the reading revolution and the campaigns of social groups such as Quakers, the impetus for the second wave has come from a variety of other sources. The persecution of Jews and Gypsies (Roma) during the Second World War put the protection of the rights of ethnic and religious minorities at the top of the international public agenda. The spread of television from the 1950s brought images of suffering from around the world directly into people's homes, sensitising them to global issues like the Vietnam War and the famine in Biafra. The shift from class-based politics to 'identity'-based politics helped give rise to the gay rights and women's movements, and efforts to end discrimination against people with disabilities. All these factors opened the way for the post-war surge in collective empathy and the growing recognition of the common humanity of all peoples.

The organisations and movements behind the second wave discovered that the possibility for creating mass empathy depends on the presence of specific conditions that enable people to convert emotional engagement into practical action. It helps if there are clear things we can do to make a difference, as was the case in the aftermath of the Asian tsunami in 2004, where all it took was clicking the 'donate' button on a website. We are more likely to take action if we have experienced similar suffering ourselves: if you survived having bowel cancer, this increases the probability that you will lend support to a bowel cancer charity. It helps too if we have a relational connection to the issue: you will march for gay rights if your best friend happens to be a lesbian, even if you are not. We are also more likely to come to people's aid if we do not believe they are to blame for their misfortune.[25] Such conditions and contexts can 'tip' or 'nudge' us from feeling empathy for someone to acting on their behalf.

According to psychologist Paul Bloom, empathy is an unreliable guide to moral action since we more readily extend our empathy to single, identifiable victims in our immediate vicinity than to masses of strangers, whether they are victims of human rights abuses in other countries or poor children facing malnutrition in our own. Instead, he believes that we should base our ethical thinking on the use of reason: 'a reasoned, even counter-empathetic analysis of moral obligation and likely consequences is a better guide to planning for the future than the gut wrench of empathy.' We need to appreciate, he argues, that 'even if we don't empathize with distant strangers, their lives have the same value as the lives of those we love'.[26]

What Bloom is missing here is an historical understanding of the link between empathy and reason. As the first and second waves of empathy demonstrate, the explanation for *why* we believe all humans should be treated and valued equally – a key belief of the Age of Reason – and *why* we enshrine such ideals in laws and rights conventions, is because empathy has made us care about the plight of strangers outside our local community. From the reading revolution and the Quaker movements that helped bring down slavery, to the photography of Lewis Hine that inspired child labour laws and the civil rights activism of the 1960s, empathy has been a driving force for extending universal rights to all human beings. Without it, we might still be living in a world without adequate social protection for children or any gay rights legislation whatsoever. As the political thinker Matthew Taylor has argued, 'the emotional foundation of universalism is empathy.'[27] Empathy and reason are not polar opposites, as critics like Bloom would have us believe, but rather mutually reinforcing ideals on which we can build a more humane civilisation. Indeed, it is 'the gut wrench of empathy' that wrenches open the door of our common concern – and only then does reason have a chance to wedge it open with laws and rights.

In 1975, during an address to a Harvard graduation class, Muhammad Ali was asked for a poem by a member of the audience. His pithy reply: 'Me, We.' It was not just one of the shortest poems in history, but a message about empathy – that we are each part of a greater whole, and only fully realise our humanity by creating bonds with others. Highly empathic people understand this philosophy of 'Me, We'. It calls on us to contribute to the task of creating mass empathy by taking part in social movements ourselves and by motivating others to join us. We can go on a demonstration, organise a meeting, and donate time as well as money to the causes we care about, whether it is immigrants' rights, criminal justice reform, or the loneliness of the elderly. It is through such acts of will that we transform politics into far more than a playground for professional politicians, and inject public life with a surge of collective empathic passion.

The Third Wave: deepening personal relationships in the age of neuroscience

The social struggles of the first and second waves of collective empathy remain with us. Slavery may have been abolished in the West in the nineteenth century, but some of its modern offspring such as debt bondage and sexual slavery continue in many countries. There are volumes of laws banning racial discrimination against ethnic minorities but inequities still abound, for instance in police racism and workplace discrimination.

While these struggles go on, a third wave of collective empathy has emerged since the 1990s, and is having a global resonance. Unlike the earlier waves, its emphasis has been less on expanding rights to previously neglected social groups than on harnessing the power of empathy to deepen and restore the quality of relationships between individuals. The term 'empathy' has also been used more prominently in public messaging and highlighted as a catalyst for change in and of itself. This latest wave has made its mark in three promising new realms: the teaching of empathy skills to schoolchildren; resolving and mediating conflict situations; and generating empathy for future generations to help tackle climate change. Although still just taking off, it has been fuelled by the research in neuroscience and evolutionary biology that has raised awareness of our empathic brains, and by the growing evidence from child and educational psychology that empathy can be learned and nurtured throughout our lives.

Walk into a primary or secondary school in a Western country today, and there is a good chance that you will find pupils learning empathy skills. Some of the world's first empathy classes took place in Finland in the 1980s, but it was only in the following decade that the idea of teaching empathy in schools began to enter the mainstream. It is astonishing that over half a million children have taken the Roots of Empathy programme – in which the teacher is a baby – and that it has spread from Canada to New Zealand, Germany and other nations. This is not the only initiative on offer. In Britain in 2005, the government created the Social and Emotional Aspects of Learning (SEAL) programme, which puts a focus on teaching empathy alongside other emotional skills like self-awareness and managing feelings. By 2010, around 80 per cent of primary and secondary schools were running SEAL, even though it was not a compulsory part of the curriculum. Amongst the teaching materials is a unit on bullying, where the students discuss what it might feel like to be bullied and do role plays to expand perspective-taking abilities. Empathy also has a central role in the International Baccalaureate (IB) Primary Years Programme. When I visited the International School of Amsterdam to see it in action, Year 5 students (aged ten and eleven) were engaged in an eight-week learning unit called 'Different People, Different Lives' to develop empathy, respect and tolerance. One activity involved a trip to a museum of blindness (where they are immersed in darkness with blind guides), then doing a project designing their own mini-museum to give people the experience of stepping into the shoes of those who have a visual impairment.[28]

The third wave is also having an impact through a growing number of peace-building and mediation projects that explicitly use empathy to help resolve conflict situations, and that are scaling it up into a powerful collective force. One of the most innovative – and controversial – is the Parents Circle-Families Forum, which brings together Israelis and Palestinians whose family members have been killed in the conflict. Its core activity is holding meetings where individuals from both sides share their personal stories of pain and loss. The organisation, which comprises over six hundred families, has been fiercely criticised by Israeli politicians, religious groups and the mainstream media for its attempts to create grass-roots dialogue between Israelis and Palestinians. The Israeli Education Ministry has even tried to ban its meetings, claiming that they 'legitimise terrorists', and has prohibited some Palestinian members from giving public talks. This has not stopped the group from embarking on a range of pioneering reconciliation projects.

One initiative began with a wrong phone number. In 2000, during the Second Intifada, an Israeli woman named Natalia Wieseltier dialled a Jewish friend in Tel Aviv, but found herself talking to a Palestinian named Jihad who was living in the Gaza Strip. Instead of hanging up she started a conversation in which they spoke about their very different lives. Soon Natalia was getting phone calls from Jihad's family, and she then put them in touch with her own network of friends. The idea was taken up by the Parents Circle, which established the Hello Peace telephone line. Members of the public could dial a free phone number: if you were Israeli you were put through to a Palestinian to talk with them for up to half an hour, and if you were Palestinian you spoke to an Israeli. Between 2002 and 2009 there were over a million conversations between the two sides. While some calls began as screaming matches, others led to lasting friendships. One Israeli family ended up regularly meeting their Palestinian counterparts at a border crossing to hand over insulin for a diabetic son who was unable to get enough of the drug from Palestinian hospitals.

For a later project, named Blood Relations, bereaved Israelis travelled to a hospital in Ramallah and donated blood for Palestinian victims, while bereaved Palestinian families went to Jerusalem and donated blood to the Israeli Red Cross. The aim of the project was captured in a single question: 'Could you hurt someone who has your blood running through their veins?' The Parents Circle also operates a schools programme, in which an Israeli and a Palestinian team up and give talks to Israeli teenagers about to enter military service, simply telling them the story of their personal loss. At the centre of all their projects is a belief in the power of conversation, reflected in the group's motto, 'It won't stop until we talk'. As one Parents Circle activist stresses, empathic dialogue is the key to ending the conflict: 'We must be prepared to listen to "the other". Because if we will not listen to the other's story we won't be able to understand the source of their pain and we should not expect the other to understand our own.'[29]

Another trailblazing peace initiative is a Rwandan radio soap opera called Musekeweya or New Dawn, which is broadcast across the country every Wednesday afternoon and is listened to by nine-tenths of the population. Its storyline – which concerns Tutsis and Hutus living in adjacent villages – is specifically written to promote the importance of empathy. Although the two villages are fictional, the tensions between them mirror those present in the run-up to the 1994 genocide. The aim of the soap opera is to foster community healing and national reconciliation, and reduce the possibilities of a revival of ethnic violence.[30] What this and other conflict resolution programmes share is a recognition that new laws and peace agreements negotiated at the political level are not enough: long-term peace requires rebuilding personal relationships from the ground up – and empathy is the tool to do it.

Actors play out ethnic tensions in the Rwandan radio soap Musekeweya, which is listened to by millions of people every week.

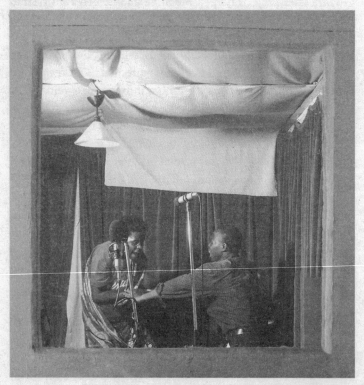

The greatest contemporary challenge for empathy is in helping to confront climate change. The magnitude of the climate crisis is extreme. The latest report of the UN's Intergovernmental Panel on Climate Change, which brings together the work of thousands of the world's leading climate scientists, is absolutely clear in its main conclusions: global warming is a scientific reality, the primary driver is human activity, and greenhouse-gas emission levels continue to rise beyond safe levels. Data from 2012 reveals that there is only one fifth as much sea ice in the Arctic as there was in 1980. International agreements to prevent the increase of carbon emissions have so far failed, and in mid-2013 carbon dioxide concentration in the atmosphere tipped over the danger mark of 400 parts per million (safe levels are around 350 ppm). Just 14 per cent of the world's population – from wealthy countries like the United States, Japan and Western Europe – are responsible for 60 per cent of the emissions since 1850.[31] Despite such statistics, the amount of action being taken by individuals, governments and businesses to stem global warming is perilously limited, and we are pushing ourselves towards ecological catastrophe.

We need to shake up our thinking to understand how empathy could contribute to alleviating the crisis. If you read the newspapers, the issue of global warming is usually framed as one requiring technological solutions, for example carbon capture and storage, or government regulations on emission levels. So let me explain just why it is so essential that we also consider empathy as part of the mosaic of strategies we should adopt, and then reveal some of the practical action that is already under way.

For a start, we need to generate more empathy *across space*. We are largely ignoring the plight of those whose lives are being devastated today by the consequences of our high emission levels, especially people living in developing countries. Whether it is floods in West Bengal, drought in Ethiopia, or rising sea levels in

Tuvalu, climate change related weather events are having major human impacts, forcing communities to surround their villages with flood defences, sell their livestock in the face of drought, or leave behind the only home they have ever known. Yet how much effort do we make to picture the reality of their lives, and see the individuals behind the headlines and statistics? How might we act differently if we empathised with women like Annapurna Beheri, whose home and small family shop selling biscuits in Orissa, India, were washed away in flash floods a few years ago?[32]

There is an equally severe empathy deficit *through time*. We are failing to take the perspective of future generations who will have to live with the detrimental effects of our continuing addiction to high-carbon lifestyles. We would hardly treat our immediate family members with such callous disregard and keep acting in ways that we knew would harm them. But the idea of making personal sacrifices now for the benefit of people who do not yet exist and who we will never meet is a challenging one. This is partly due to the short-term thinking that pervades Western culture, where politicians can barely see beyond the next election, and corporations beyond the next quarterly results. We lack the wisdom of the Iroquois maxim, 'In every deliberation, we must consider the impact on the seventh generation . . . even if it requires having skin as thick as the bark of a pine.' But we also succumb to short-termism because not everyone is our progeny. We are biologically wired to worry about the future welfare of our own children and grandchildren, but find it far harder to take interest in the prospects for the descendants of our neighbours, let alone of people living in distant lands.[33]

Many climate change activists, environmental organisations and policy makers are starting to realise that expanding empathy across space and through time can ratchet up our moral concern to new levels and spur us to take concrete action. They understand that we must become experts at imagining ourselves into the lives and thoughts of the current and future victims of global warming. Amongst the many powerful efforts to develop empathy across space is the Hard Rain Project exhibition, which has been touring the world since 2006. It contains moving photos related to climate change, habitat loss, poverty, and human rights, combined with lyrics from the Bob Dylan song 'A Hard Rain's A-Gonna Fall'.[34] A number of the photos, such as an Inuit hunter standing on a tiny, melting piece of ice, draw on empathic perspective-taking, and personalise the reality of global warming in developing countries and remote regions. In 2007, the development agency Oxfam took an innovative step to raise public awareness about climate change. In June that year Jenna Meredith, a resident of the city of Hull, lost her uninsured home in the worst floods Britain had seen in sixty years. After becoming a community spokesperson to get the government to boost relief efforts, Oxfam took her to visit flood victims in eastern India, where millions had been made homeless. 'It was heartbreaking,' she said after returning from her one-week trip. 'I have been flooded out and lost everything so I know what it is like for the people in India. But in comparison I feel lucky. We can go and buy food from the shops, but the people I've met have lost their crops. They haven't got anything.' Having made an empathic connection, Jenna's experience transformed her into a vocal public advocate for taking action on climate change in the developing world.[35]

The really difficult task lies in generating empathy through time. The positive news is that creative minds have been at work to find ways to transport us into the shoes of future generations. An example is the 2009 film *The Age of Stupid*, in which the story is told from the perspective of an old man living in the devastated world of 2055, looking back at 'archive' footage and asking, 'Why didn't we stop climate change when we had the chance?' It is just the kind of film that can make us understand that our everyday consumer habits might be viewed as 'carbon crimes' by future generations. Do we really want to act like criminals? Oxfam has produced a teaching resource called Climate Chaos, for use amongst primary schoolchildren. One exercise, 'From My Grandchild', asks pupils to imagine what life could be like in the UK in fifty years' time, when they may have a grandchild the age they are now, if the climate continues to change. They then write a story from the viewpoint of their own grandchild.[36] We should be campaigning to put such activities at the heart of all our children's education.

Where we need to think harder is in using conversational empathy to catapult us into future lives. Many child- and youth-led organisations, such as Children in a Changing Climate, are attempting to alert adults to their concerns about global warming and engage them in dialogue.[37] Yet we urgently require initiatives that do more to capture the public imagination. My own suggestion, based on my experience organising Conversation Meals at The Oxford Muse, is to hold 'Climate Street Banquets'. In nineteenth-century France there were conversation banquets that brought together people from different classes to help bridge social divides. We need something similar for climate change – not across classes, but across generations. Policy-makers and politicians hear far more from each other than from the children and youths whose lives will be most affected by global warming, and whose views represent the perspectives of future generations more than any other group in society. So I propose that on an agreed day each year, every major city holds a cross-generational Climate Banquet, which invites a thousand young people to sit down opposite a thousand older people to discuss the future impacts of global warming. Among the adults would be politicians, oil company executives, climate change sceptics and people who take regular short-haul plane flights for their holidays. Just picture a mile-long line of trestle tables snaking through the city streets, with a thousand conversations happening at once.

These are the kinds of projects that can help rouse us into action, whether it is protesting on the streets, travelling by train not plane, or joining a low-carbon-living community. By choosing to play a role, we will become agents in spreading the third wave of collective empathy. The gargantuan task of confronting the climate crisis leaves many people paralysed with despair. I prefer hope. A few years ago I was at a climate change rally in London with around 40,000 other people. An elderly grandmother next to me had a photograph of a tiny baby hanging around her neck, contained in a plastic sleeve. Underneath it said, 'I'm here for Alice, aged one month.' This photograph, for me, was a small and moving sign of hope that we all understand the importance of empathy for the fate of humankind.

The prospects for bioempathy

Climate change is only part of the ecological crisis we face. Alongside it, biodiversity loss, natural resource depletion and environmental pollution are putting the planet under immense pressure. Species extinction has accelerated exponentially over the past hundred years. If everyone on the planet consumed natural resources at the rate of the average European, we would need two planet Earths to sustain us – and if we consumed at the US rate, we would require nearly five.[38] The pressures are being exacerbated by a growing global middle class and an expanding global population that may reach nine billion people by 2050.

Why are we not doing more to prevent the decimation of our fragile environment? Perhaps the problem is that we simply do not care enough about nature, both as something valuable in itself, and as the life-support system for human beings. If only we cared more, and truly recognised our interdependence with the natural world, then we would act to stem the tide of destruction. That is why a growing chorus of voices, from deep ecologists to animal rights activists, argue that we urgently need to expand our empathy to include animals, plant life and the Earth itself, with the aim of creating what Jeremy Rifkin calls a 'global empathic consciousness'.[39]

The attempt to extend the boundaries of the third wave of empathy across species is proving controversial, since for the last century psychologists have almost exclusively thought about empathy as a purely human-to-human phenomenon. But could it be that we possess a hidden capacity for 'bioempathy'?

There is strong evidence that we can empathise with certain animal species, especially those that seem to display similar emotional traits to human beings, such as chimpanzees, bonobos, and gorillas.[40] When the primatologist Dian Fossey spent thirteen years studying mountain gorillas in Rwanda, she developed strong empathic attachments to many of them, particularly those whom she had watched grow up. She observed their fear when confronted with physical danger, their joy when playing together, and noticed when they became angry or agitated. It was evident to her that the gorillas experienced a whole range of human-like emotions – which she would often mirror empathically in her own responses to them. Fossey's cross-species emotional connection was never clearer than when one of her favourites, a gorilla named Digit she had known for ten years, was found with his head and hands hacked off by poachers:

> There are times when one cannot accept facts for fear of shattering one's being . . . From that moment on, I came to live within an insulated part of myself . . . I have tried not to allow myself to think of Digit's anguish, pain, and the total comprehension he must have suffered in knowing what humans were doing to him.[41]

Animal empathy does not only happen in the mountains of central Africa. The sight of a dog whimpering and recoiling because it is about to be hit by someone triggers a visceral response in most of us. We may physically flinch and feel a desperate concern for its plight (especially if it is our dog). In such cases, our empathy is based on a fundamental characteristic we share with many species: a preference to avoid pain and preserve our own life. We know that the dog – just like us – does not want to be beaten or killed. This kind of empathic sensitivity has motivated people to alleviate the suffering of other creatures ever since the foundation of the Society for the Prevention of Cruelty to Animals in England in 1824.[42] Only a generation ago it seemed eccentric to attribute rights to animals, but this is now commonplace. We need a similar attitudinal shift today so that the idea of cross-species empathy becomes an accepted cultural norm.

But there are of course limits to our ability to empathise with animals. People often claim that they can see guilt or sadness on the face of their pet dog. There is a risk, however, that we are anthropomorphising – attributing human emotions to animals that we cannot be certain they are experiencing. The case for animal empathy becomes even more murky when we consider species that have minimal biological resemblance to humans. How easily can we understand the perspective of a mosquito, an earthworm, or a tiny Paedocypris fish, which is around 8 mm long? Can we mirror their emotional states (if they have any)? There are some organisms whose state of being remains a mystery to us, on both a cognitive and affective level. Such creatures are outside the purview of our empathic capacities. The same is true for plants. There is no established evidence that sunflowers or oak trees possess consciousness or engage in purposeful thought (they lack a nervous system).[43] And that rules out the strict definition of empathy, for we cannot step into the mind of an organism that does not have one: there is no perspective for us to grasp, no imagination to comprehend.

This is not to say that human beings are biologically or emotionally detached from nature. Far from it. Like many people, I have wept while watching one of my favourite trees being chopped down, and feel a pang of sadness every time I cycle past the churchyard in central Oxford where it had stood for over a century. Studies of hospital patients show that those who can view plant life through their window recover from operations more rapidly, and require fewer painkillers, than those who are staring out on a brick wall. Children with attention deficit disorder experience a reduction of symptoms when they step into the wild.[44] And most of us have experienced the strange sense of mental calm that certain habitats can evoke in us, like when walking through a beech forest on a fresh spring morning. What is going on in such cases? The leading explanation is that these are all examples of 'biophilia', a term invented by the evolutionary biologist Edward O. Wilson, which refers to our 'innate tendency to focus on life and life-like forms and, in some instances, to affiliate with them emotionally'.[45] The idea is that our very existence is intimately intertwined with our natural surroundings, and being divorced from nature can erode our physical and mental health. Why else do we fill our offices and homes with pot plants?

The real question is how, if at all, biophilia and empathy might be connected. Could it be that our emotional response to nature – for instance when we feel wilted and depressed upon seeing a wilting plant – might involve some of the same mirror neuron processes associated with human-to-human empathy? At this point in time any relationship between biophilia and empathy remains speculative. Exploring the link between them is one of the most exciting future challenges for those working at the frontiers of neuroscience research, and is the next step in our quest towards developing a global empathic consciousness. There is already scientific work being done on the way that exposure to plant life can alter human moods, and trigger emotions and memories – something that poets and naturalists have recognised since the romantic era in the eighteenth century.[46] It is not such a large step to suppose that nature can induce some form of empathic response too. My hunch is that we are on the brink of discovering a human capacity for 'bioempathy'.

Even if it turns out that we cannot, in a strict sense, extend empathy to all life on earth, we can still use the *skills* of empathising to deepen our care for nature and appreciation of our symbiotic relationship with it. Just as we might cultivate curiosity about the strangers living in our neighbourhood, we can apply our curiosity to the plants and animals that we typically walk straight past in the local park, exploring their unique beauties and expanding our sense of wonder about them. Just as we may try experiential immersions like George Orwell's trips on the streets of East London, we can immerse ourselves in wilderness and see how the experience changes us – camping on a mountaintop, swimming in a stream, or rambling through a wood and suddenly coming face-to-face with a roaming deer. I once asked the British ecologist and hedgehog expert Hugh Warwick whether it was possible to empathise with animals like the humble hedgehog. His reply, both playful and serious, helped me understand that the empathic ability to look from another person's perspective is the ultimate transferable skill, and has the power to bond us to the natural world:

It is impossible to know exactly what it feels like to be a hedgehog. But what I ask people to do is to change their perspective. Literally. Get down at hedgehog level, get nose-to-nose with a hedgehog and then look at their world from this position. This will give you an insight into the complications we have thrown in the path of hedgehogs. Whether it is the cars on the roads that not only threaten extinction, but also fragment the environment by preventing movement, to the litter that collars and kills hedgehogs, to the gardens given over to car-ports, decking and patios, and the borders cleansed of life with agro-toxins – we get to see those anthropogenic threats all the more clearly. But for me the most important thing is the contact of the eyes – looking at a hedgehog looking at me – eyes meeting and there being this almost intangible spark of wildness. Gaze at a hedgehog and let yourself fall in love with nature.[47]

Riding the revolutionary wave

Looking back at the historical record, we cannot tell the story of the human journey without including a hefty chapter on the power of empathy. For three hundred years, due to the work of social activists and the movements they have founded, waves of collective empathy have been transforming the cultural and political landscape.

When I began researching, writing about, and experimenting with empathy over a decade ago, I could scarcely have imagined how popular the concept was going to become. Long confined to academic psychology and therapy circles, it is now a familiar idea to brain scientists, policy makers, happiness experts and educators. The latest empathy wave is producing ground-breaking initiatives around the world, from the Roots of Empathy school classes to the peace projects of the Parents Circle, from interfaith dialogues promoting tolerance amongst people of different religions, to restorative justice programmes in prisons where victims of crime sit down and talk face-to-face with the perpetrators. A growing interest in empathy can be found amongst designers and architects, many of them inspired by innovators like Patricia Moore, and amongst social entrepreneurs who understand that the primary purpose of stepping into someone else's shoes is not to sell them more products but to promote their wellbeing. Empathy is, moreover, becoming the watchword for a new generation of activists campaigning on issues such as economic inequality, disability rights, climate change, and gender justice. In 2012 Occupy protesters in the United Kingdom and North America were attending empathy training workshops, and holding discussions in 'Empathy Tents' and around 'Empathy Tables'.

The unprecedented popularity of empathy is reflected in data showing that between 2004 and 2013 the use of the word 'empathy' as an internet search term doubled, while over the same decade searches for 'sympathy' dropped by around 30 per cent.[48] Although this might seem like linguistic fashion, it reveals how we have become more interested in understanding other people, rather than merely pitying them. Almost exactly a century after the word empathy entered the English language, it has become the concept of choice for the socially minded.

None of this could have happened without collective efforts to launch the empathy revolution into every corner of social and political life. Each of us now has an opportunity to join with others and contribute to an historic third wave of empathy that leaves an indelible mark of humanity on the world.

THE FUTURE OF EMPATHY

From early on I have suspected that so important-sounding task 'Know Thyself' is a ruse of a cabal of priests. They are trying to seduce man from activity in the outside world, to distract him with impossible demands; they seek to draw him into a false inner contemplation. Man only knows himself insofar as he knows the world.

– Johann Wolfgang von Goethe

How to live? What to do? Every culture has offered schemes and solutions for the art of living. The ancient Greeks extolled the virtues of courage, wisdom and temperance. Early Christianity urged believers to imitate the life of Christ in order to achieve communion with God. In the Enlightenment we were advised to sublimate our passions to the dictates of reason. Since the end of the Second World War, the dominant message has been to pursue our personal desires and self-interest, based on the assumption that we are in essence selfish creatures, and that the good life lies in consumer pleasures and material wealth.

We now have an alternative within our grasps: empathy. There may be no more powerful way to escape the boundary of our egos, and to gain fresh perspectives on how to live, than by looking at life through the eyes of others. Just think how much empathy changed the lives of people like George Orwell, Harriet Beecher Stowe, Oskar Schindler and Patricia Moore. We need a better balance between gazing inwards and looking outwards, between introspection and outrospection. As Goethe said, we should seek to understand who we are by stepping outside ourselves and discovering the world.

The future of empathy lies not just in the choices we make as individuals to transform our own lives. If we aspire for empathy to fulfil its revolutionary potential as a force for social change, we must generate a deep cultural shift so that looking at the world through other people's eyes becomes as common as looking both ways when we cross the road. This shift is already under way thanks to the third wave of empathy and the activists behind it. But there is so much more we can do to expand its reach. So here are three ideas that can help ignite our collective imaginations and launch us into a new empathic era.

Empathy Conversations

The first way to spread the empathy revolution is through conversation. We need to become empathy gardeners, seeding millions of shoe-swapping conversations in school rooms, board rooms and war rooms, in pubs, churches, kitchens and online. I would like to see empathy conversation circles spring up across the globe, similar to the conversation circles that emerged in eighteenth- and nineteenth-century Europe to spread radical ideas about liberty and equality.[1] To that end, here is a menu of questions about the six habits of highly empathic people that you can take as a starting point for discussions with friends, family, colleagues and strangers.

THE SIX HABITS OF HIGHLY EMPATHIC PEOPLE
A menu for conversation

Habit 1: Switch on your empathic brain

- How did experiences in your childhood and youth shape your capacity to empathise?
- What do you think tips the balance between *homo self-centricus* and *homo empathicus* in human beings, and why?

Habit 2: Make the imaginative leap

- Think of a time when you really tried to step into somebody else's shoes. What difference did it make?
- What kinds of people do you have trouble empathising with, and why? How could you use empathy to start bridging the divide between you?

Habit 3: Seek experiential adventures

- What would be your ideal holiday project for immersing yourself in the life of someone from a different cultural or socio-economic background to your own?
- Think of an individual whose political or religious views you disagree with. What experiential adventure could you go on to better appreciate their viewpoint?

Habit 4: Practise the craft of conversation

- What has been the most surprising and stimulating conversation you have ever had with a stranger?
- What is the biggest source of tension or misunderstanding in your family life? How could you initiate a conversation to better understand the feelings and needs of those involved?

Habit 5: Travel in your armchair

- Which film, novel or other artwork has done most to expand your empathy and affect how you act in the world?

- How is digital culture affecting your personality – your mind, character and relationships? Would a digital diet help or hinder your ability to empathise?

Habit 6: Inspire a revolution

- Think of a social or political cause you really care about. How could you call on empathy to get more people to understand it and take action on it?

- What single change could you make in your life to deepen your empathic connection with the natural world?

And finally:

- Which of the six habits would you most like to develop more in the future, and what first practical step could you take in the next 48 hours to do so?

The Empathy Library

The Great Library of Alexandria, which was founded in Egypt in the third century BC, aspired to be a depository of all knowledge in the ancient world. Building up the global empathy movement requires a new kind of library that is perhaps less wide-ranging but equally ambitious in its vision. To get started, I have created an online Empathy Library (you can find it at www. empathylibrary.com, which aims to be a digital treasure house where people share inspiring books, films, apps and articles that spark empathic thinking and action –and to which you may add your own contribution. You could use the library materials to set up empathy film clubs or reading groups, and as a source of ideas for empathy projects in schools, community organisations or your workplace. As a taster of what you will find in the Empathy Library, here is a list of some of my own favourite empathy resources.

Non-fiction books

George Orwell, *Down and Out in Paris and London* (1933)
Find out how to survive penniless on the streets of East London, and what you can learn about life as a kitchen assistant in a fancy French hotel.

Jean-Dominique Bauby, *The Diving Bell and the Butterfly* (1997)
Enter the world of a man who is completely paralysed and can only communicate by blinking his left eye.

Frans de Waal, *The Age of Empathy: Nature's Lessons for a Kinder Society* (2009)
One of the most interesting and authoritative books on the science of empathy, written by a leading primatologist.

Adam Hochschild, *Bury the Chains: The British Struggle to Abolish Slavery* (2006)
Superb history of the rise of the world's first empathy-powered social movement.

John Howard Griffin, *Black Like Me* (1960)
A white man disguises himself as an African-American to discover the realities of daily life in the Deep South of the 1950s.

Fiction

George Eliot, *Middlemarch* (1874)
She wrote this novel with the specific intention of inspiring her readers with empathy for its troubled characters. Did she succeed?

Rohinton Mistry, *A Fine Balance* (1995)
Get caught up in the lives of four people whose paths criss-cross in a labyrinth of caste, class and religion in Mumbai.

Zadie Smith, *White Teeth* (2000)
Bangladeshi curry-house waiter and his English friend take us on a journey through the realities and complexities of multiculturalism and immigration in Britain.

Christopher Wakling, *What I Did* (2012)
Immerse yourself in the mind of a six-year-old boy whose family is sucked into an investigation by social services.

Ursula le Guin, *Vaster Than Empires and More Slow* (1971)
A short story about a man sent to an alien world due to his singular gift – the power of empathy. Try also Le Guin's 1973 story *The Ones Who Walk Away from Omelas*.

Films

All Quiet on the Western Front (1930)
Anti-war film from the perspective of a German soldier in the First World War, based on the novel by Erich Maria Remarque.

Gandhi (1982)
Admire Ben Kingsley's portrayal of the empathy master who spent years living on ashrams as a poor peasant – as well as being a fine political troublemaker.

Flags of Our Fathers (2006) and *Letters from Iwo Jima* (2006)
Clint Eastwood directed this pair of films about the Battle for Iwo Jima in the Second World War, one from the US perspective, the other – in Japanese – from the Japanese perspective.

Love, Hate and Everything in Between (2012)
Documentary on the global empathy movement by Alex Gabbay, featuring interviews with top empathy thinkers such as Jeremy Rifkin and Mary Gordon.

Schindler's List (1993)
Why did Nazi sympathiser Oskar Schindler become one of the greatest Holocaust rescuers? Based on *Schindler's Ark*, the Booker Prize-winning novel by Thomas Keneally.

Websites

Parents Circle-Families Forum www.theparentscircle.com
Grass-roots peace-building organisation that brings together Palestinians and Israelis who have lost family members in the conflict.

Roots of Empathy www.rootsofempathy.org
Canadian organisation that has pioneered teaching empathy in schools – using babies.

Reading the Mind in the Eyes www.glennrowe.net/baroncohen/faces/eyestest.aspx
One of the best online empathy tests, developed by Cambridge psychologist Simon Baron-Cohen.

Start Empathy www.startempathy.org
Movement founded by the Ashoka organisation to kick-start the empathy revolution in the education sector.

Empathy Cafe Magazine www.scoop.it/t/empathy-and-compassion
The latest empathy news from around the world, curated by Edwin Rutsch, founder of the Center for Building a Culture of Empathy.

The Empathy Museum

The great challenge for the twenty-first century is to expand the third wave of empathy so it has the power to wipe out the empathy deficits that plague contemporary society. Empathy conversations and the Empathy Library will certainly help. But we will also need something more daring. That is why my ambition is to found the world's first Empathy Museum.

Just as many major cities now have Holocaust Museums, it is time that they established Empathy Museums too. Their purpose would be nothing less than to generate an upsurge of global empathic awareness by creating an experiential adventure space where you can explore how to view life from the perspective of other people. If museums make you think of dusty exhibits inside glass cases, think again. An Empathy Museum would be a mind-melding playground rivalling the finest galleries and tourist attractions that a city has to offer. It will excite imaginations as did the first public museums in the seventeenth century, whose collections of curiosities revealed the wonders of nature and human civilisation for the first time.

What might you find in the Empathy Museum? It may start life as a series of 'pop-up' exhibits in different cities, along with an online gallery that can be visited from anywhere. Ultimately, however, I envisage the Empathy Museum as a permanent exhibition space. Let me take you on a tour of what it could look like.

Human Library

Parked in the museum forecourt you will find the Human Library bus. On its seats are open-minded volunteers who you can 'borrow' for conversation, just as you might borrow a book. They could be Sikh teenagers or management consultants, off-duty soldiers or mental health nurses. Sit down beside one of them and get talking to somebody whose world you would rarely get to enter in your daily life. The ceiling of the bus is covered with questions to stimulate your discussion, on topics such as love, belief, fear and curiosity.

Labour Behind the Label

In this room there are rows of sewing machines and a team of former sweatshop factory workers from Vietnam who will teach you how to make a shirt under the working conditions of your favourite fashion label. At the end you will be paid the equivalent amount that a garment factory worker in a developing country receives per shirt. Unfortunately it will not be nearly enough for a cup of tea in the café, although it might prompt you to write to the companies whose clothes you buy to improve pay and conditions for their workers.

All the World's a Stage

Professional actors will guide you in dramatic role plays, improvisations and other acting exercises to help you discover the secrets of stepping into the life of another person. You may be invited to take on the role of a fashion model or a Buddhist monk, and wander the room talking to other visitors in imaginary roles, making sure you ask and answer questions in character. There are also video displays where famous method actors discuss their art, using clips from their films.

Storytelling Hub

Here you can find audio and video recordings of individuals from many walks of life and periods in history talking about moments when empathy (or an absence of it) changed their lives. Subjects include wealthy Tokyo bankers, school teachers from the early years of the Cuban revolution, and prisoners on death row. There are facilities for visitors to make recordings of their own empathy experiences, which will become part of a publicly accessibly digital archive.

Water Walk

Step into this circular room and you will immediately be struck by the dry heat and dust. Around the walls are video projections of a parched African landscape, with women walking across a plain with large, heavy water jugs balanced on their heads. You hear them talking about the climate change-induced drought they are facing, and how far they have to walk each day to find water for their families. A circular pathway is marked on the floor. You can see other visitors picking up jugs of water and placing them on their heads, then walking in circles around the room in step with the African women (don't try this at home). Some of them are sweating in the heat as they hold their jugs steady, others straining under the weight. Are you ready to join them? Can you imagine this being your daily routine?

Dressing-Up Box

Come through the door and you will see racks of clothes you can dress up in to experience lives you have never lived. There is all the gear you need to go and beg for an hour at the entrance to the Empathy Museum, or help sweep and mop the floors and toilets. Put on the popular waiter or waitress outfit and you will have a chance to serve the public by clearing the tables in the café (just watch out for the hectic lunchtime slot).

How Empathic is Your Brain?

The latest neuro-imaging device will record your empathy levels across different brain regions. Your neural responses will be tested while watching films of people experiencing both pleasure and pain, such as having their finger trapped in a door. You will also be shown images of suffering animals in factory farms and trees being felled in the Amazon, as part on an ongoing research project on human empathy with the natural world. At the end you will be presented with a map showing the empathic hotspots of your brain.

Outrospection Café

When you buy lunch from the café, the cashier registers it with a special scanner and takes your table number. Once you sit down, the screen on your table begins playing a video showing an interview with the workers who produced the items you just purchased. If you bought fair trade coffee, there may be a Mexican coffee picker talking about the new health clinic that has just opened on the cooperative plantation where he is employed. If you chose the standard coffee, it could be a Brazilian worker explaining how her wage is so low that she cannot afford to send her children to school. In the evenings the café is converted into a 'restaurant in the dark'. Blind waiters and waitresses will present you with a meal that you eat in complete darkness.

The Empathy Shoe Shop

As you leave the museum a touch screen invites you to pledge online the empathic adventures that you plan for the coming weeks. You then enter a unique shoe shop. On sale are the museum's line of canvas Empathy Shoes, with questions to stimulate empathic conversations printed all over them. When wearing them out and about, you will be recognised as a walking ambassador of the empathy revolution – someone who is dedicated to the art of stepping into the shoes of others and seeing the world from their perspective.

The word 'museum' comes from the Muses of Greek mythology, whose job was to inject a divine spark into everyday life. My hope is that in the future the source of this spark will be a global network of Empathy Museums that will reinvent the very meaning of public culture and leave their visitors changed forever. Together with the Empathy Library, empathy conversations, and the ongoing work of empathy activists around the planet, they will be fuelling the revolution of human relationships that we so urgently need.

NOTES

The radical power of empathy

1 See Baron-Cohen (2011, 11) and Gordon (2005, 30) for related definitions.
2 Interview 25/10/12; Moore 1985, 160; http://www.youtube.com/watch?v=Xr3ibtQuf2o
3 Rifkin 2010, 42–43.
4 Hanh 1987, 87.
5 Estimates of 'zero degrees of empathy' typically range between 1 per cent and 4 per cent of the population, with 2 per cent being the most widely accepted figure. See Baron-Cohen (2011, 29–64); Olson (2010, 11); http://www.autism.org.uk/about-autism/myths-facts-and-statistics/statistics-how-many-people-have-autism-spectrum-disorders.aspx.
6 http://www.northwestern.edu/observer/issues/2006/06/22/obama.html
7 Konrath, O'Brien and Hsing 2011; http://www.scientificamerican.com/article.cfm?id=what-me-care; Twenge and Campbell 2009.
8 http://www.oecd.org/els/socialpoliciesanddata/dividedwestandwhyinequalitykeepsrising.htm; Piff et al 2012; http://www.scientificamerican.com/article.cfm?id=how-wealth-reduces-compassion&print=true
9 Pinker 2011, 175. See also Hunt (2007).
10 Layard 2007, 20; 2005, 234; Covey 2004, 236. See also Batson (2011, 185–187). http://greatergood.berkeley.edu/article/item/feeling_like_partners/; http://www.mentalhealth.org.uk/content/assets/PDF/publications/the_lonely_society_report.pdf; http://greatergood.berkeley.edu/topic/empathy/definition#what_is
11 Slote 2007.
12 Interview 25/10/12.
13 http://www.ianmcewan.com/bib/articles/love-oblivion.html
14 Mukherjee 1993, 91.
15 Hollan and Throop 2011, 10–11, 25–29.
16 Krznaric 2012a.

17 Dworkin 2012.

18 Singer 1997, 244–253.

19 http://nymag.com/news/features/45938/

20 http://new.bostonreview.net/BR24.3/schor.html

21 Ben-Shahar 2008, 125–126; http://www.thecrimson.com/article/2006/2/15/the-science-of-smiling-strongcorrection-appendedstrongbrbr845/

22 Seligman 2003, 148.

23 http://psychcentral.com/blog/archives/2011/09/06/statistics-europeans-have-mental-health-issues-too/

24 This image is a video still from my RSA Animate, *The Power of Outrospection* (Krznaric 2012a).

25 Bloom 2013.

Habit 1: Switch on your empathic brain

1 http://www.gallup.com/poll/18802/gallup-panel-people-cant-trusted.aspx; Brewer and Steenbergen 2002.

2 Thanks to Alfie Kohn for this example (Kohn 1990, 3).

3 Friedrich von Hayek interview in Adam Curtis's documentary film *The Trap* (episode 1).

4 Galbraith 1977, 45.

5 Richard Dawkins interview in Adam Curtis's documentary film *The Trap* (episode 2).

6 Freud 1962, 58–59.

7 Smith 1976, 499–502.

8 Rifkin 2010, 90–92.

9 Allport 1937, 530–531.

10 Kringelbach and Phillips 2014, 104–105.

11 Baron-Cohen 2004, 1, 70–1, 95.

12 Baron-Cohen 2004, 200–5. For critiques of standard empathy measures, see http://www.romankrznaric.com/outrospection/2010/01/30/359

13 Gerhardt 2010, 57; Rifkin 2010, 69.

14 Quoted in Rifkin (2010, 70).

15 Gerhardt 2010, 66–67, 170; Rifkin 2010, 74.

16 Gerhardt 2010, 56.

17 Quoted in Rifkin (2010, 78).

18 Gerhardt 2010, 168.

19 Bowlby 1988, 154; Gerhardt 2004, 195.

20 Kropotkin 1998, 53.

21 Interview 14/11/9.

22 http://greatergood.berkeley.edu/article/item/the_evolution_of_empathy

23 De Waal 2010, 91; http://greatergood.berkeley.edu/article/item/the_evolution
   _of_empathy

24 Masserman *et al.* 1964.

25 http://greatergood.berkeley.edu/article/item/the_evolution_of_empathy

26 Nowak and Highfield 2011, xiii.

27 Quoted in Olson (2010, 14).

28 http://greatergood.berkeley.edu/article/item/the_evolution_of_empathy

29 Quoted in Keysers 2011, 11; Rifkin 2010, 82.

30 Interview 21/7/11.

31 Pinker 2011, 577. See also Hickok (2008).

32 Baron-Cohen 2011, 19, 26–27; Kringelbach and Phillips 2014, 106.

33 Jackson et al 2006.

34 Zak 2012, 63-64; Kringelbach and Phillips 2014, 115–7.

35 Even Keysers (2011, 54) recognises the gaps in our understanding: 'What we
   still do not understand is *how* a score on a Perspective Taking Scale is linked
   to activity in your mirror system.' See also Singer and Lamm (2009, 92–3).

36 Baron-Cohen 2011, 87, 118; Klimecki, Leiberg, Lamm and Singer 2012.

37 Galinsky and Moskowitz 2000.

38 Batson *et al.* 1997, 508; Batson 1991, 121–138; Batson 2011, 11, 176; Pinker
   2011, 586.

39 http://well.blogs.nytimes.com/2012/06/21/can-doctors-learn-empathy/;
   Reiss *et all.* 2012.

40 Klimecki *et al.* 2013; Leiberg *et al.* 2011.

41 Gordon 2005, 245–8; Gordon 2002, 242; Roots of Empathy 2008; Schonert-
   Reichl 2008; Santos *et al.* 2011; http://engageforeducation.org/news/roots-
   of-empathy-pioneering-anti-bullying-programme-offered-scotland-wide/;
   http://www.itv.com/news/london/story/2012-11-23/baby-tackles-bullying/;
   http://greatergood.berkeley.edu/article/item/taking_lessons_from_a_baby;
   personal communication with Mary Gordon 8/6/8.

42 Gordon 2005, xvi–xvii, 6, 9; Krznaric 2008, 24–5.

43 Lakoff 2005, xv, 3.

44 http://www.youtube.com/watch?v=u6XAPnuFjJc

Habit 2: Make the imaginative leap

1 Quoted in Phillips and Taylor (2009, 97).

2 Clark 1997, 34–5.

3 http://www.theaustralian.com.au/news/features/our-better-selves/story-
  e6frg8h6-1226535324061

4 http://www.romankrznaric.com/outrospection/2010/09/12/609
5 Gladwell 2005, 61–66, 84–6.
6 http://www.sbs.com.au/news/article/1761364/Analysis-Illegals-and-the-erosion-of-empathy
7 Arendt 1994, 135.
8 Blass 2004, 102–3.
9 Burger 2009.
10 Blass 2004, 87–9, 96–9, 108–111, 124, 307–9; Blass 1999, 967.
11 Blass 2004, 103.
12 http://www.youtube.com/watch?v=onsIdBanynY; Slote 2007, 22.
13 Smith 1976, 233–234.
14 http://www.romankrznaric.com/outrospection/2010/05/14/475.
15 http://www.guardian.co.uk/science/2013/jan/04/barack-obama-empathy-deficit. See also Bloom (2013) and Prinz (2011).
16 Moyn 2006, 400–401.
17 Sontag 1979, 20.
18 Cohen 2001, 1.
19 Levinas 2006.
20 Keneally 1994, 35–7, 52, 139–147, 189–190, 220, 277, 318, 339, 355, 372, 423; Keneally 2008, 17, 23, 25, 46, 118, 125, 153, 191.
21 Keneally 2008, 152.
22 Oliner and Oliner 1992; Monroe 2004; Fogelman 1994.
23 http://www.michaeldvd.com.au/Articles/WhoIsOskarSchindler/WhoIsOskarSchindler.html
24 Batson 2011, 178–9.
25 Buber 1965, 70–71.
26 Armstrong 2011, 139.
27 Smith 1976, 66, 502.
28 Eisner 1994, 6, 33.
29 Hedrick 1994, 110.
30 Hedrick 1994, 193, 201, 237.
31 Armstrong 2007, xiv, 390.
32 Fletcher 1966, 117.
33 http://www.theatlantic.com/international/archive/2013/01/signing-off/266925/
34 Reynolds 1995; Said 2003.
35 Armstrong 2011, 103–4.
36 Gandhi 1984.
37 Armstrong 2011, 5.

38 Hanh 1987, 62.

39 Batchelor 1997, 85–6.

40 Krznaric 2003; Krznaric 2010a.

41 Nagel 1991, 169.

Habit 3: Seek experiential adventures

1 Interview with Sophie Raworth, Andrew Marr Show, BBC, http://www.bbc. co.uk/news/entertainment-arts-21572983; McDonald 2013, 164–5; Stanislavski 1937.

2 Rousseau 1963, 9; Dewey 1997, 25; Krznaric 2012b, 128.

3 Eide 2007.

4 Seymour-Jones 1993, 132, 154–62; Webb 1971, 344–5; Webb 1888.

5 Orwell 1966, 179–80, 189; 1962, 120, 130.

6 Griffin 2009, 21, 28, 46, 51–2, 61–2, 159–67, 179, 180, 185, 211, 216–9, 226; Bonazzi 1997; Terkel 1982, 335–9.

7 Wallraff 1988, 2, 71, 76, 177; Wallraff 1978; Pilger 2004, 159.

8 Interview 3/3/12; http://rs100aday.com/

9 Mandela 1995, 536.

10 http://www.dialogue-in-the-dark.com/wp-content/uploads/Wall_street_ journal_intemplate.pdf; http://www.nytimes.com/2011/08/19/arts/design/ dialog-in-the-dark-at-south-street-seaport-exhibition-review.html?_r=2&; http://www.icubed.us/career-interviews-list/node/1809

11 Anderson 1997, 50.

12 Anderson 1997, 65, 76, 78; Guevara 1996, 60.

13 http://www.marxists.org/archive/guevara/1960/08/19.htm

14 http://news.nationalgeographic.co.uk/news/2004/10/1014_041014_ motorcycle_diaries.html

15 Anderson 1997, 96.

16 Anderson 1997, 386–8.

17 Anderson 1997, 126, 135; Granado 2003, xi.

18 http://www.telegraph.co.uk/news/features/3634426/How-Nelson-Mandela-won-the-rugby-World-Cup.html

19 Mandela 1995, 183, 194.

20 The Mandela case created intense debate within the Amnesty International movement at the time about whether to suspend the rule that 'prisoners of conscience' could not advocate or use violence. Although the rule was not suspended, Amnesty did campaign for Mandela to be given a fair trial.

21 Mandela 1995, 549, 680, 745.

22 Krznaric 2011, 176.

23 Sennett 2012, 6.

24 Solnit 2010, 4.

25 Solnit 2010, 188, 194, 206.

26 Solnit 2010, 2, 8.

27 Krznaric 2011, 60–64.

28 http://www.guardian.co.uk/music/2008/jul/13/classicalmusicandopera.
    israelandthepalestinians

29 http://jewishquarterly.org/2010/11/said-barenboim-and-the-west-east-
    divan-orchestra/; Zaki 2012.

30 Barenboim and Said 2004, 10; http://www.guardian.co.uk/music/2008/
    jul/13/classicalmusicandopera.israelandthepalestinians

31 Malone 2012, ebook location 2967 of 3241.

32 Malone 2012, ebook location 2992 of 3241.

33 http://www.radiotimes.com/news/2012-09-20/gareth-malone-on-the-choir-
    sing-while-you-work-military-wives-and-getting-competitive

34 Crouch and Ward 1988, 94–109.

35 Sennett 1999, 136–140.

36 Kropotkin 1998, 184, 217–8; http://libcom.org/library/anarchy-milton-keynes-
    music-colin-ward

37 Armstrong 2011, 147.

Habit 4: Practise the craft of conversation

1 Gatenby 2004; Tannen 1999, 211.

2 Zeldin and Krznaric 2004, 1.

3 Rowson 2012, 35; Warner 2013, 2, 4; Zeldin 1995, 191.

4 Zeldin 1995, 198–202.

5 Rowson 2012, 3.

6 Sennett 2012, 23.

7 Diamond 2012, 49–50.

8 Krznaric 2011, 45–6.

9 Parker 1996, 5.

10 Dibb 1985/6.

11 Parker 1996, 21, 126.

12 Dibb 1985/6.

13 Parker 1996, 21, 164–6.

14 Parker 1996, 166.

15 Parker 1996, 52.

16 Cain 2013, 13; 137–8.

17 Krznaric, Whalen and Zeldin 2006 xvii-xviii; http://www.oxfordmuse.com/ ?q=portrait-of-oxford-project#oxford-unmasked

18 Covey 2004, 237–8.

19 Rosenberg 2003, 2.

20 Rosenberg 2003, 91, 127.

21 Rosenberg 2003, 54.

22 Rosenberg 2003, 13–14.

23 Obama 2007, 66–8.

24 Rosenberg 2003, 96–100.

25 Faber and Mazlish 2013, Chapter 1.

26 Hoffman 2000, 197–205.

27 Anonymous testimony.

28 Baron-Cohen 2011, 13, 18; see also Singer and Lamm (2009), and Klimecki, Leiberg, Lamm and Singer (2012).

29 Personal communications, 18/2/13, 10/7/13.

30 Zeldin 2003.

31 Interview with Brené Brown, London, 3/10/12; http://www.romankrznaric. com/outrospection/2012/10/16/1729.

32 Brown 2012, 34–37.

33 James 2013, 3–4.

34 Brown 2012, 185–6.

35 Rosenberg 2003, 40.

36 Patnaik 2009; Goleman 1999.

37 Drayton 2006, 6; http://empathy.ashoka.org/rationale.

38 Brown 2012, 74–5.

39 Borg 2010, 8.

40 http://www.psandman.com/col/empathy2.htm

41 http://www.empathytraining.co.uk/pages/emp_training_courses.html; http://abbykerr.com/empathy-marketing/

42 Olson 2013, 61.

43 See also Ewan (1996, 3–4, 159–73).

44 Quoted in Olson (2013, 62); http://tobaccocontrol.bmj.com/content/3/3/ 270.full.pdf

45 Quoted in Schlosser 2002, 41.

46 Olson 2013, 54.

47 Patnaik 2009, 166–70.

48 Zeldin 1998, 14.

49 Mehl, Vazire, Holleran and Clark 2010.

50 http://theforgivenessproject.com/stories/jo-berry-pat-magee-england/

51 Rosenberg 2003, 103–4, 129–140; Neff 2003, 90; Niezink and Rutsch 2013.
52 Neff 2003, 85; see also Armstrong 2011, 67–81.
53 Krznaric 2011, 10–11.

Habit 5: Travel in your armchair

1   http://www.guardian.co.uk/books/2012/jun/29/my-life-as-bibliophile-julian-
    barnes
2   Pinker 2011, 589; Keen 2007.
3   http://www.nybooks.com/articles/archives/2006/oct/19/death-at-marathon/
    ?pagination=false; Mendelsohn 2006.
4   Armstrong 2011, 87–8.
5   http://www.npr.org/templates/story/story.php?storyId=6781357
6   Terkel 2007, 7; Kelly 1998, 158–161.
7   Kelly 1998, 2, 160; Terkel 2007, 7.
8   Kelly 1998, 122–3.
9   Olson 2013, 6–10, 92.
10 Olson 2013, 90-92; http://www.nybooks.com/articles/archives/2010/mar/
    25/the-wizard/?pagination=false
11 Bennett 2005, 36.
12 Freedberg and Gallese 2007, 202.
13 http://query.nytimes.com/mem/archive-free/pdf?res=9D00E5DF133AE733
    A25754C2A9679D946597D6CF
14 Freedman 1994, 72.
15 Trachtenberg 1989, 203, 205.
16 Freedman 1994, 93, dust jacket text; http://www.archives.gov/education/
    lessons/hine-photos/.
17 Linfield 2010, 7, 127–32.
18 Sontag 1979, 20–21.
19 Olson 2013, 86.
20 Olson 2013, 90.
21 Linfield 2010, 22, 39.
22 Keen 2007, 37–8.
23 http://www.st-andrews.ac.uk/~jfec/ge/eliot.html; Keen 2010, 54.
24 Oatley 2011, 63; Nussbaum 1995, xvi, 10, 66; Pinker 2011, 175–6.
25 Keen 2007, vii, xx, 53, 55, 70–74, 102, 131, 140.
26 Keen 2007, 52.
27 http://www.romankrznaric.com/outrospection/2011/10/13/821
28 Elderkin and Berthoud 2013.
29 http://www.bbc.co.uk/news/technology-22464368

30 Rifkin 2010, 472, 580.
31 http://www.coffeetrust.org/category/ask-a-coffee-farmer
32 Turkle 2011, 225.
33 Aboujaoude 2012, 106–8.
34 http://www.polygon.com/2013/5/9/4313246/gamings-new-frontier-cancer-depression-suicide
35 Belman and Flanagan 2010, 12; http://www.changemakers.com/competition/entrepreneuring-peace/entries/peacemaker-video-game-promote-peace
36 Lanier 2011, 36.
37 Lanier 2011, 16, 48.
38 Smith 2010.
39 Chatfield 2012, 42.
40 Aboujaoude 2012, 21, 45.
41 Chatfield 2012, 39.
42 Aboujaoude 2012, 21, 40, 107–8.
43 http://www.pewinternet.org/Media-Mentions/2007/Do-You-Use-Google-For-Vanity-Searching-Youre-Not-Alone.aspx
44 Aboujaoude 2012, 68–74; http://www.sciencedirect.com/science/article/pii/S0191886911005332
45 http://www.guardian.co.uk/world/2012/jan/03/how-the-revolution-went-viral
46 Rifkin quoted in Gabbay (2012).
47 Chatfield 2013, 134.

Habit 6: Inspire a revolution

1   Holman 1995, 72.
2   Taylor 1967, 455.
3   Titmuss 1950, 393.
4   Isaacs 1941, 9.
5   Titmuss 1950, 388; Holman 1995, 97.
6   Barnett House Study Group 1947, 107.
7   *The Economist*, 1 May, 1943, 545; Titmuss 1950, 516.
8   Women's Group on Public Welfare 1944, xiii.
9   Quoted in Holman (1995, 140).
10 Holman 1995, 128–135; Titmuss 1950, 510–516.
11 Taylor 1967, 455, 503.
12 Krznaric 2007.
13 Rifkin 2010, 10; Rifkin quoted in Gabbay (2012); Pinker 2011, 572, 590.
14 Pinker 2011, 129–133; 415–6.

15 Phillips and Taylor 2009, 27.

16 Pinker 2011, 133.

17 Pinker 2011, 143.

18 Hunt 2007, 32, 38–9, 40, 80. See also Knott (2009).

19 Zeldin 1995, 330.

20 Woolman 1800, 179; Krznaric 2011, 140–1.

21 Hochschild 2006, 5, 78, 118, 155, 197–8, 222, 366.

22 Journal 30th November, 1808, quoted in Skidmore (2005, 80).

23 Zeldin 1995, 330–1.

24 Rifkin 2010, 26.

25 Clark 1997, 41, 84, 111–115.

26 Bloom 2013.

27 Taylor 2010, 16.

28 Krznaric 2008.

29 http://www.theparentscircle.org/Story.aspx?ID=415;   http://adage.com/article/goodworks/blood-relations-uniting-israelis-palestinians/229960/; http://news.bbc.co.uk/1/hi/world/middle_east/6948034.stm; http://www.theparentscircle.org/MediaPage.aspx?ID=357

30 http://www.labenevolencija.org/2010/12/the-task-of-la-benevolencija-in-rwanda/

31 http://www.ipcc.ch/; http://www.nybooks.com/articles/archives/2013/may/09/some-like-it-hot/; http://www.guardian.co.uk/environment/blog/2013/may/30/carbon-milestone-newspapers; http://arxiv.org/abs/0804.1126;Krznaric 2011, 219.

32 Krznaric 2010b, 153–4.

33 Krznaric 2010c, 130.

34 http://www.hardrainproject.com

35 Krznaric 2010b.

36 http://www.oxfam.org.uk/education/resources/climate_chaos/day_two/files/afternoon3_from_my_grandchild.pdf

37 http://www.childreninachangingclimate.org/home.htm

38 Krznaric 2011, 219, 223.

39 Rifkin 2010, 42.

40 Kellert and Wilson 1993; Schultz 2000.

41 Fossey 1985, 206; Coetzee 1999, 114; http://www.vanityfair.com/society/features/1986/09/fatal-obsession-198609

42 Bourke 2011, 68, 174–5.

43 http://www.scientificamerican.com/article.cfm?id=do-plants-think-daniel-chamovitz&page=3

44 Louv 2005; Krznaric 2011, 216–7.
45 Wilson 1984, 1; Barbiero 2011, 13.
46 Haviland-Jones et al 2005.
47 http://www.romankrznaric.com/outrospection/2010/04/10/422
48 http://chewychunks.wordpress.com/2013/01/09/empathy-replaces-sympathy-rsa-animate/

The future of empathy

1 The first circles have already formed: http://www.lidewijniezink.com/projects

BIBLIOGRAPHY

Aboujaoude, Elias (2012) *Virtually You: The Dangerous Powers of the E-Personality* (New York, Norton).

Allport, Gordon (1937) *Personality: A Psychological Interpretation* (London, Constable).

Anderson, Jon Lee (1997) *Che Guevara: A Revolutionary Life* (London, Bantam).

Arendt, Hannah (1994) *Eichmann in Jerusalem: A Report on the Banality of Evil* (London, Penguin).

Armstrong, Karen (2007) *The Great Transformation: The World in the Time of Buddha, Socrates, Confucius and Jeremiah* (London, Atlantic).

Armstrong, Karen (2011) *Twelve Steps to a Compassionate Life* (London, Bodley Head).

Barbiero, Giuseppe (2011) 'Biophilia and Gaia: Two Hypotheses for an Affective Ecology', *Journal of Biourbanism*, No.1: 11–27.

Barenboim, Daniel and Edward Said (2004) *Parallels and Paradoxes: Explorations in Music and Society* (London, Bloomsbury).

Barnett House Study Group (1947) *London Children in War-time Oxford* (London, Oxford University Press).

Baron-Cohen, Simon (2004) *The Essential Difference* (London, Penguin).

Baron-Cohen, Simon (2011) *Zero Degrees of Empathy: A New Theory of Human Cruelty* (London, Allen Lane).

Batchelor, Stephen (1997) *Buddhism Without Beliefs: A*

Contemporary Guide to Awakening (New York, Riverhead Books).

Batson, C. Daniel (1991) *The Altruism Question: Toward a Social-Psychological Answer* (Hillsdale NJ, Erlbaum Associates).

Batson, C. Daniel (2011) *Altruism in Humans* (New York, Oxford University Press).

Batson C. Daniel, Karen Sager, Eric Garst, Misook Kang, Kostia Rubchinsky and Karen Dawson (1997) 'Is Empathy-Induced Helping Due to Self-Other Merging?', *Journal of Personality and Social Psychology*, Vol. 73 No. 3: 495–509.

Belman, Jonathan and Mary Flanagan (2010) 'Designing Games to Foster Empathy', *Cognitive Technology* Vol. 14, No. 2: 5–15.

Ben-Shahar, Tal (2008) *Happier: Can you learn to be happy?* (Maidenhead, McGraw-Hill).

Bennett, Jill (2005) *Empathic Vision: Affect, Trauma, and Contemporary Art* (Stanford, Stanford University Press).

Blass, Thomas (2004) *The Man Who Shocked the World: The Life and Legacy of Stanley Milgram* (New York, Basic Books, uncorrected proof).

Bloom, Paul (2013) 'The Baby in the Well: The Case Against Empathy', *The New Yorker*, May 20.

Bonazzi, Robert (1997) *Man in the Mirror: John Howard Griffin and the Story of Black Like Me* (Maryknoll, Orbis Books).

Borg, James (2010) *Persuasion: The Art of Influencing People* (London, Prentice Hall).

Bourke, Joanna (2011) *What it Means to Be Human: Reflections from 1791 to the Present* (London, Virago).

Bowlby, John (1988) *A Secure Base: Clinical Applications of Attachment Theory* (Abingdon, Routledge).

Brewer, Paul and Marco Steenbergen (2002) 'All Against All: How Beliefs About Human Nature Shape Foreign Policy Options', *Political Psychology* Vol. 23 No.1: 39–58.

Brown, Brené (2012) *Daring Greatly: How the Courage to Be*

Vulnerable Transforms the Way We Live, Love, Parent, and Lead (New York, Gotham).

Buber, Martin (1965) 'Distance and Relation' in *The Knowledge of Man* (New York, Harper and Row).

Burger, Jerry (2009) 'Replicating Milgram: Would People Still Obey Today?', *American Psychologist*, Vol. 64 No.1: 1–11.

Cain, Susan (2013) *Quiet: The Power of Introverts in a World That Can't Stop Talking* (London, Penguin).

Chatfield, Tom (2012) *How to Thrive in the Digital Age* (London, Macmillan).

Chatfield, Tom (2013) *Netymology: From Apps to Zombies – A linguistic celebration of the digital world* (London, Quercus).

Clark, Candace (1997) *Misery and Company: Sympathy in Everyday Life* (Chicago, University of Chicago Press).

Coetzee, J. M. (1999) *The Lives of Animals* (Princeton, Princeton University Press).

Cohen, Stanley (2001) *States of Denial: Knowing About Atrocities and Suffering* (Cambridge, Polity).

Covey, Stephen (2004) *The Seven Habits of Highly Effective People* (London, Simon and Schuster).

Crouch, David and Colin Ward (1988) *The Allotment: Its Landscape and Culture* (London, Faber and Faber).

De Waal, Frans (2010) *The Age of Empathy: Nature's Lessons for a Kinder Society* (London, Souvenir Press).

Dewey, John (1997) *Experience and Education* (New York, Touchstone).

Diamond, Jared (2012) *The World Until Yesterday: What Can We Learn from Traditional Societies?* (London, Allen Lane).

Dibb, Mike (1985/6) *Studs Terkel's Chicago*, documentary film (London, BBC).

Drayton, Bill (2006) 'Everyone a Changemaker: Social Entrepreneurship's Ultimate Goal', *Innovations*, Winter 2006, MIT Press.

Dworkin, Ronald W. (2012) 'Psychotherapy and The Pursuit of Happiness', *The New Atlantis*, Spring.

Eide, Elisabeth (2007) '"Being the Other' – or Tourist in her Reality? Reporters' and Writers' Attempts at Cross-Identification', *Social Identities*, Vol. 13 No.1: 3–17.

Eisner, Bruce (1994) *Ecstasy: The MDMA Story* (Berkeley, Ronin Publishing).

Elderkin, Susan and Ella Berthoud (2013) *The Novel Cure: An A to Z of Literary Remedies* (Edinburgh, Canongate).

Ewan, Stuart (1996) *PR! A Social History of Spin* (New York, Basic Books).

Faber, Adele and Elaine Mazlish (2013) *How to Talk So Kids Will Listen and Listen So Kids Will Talk* (London, Piccadilly Press).

Fletcher, Joseph (1966) *Situation Ethics: The New Morality* (Louisville, Westminster John Knox Press).

Fogelman, Eva (1994) *Conscience and Courage: Rescuers of Jews During the Holocaust* (New York, Anchor Books).

Fossey, Dian (1985) *Gorillas in the Mist* (London, Penguin).

Freedberg, David and Vittorio Gallese (2007) 'Motion, emotion and empathy in esthetic experience', *Trends in Cognitive Sciences*, Vol. 11 No.5: 197–203.

Freedman, Russell (1994) *Kids at Work: Lewis Hine and the Crusade Against Child Labor* (New York, Clarion Books).

Freud, Sigmund (1962) *Civilization and its Discontents* (New York, Norton).

Gabbay, Alex (2012) *Love Hate and Everything In Between*, documentary film (London, Monkey and Me Films).

Galbraith, John Kenneth (1977) *The Age of Uncertainty* (London, BBC Books and Andre Deutsch).

Galinsky, Adam and Gordon Moskowitz (2000). 'Perspective-Taking: Decreasing Stereotype Expression, Stereotype Accessibility, and In-Group Favouritism', *Journal of Personality and Social Psychology*, Vol. 78 No.4: 708–724.

Gandhi, Mahatma (1984) *An Autobiography, or The Story of My Experiments with Truth* (Ahmedabad, Navajivan Publishing House).

Gatenby, Reg (2004) 'Married Only At Weekends? A Study of the Amount of Time Spent Together by Spouses (London, Office for National Statistics).

Gerhardt, Sue (2004) *Why Love Matters: How affection shapes a baby's brain* (London, Routledge).

Gerhardt, Sue (2010) *The Selfish Society: How we all forgot to love one another and made money instead* (London, Simon and Schuster).

Gladwell, Malcolm (2005) *Blink: The Power of Thinking Without Thinking* (London, Penguin).

Goleman, Daniel (1999) *Working With Emotional Intelligence* (London, Bloomsbury).

Gordon, Mary (2002) 'Roots of Empathy: responsive parenting, caring societies', *Keio Journal of Medicine*, Vol. 52 No.4: 236–243.

Gordon, Mary (2005) *Roots of Empathy: Changing the World Child By Child* (Toronto, Thomas Allen).

Granado, Alberto (2003) *Travelling with Che Guevara: The making of a revolutionary* (London, Pimlico).

Griffin, John Howard (2009) *Black Like Me* (London, Souvenir Press).

Guevera, Che (1996) *The Motorcycle Diaries: A Journey Around South America* (London, Fourth Estate).

Hanh, Thich Nhat (1987) *Being Peace* (London, Rider).

Haviland-Jones, Jeannette, Holly Hale Rosario, Patricia Wilson and Terry McGuire (2005) 'An Environmental Approach to Positive Emotions: Flowers', *Evolutionary Psychology*, Vol. 3: 104–32.

Hedrick, Joan D. (1994) *Harriet Beecher Stowe: a Life* (New York, Oxford University Press).

Hickok, Gregory (2008) 'Eight Problems for the Mirror Neuron

Theory of Action Understanding in Monkeys and Humans', *Journal of Cognitive Neuroscience*, Vol. 21 No.7: 1229–1243.

Hochschild, Adam (2006) *Bury the Chains: The British Struggle to Abolish Slavery*, (London, Pan).

Hoffman, Martin (2000) *Empathy and Moral Development: Implications for Caring and Justice* (Cambridge, Cambridge University Press).

Hollan, Douglas and Jason Throop (eds) (2011) *The Anthropology of Empathy: Experiencing the Lives of Others in Pacific Societies* (New York, Berghahn Books).

Holman, Bob (1995) *The Evacuation: A Very British Revolution* (Oxford, Lion).

Hunt, Lynn (2007) *Inventing Human Rights: A History* (New York, Norton).

Isaacs, Susan (ed) (1941) *The Cambridge Evacuation Survey: A Wartime Study in Social Welfare and Education* (London, Methuen).

Jackson, Philip, Eric Brunet, Andrew Meltzoff and Jean Decety (2006) 'Empathy examined through the neural mechanisms involved in imagining how I feel versus how you feel pain', *Neuropsychologia* Vol. 44: 752–761.

James, Oliver (2013) *Office Politics: How to Thrive in a World of Lying, Backstabbing and Dirty Tricks* (London, Vermilion).

Keen, Suzanne (2007) *Empathy and the Novel* (Oxford, Oxford University Press).

Kellert, Stephen R. and Edward O. Wilson (eds) (1993) *The Biophilia Hypothesis* (Washington, Island Press and Shearwater Books).

Kelly, Andrew (1998) *All Quiet on the Western Front: The Story of a Film* (London, I.B. Tauris).

Keneally, Thomas (1994) *Schindler's List* (original title *Schindler's Ark*), (London, BCA).

Keneally, Thomas (2008) *Searching for Schindler* (London, Sceptre).

Keysers, Christian (2011) *The Empathic Brain: How the discovery of mirror neurons changes our understanding of human nature* (Christian Keysers, Amazon Kindle).

King, Martin Luther, Jr. (1964) *Why We Can't Wait* (New York, Signet Books).

Klimecki, Olga, Susanne Leiberg, Claus Lamm and Tania Singer (2012) 'Functional Neuro Plasticity and Associated Changes in Positive Affect After Compassion Training', *Cerebral Cortex* (advance access published 1 June 2012).

Klimecki, Olga, Susanne Leiberg, Matthieu Ricard and Tania Singer (2013) 'Differential Patter of Functional Brain Plasticity After Compassion and Empathy Training', *Social Cognitive and Affective Neuroscience* (advanced access published 9 May 2013), doi:10.1093/scan/nst060.

Knott, Sarah (2009) *Sensibility and the American Revolution* (Chapel Hill, University of North Carolina Press).

Kohn, Alfie (1990) *The Brighter Side of Human Nature: Empathy and Altruism in Everyday Life* (New York, Basic Books).

Konrath, Sara, Edward O'Brien and Courtney Hsing (2011) 'Changes in Dispositional Empathy in American College Students Over Time: A Meta-Analysis', *Personality and Social Psychology Review*, Vol. 15 No.2: 180–198.

Kringelbach, Morten and Helen Phillips (2014) *Emotion: pleasure and pain in the brain* (Oxford, Oxford University Press).

Kropotkin, Peter (1998) *Mutual Aid: A Factor of Evolution* (London, Freedom Press).

Krznaric, Roman (2003) *The Worldview of the Oligarchy in Guatemalan Politics* (PhD Thesis, University of Essex).

Krznaric, Roman (2007) 'How Change Happens: Interdisciplinary Perspectives for Human Development', Oxfam GB Research Report (Oxford, Oxfam).

Krznaric, Roman (2008) 'You Are Therefore I Am: How Empathy Education Can Create Social Change', Oxfam GB Research Report (Oxford, Oxfam).

Krznaric, Roman (2010a) 'Empathy with the Enemy', *The Pedestrian*, No.1: 117-130.

Krznaric, Roman (2010b) 'Empathy and Climate Change: Proposals for a Revolution of Human Relationships' in Stefan Skrimshire (ed) *Future Ethics: Climate Change and Apocalyptic Imagination* (London, Continuum).

Krznaric, Roman (2010c) 'Five Lessons for the Climate Crisis: What the History of Resource Scarcity in the United States and Japan Can Teach Us' in Mark Levene, Rob Johnson and Penny Roberts (eds), *History at the End of the World? History, Climate Change and the Possibility of Closure* (Penrith, Humanities E-Books).

Krznaric, Roman (2011) *The Wonderbox: Curious Histories of How to Live* (London, Profile Books).

Krznaric, Roman (2012a) *The Power of Outrospection*, RSA Animate video (London, Royal Society of the Arts).

Krznaric, Roman (2012b) *How to Find Fulfilling Work* (London, Macmillan).

Krznaric, Roman, Christopher Whalen and Theodore Zeldin (eds) (2006) *Guide to an Unknown University* (Oxford, The Oxford Muse).

Lakoff, George (2005) *Don't Think of an Elephant! Know your values and frame the debate* (Melbourne, Scribe Short Books).

Lanier, Jaron (2011) *You Are Not a Gadget* (London, Penguin).

Layard, Richard (2005) *Happiness: Lessons from a New Science* (London, Allen Lane).

Layard, Richard (2007) 'Happiness and the Teaching of Values', *CentrePiece*, Summer: 18-23.

Leiberg, Susanne, Olga Klimecki and Tania Singer (2011) 'Short-Term Compassion Training Increases Prosocial Behaviour in a New Developed Prosocial Game', *PloS ONE*, Vol. 6, No.3.

Levinas, Emmanuel (2006) *Humanism of the Other* (Urbana, University of Illinois Press).

Linfield, Susie (2010) *The Cruel Radiance: Photography and Political Violence* (Chicago, University of Chicago Press).

Louv, Richard (2005) *Last Child in the Woods: Saving Our Children from Nature-Deficit Disorder* (London, Atlantic Books).

Malone, Gareth (2012) *Choir* (London, Collins, ebook).

Mandela, Nelson (1995) *Long Walk to Freedom* (London, Abacus).

Masserman, Jules, Stanley Wechkin and William Terris (1964) 'Altruistic Behaviour in Rhesus Monkeys', *American Journal of Psychiatry*, Vol. 121 (December): 584–585.

McDonald, Paul (2013) *Hollywood Stardom* (Chichester, Wiley-Blackwell).

McMahon, Darrin (2006) *Happiness: A History* (New York, Grove Press).

Mehl, M.R., S. Vazire, S.E. Holleran and C.S. Clark (2010) 'Eavesdropping on happiness: Well-being is related to having less small talk and more substantive conversations', *Psychological Science*, 21: 539–541.

Mendelsohn, Daniel (2006) 'September 11 at the Movies', *New York Review of Books*, September 21: 43–46.

Monroe, Kristen Renwick (2004) *The Hand of Compassion: Portraits of Moral Choice During the Holocaust* (Princeton, Princeton University Press).

Moore, Patricia (1985) *Disguised* (Waco, World Books).

Moyn, Samuel (2006) 'Empathy in History, Empathizing with Humanity', *History and Theory*, Vol. 45 (October): 397–415.

Mukherjee, Rudrangshu (ed) 1993, *The Penguin Gandhi Reader* (New Delhi, Penguin Books).

Nagel, Thomas (1991) *Mortal Questions* (Cambridge, Cambridge University Press).

Neff, Kristin (2003) 'Self-Compassion: An Alternative Conceptualization of a Healthy Attitude Towards Oneself', *Self and Identity*, Vol. 2: 85–101.

Niezink, Lidewijn and Edwin Rutsch (2013). 'Empathy Circles: An instrument to practice empathy.' www.lidewijniezink. com/projects

Nowak, Martin with Roger Highfield (2011) *Supercooperators: Evolution, Altruism and Human Behaviour or Why We Need Each Other to Succeed* (Edinburgh, Canongate).

Nussbaum, Martha (1995) *Poetic Justice: The Literary Imagination and Public Life* (Boston, Beacon Press).

Oatley, Keith (2011) 'In the Minds of Others', *Scientific American Mind*, November/December: 63–67.

Obama, Barack (2007) *The Audacity of Hope: Thoughts on Reclaiming the American Dream* (Edinburgh, Canongate).

Oliner, Samuel P. and Pearl M. Oliner (1992) *The Altruistic Personality: Rescuers of Jews in Nazi Europe* (New York, Free Press).

Olson, Gary (2010) 'Empathy and Neuropolitics: This is your brain on neoliberal culture. Any questions?', Department of Political Science, Moravian College, Bethlehem, Pennsylvania.

Olson, Gary (2013) *Empathy Imperiled: Capitalism, Culture and the Brain* (New York, Springer).

Orwell, George (1962) *The Road to Wigan Pier* (Harmondsworth, Penguin).

Orwell, George (1966) *Down and Out in Paris and London* (Harmondsworth, Penguin).

Parker, Tony (1996) *Studs Terkel: A Life in Words* (New York, Henry Holt).

Patnaik, Dev (2009) *Wired to Care: How Companies Prosper When They Create Widespread Empathy* (Upper Saddle River, NJ, FT Press).

Phillips, Adam and Barbara Taylor (2009) *On Kindness* (London, Hamish Hamilton).

Piff, Paul, Daniel Stancato, Stéphane Côté, Rodolfo Mendoza-Denton, Dacher Keltner (2012) 'Higher Social Class Predicts

Unethical Behaviour', *Proceedings of the National Academy of Sciences*, February 27.

Pilger, John (ed) (2004) *Tell Me No Lies: Investigative Journalism and its Triumphs* (London, Jonathan Cape).

Pinker, Steven (2011) *The Better Angels of our Nature: The Decline of Violence in History and its Causes* (London, Allen Lane).

Prinz, Jesse (2011) 'Is empathy necessary for morality?' in Peter Goldie and Amy Coplan (eds) *Empathy: Philosophical and Psychological Perspectives* (Oxford, Oxford University Press).

Reynolds, Henry (1995) *The Other Side of the Frontier: Aboriginal Resistance to the European Invasion of Australia* (Ringwood, Victoria, Penguin).

Riess, Helen, John M. Kelley, Robert W. Bailey, Emily J. Dunn and Margot Phillips (2012) 'Empathy Training for Resident Physicians: A Randomized Controlled Trial of a Neuroscience-Informed Curriculum', *Journal of General Internal Medicine*, 2 May, DOI: 10.1007/s11606-012-2063-z.

Rifkin, Jeremy (2010) *The Empathic Civilization: The Race to Global Consciousness in a World in Crisis* (Cambridge, Polity).

Roots of Empathy (2008) 'Roots of Empathy: A Summary of Research Studies Conducted 2000–2007', March, Roots of Empathy, Toronto.

Rosenberg, Marshall (2003) *Nonviolent Communication: A Language of Life* (Encinitas, CA, PuddleDancer Press).

Rousseau, Jean-Jacques (1963) *Émile* (London, J.M. Dent & Sons).

Rowson, Jonathan (2012) 'The Power of Curiosity: How Linking Inquisitiveness to Innovation Could Help to Address Our Energy Challenges' (London, Royal Society of the Arts).

Said, Edward (2003) *Orientalism* (London, Penguin).

Santos R. G., M. J. Chartier, J. C. Whalen, D. Chateau and L. Boyd (2011) 'Effectiveness of school-based violence prevention for children and youth: Cluster randomized controlled field trial of the Roots of Empathy program with replication and three-year follow-up', *Healthcare Quarterly*, Vol. 14: 80–91.

Schlosser, Eric (2002) *Fast Food Nation: What the All-American Meal is Doing to the World* (London, Penguin).

Schonert-Reichl, Kimberly (2008) 'Effectiveness of Roots of Empathy Program: Research Summary, 2000–2008', Child and Adolescent Development Laboratory, Faculty of Education, Department of Educational and Counselling Psychology, and Special Education, University of British Columbia, Vancouver.

Schultz, P. Wesley (2000) 'Empathizing With Nature: The Effects of Perspective Taking on Concern for Environmental Issues', *Journal of Social Issues*, Vol.56 No.3: 391–406.

Seligman, Martin (2003) *Authentic Happiness: Using the New Positive Psychology to Realize Your Potential for Lasting Fulfillment* (London, Nicholas Brealey).

Sennett, Richard (1999) *The Corrosion of Character: The Personal Consequences of Work in the New Capitalism* (New York, Norton).

Sennett, Richard (2012) *Together: The Rituals, Pleasures and Politics of Cooperation* (London, Allen Lane).

Seymour-Jones, Carole (1993) *Beatrice Webb: Woman of Conflict* (London, Pandora Press).

Singer, Peter (1997) *How Are We To Live?: Ethics in an Age of Self-Interest* (Oxford, Oxford University Press).

Singer, Tania and Claus Lamm (2009) 'The Social Neuroscience of Empathy', *The Year in Cognitive Neuroscience 2009*, New York Academy of Sciences 1156: 81–96.

Skidmore, Gil (2005) *Elizabeth Fry: A Quaker Life – Selected Letters and Writings* (Oxford, Altamira Press).

Slote, Michael (2007) *The Ethics of Care and Empathy* (London, Routledge).

Smith, Adam (1976) *The Theory of Moral Sentiments* (Indianapolis, Liberty Classics).

Smith, Zadie (2010) 'Generation Why?, *New York Review of Books*, November 25.

Solnit, Rebecca (2010) *A Paradise Built in Hell: The extraordinary communities that arise in disaster* (London, Penguin).

Sontag, Susan (1979) *On Photography* (London, Penguin).

Stanislavski, Constantin (1937) *An Actor Prepares* (London, Geoffrey Bles).

'Taking on Concern for Environmental Issues', *Journal of Social Issues*, Vol.56, No.3: 391–406

Tannen, Deborah (1999) 'Women and Men in Conversation' in Rebecca S. Wheeler (ed), *The Workings of Language: From Prescriptions to Perspectives* (Wesport, Conn., Praeger).

Taylor, A.J.P. (1967) *English History 1914–45* (London, Readers Union and Oxford University Press).

Taylor, Matthew (2010) 'Twenty-first Century Enlightenment' (London, Royal Society of the Arts).

Terkel, Studs (1982) *American Dreams: Lost and Found* (London, Granada).

Terkel, Studs (2007) *Touch and Go: A Memoir* (New York, New Press).

Titmuss, Richard (1950) *Problems of Social Policy* (London, H.M.S.O. and Longmans, Green & Co.).

Trachtenberg, Alan (1989) *Reading American Photographs: Images as History, Matthew Brady to Walker Evans* (New York, Hill and Wang).

Turkle, Sherry (2011) *Alone Together: Why we expect more from technology and less from each other* (New York, Basic Books).

Twenge, Jean and Keith Campbell (2009) *The Narcissism Epidemic: Living in the Age of Entitlement* (New York, Atria).

Wallraff, Günter (1978) *The Undesirable Journalist* (London, Pluto Press).

Wallraff, Günter (1988) *Lowest of the Low* (London, Methuen).

Warner, Marina (2013) 'Contradictory Curiosity', unpublished manuscript, January 26.

Webb, Beatrice (1888) 'Pages From a Work-Girl's Diary', *The Nineteenth Century*, Vol. 139 (September): 301–314.

Webb, Beatrice (1971) *My Apprenticeship* (Harmondsworth, Penguin Books).

Wilson, Edward O. (1984) *Biophilia: The Human Bond With Other Species* (Cambridge MA, Harvard University Press).

Women's Group on Public Welfare (1944) *Our Towns: A Close-Up* (London, Oxford University Press).

Woolman, John (1800) *The Works of John Woolman (in Two Parts)* (Philadelphia, Benjamin & Jacob Johnson).

Zak, Paul (2012) *The Moral Molecule: The New Science of What Makes Us Good and Evil* (London, Bantam Press).

Zaki, Jamil (2012) 'The Curious Perils of Seeing the Other Side', *Scientific American Mind*, 23: 20–21.

Zeldin, Theodore (1995) *An Intimate History of Humanity* (London, Minerva).

Zeldin, Theodore (1998) *Conversation* (London, Harvill).

Zeldin, Theodore (2003) 'The New Conversation', manuscript.

Zeldin, Theodore and Roman Krznaric (2004) *Guide to an Unknown City* (Oxford, The Oxford Muse).

ACKNOWLEDGEMENTS

One of the reasons I left academia over a decade ago was so I could pursue my studies of empathy, a topic that did not seem to fit neatly within any traditional disciplinary boundaries, and that required exploration far beyond the realm of university libraries. This book is the culmination of my research and thinking.

Over the years I have received enormous support from a variety of people, including scholars, activists, friends and family. Amongst those whom I would especially like to thank are: Abi Stephenson, Adam Swift, Andrew Park, Anna Krznaric, Bill Drayton, Bill McKibben, Brené Brown, Christian Keysers, Christopher Wakling, Daniel Crewe, Darren James, Edwin Rutsch, Frans de Waal, George Marshall, Hugh Warwick, Jean Knox, Jenny Raworth, Joey Katona, Lina Nahhas, Mary Gordon, Matthew Cherian, Mike Dibb, Patricia Moore, Peter Holmes à Court, Peter Krznaric, Pieter Serneels, Richard Raworth, Ryan Green, Sarah Stuart-Brown, Sue Weaver, Theodore Zeldin, and Tushar Vashisht.

A very special thanks to my crack team of interdisciplinary readers who commented on the manuscript: Darwin Franks, John-Paul Flintoff, Konstantin Dierks, Lisa Gormley, Morten Kringelbach, Philippa Perry, Quentin Spender, Sarah Knott, Sophie Howarth, Sue Gerhardt, and Tom Chatfield. I have also benefited hugely from the ideas, questions and critiques of people who have attended my talks and workshops on empathy at The School of Life, literary and music festivals, philosophy clubs, international development agencies, schools, businesses, churches and community groups.

Judith Kendra at Rider Books has been a wonderful, wise and supportive editor. Thanks also to Alice Latham, Amelia Evans, Catherine Knight, Sue Lascelles, Shona Abhyankar, Alex Cooper, Helen Pisano and others in the Rider team for all their help, as well as Two Associates for the cover design. My agent, Maggie Hanbury, has been amazing as always and has really understood how important this book is to me. Henry de Rougemont and Harriet Poland at the Hanbury Agency also deserve special thanks for bringing this book to life.

I feel lucky to live with three people who have done so much to inspire not just my thinking about empathy, but my attempts to put the ideas I write about into practice in everyday life: my partner, Kate Raworth, and our children Siri and Casimir.

The author and publisher would like to thank the following for permission to include copyright material:

PICTURE CREDITS: p.xi 'Patricia Moore (young and old)' with kind permission from Patricia Moore; p. xxviii 'Socrates in The Power of Outrospection' © 2012, Cogntive Media Limited; p.10 'Child's Eye View Exhibition' by Paul Ritter and Jean Ritter, with kind permission from Jean Ritter; p. 23 'Spider on Shoulder' © Elizabeth Best/Alamy; p. 31 'Roots of Empathy' © Roots of Empathy; p.36 'Miner Emrys Jones' © Hulton-Deutsch Collection/CORBIS; p.58 'Harriet Beecher Stowe's son Charley' © The Schlesinger Library, Radcliffe Institute, Harvard University; p.80 'Günther Wallraff cleaning toilets' © ANP Foto; p. 85 'Che Guevara and Luis Granado, 1952', Museo Che Guevara (Centro de Estudios Che Guevara en La Habana, Cuba)/ Wikimedia Commons/Public Domain; p.92 'Empathy Escapes, the next revolution in holiday travel' with kind permission from

Kate Raworth; p.108 'Studs Terkel on street' © Steve Kagan/ Time & Life Pictures/Getty Images; p.110 'Conversation Meal, Oxford Muse' with kind permission from Kate Raworth; p.131 'Jo Berry and Pat Magee' with kind permission from Brian Moody and The Forgiveness Project; p.140 'Paul in the trench, comforting dying soldier' © Bettmann/CORBIS; p.145 'Little Spinner' by Lewis Hine (1908) with kind permission from the Library of Congress; p.150 'PeaceMaker screen shot' © ImpactGames LLC; p.171 'Children waiting to evacuate Southampton' © Hulton-Deutsch Collection/CORBIS; p.177 'Simpson on the rack' © Mary Evans Picture Library; p.190 'Musekeweya Rwandan Radio Soap' © Anoek Steketee.

TEXT CREDITS: *The Atlantic* magazine for material from *Signing off* by Robert Wright (*The Atlantic*, 2013); Canongate Books for material from *The Audacity of Hope: Thoughts on Reclaiming the American Dream* by Barack Obama (Canongate, 2007); Adam Curtis and the BBC for material from *The Century of the Self*; Bill Drayton for material from 'Everyone a Changemaker: Social Entreneurship's Ultimate Goal' by Bill Drayton in *Innovations* (MIT Press, 2006); Dundurn Press Limited for material from *Roots of Empathy: Changing the World, Child by Child* by Mary Gordon (Thomas Allen Publishers). Copyright © 2005, Mary Gordon; The Forgiveness Project for material from The Forgiveness Project; Nikki Gemmell for material from 'Our Better Selves' by Nikki Gemmell (*The Australian*, December 15, 2012); Greater Good Science Center for material as adapted from *Our Inner Ape: A Leading Primatologist Explains Why We Are Who We Are* by Frans de Waal (Riverhead, 2006); *Guardian* for material from 'Bridging the Gap' by Daniel Barenboim (*Guardian* online); Harper Collins Publishers Ltd and Curtis Brown Group Ltd for material from *Choir* by Gareth Malone. Copyright © 2012, Gareth Malone; Little, Brown Book Group for material from *Long Walk to Freedom* by Nelson Mandela

(Abacus, 1995); Monkey & Me Films for material from *Love Hate and Everything in Between* by Alex Gabbay (Monkey & Me Films, 2012); Kristin Neff for material from 'Self-Compassion: An Alternative Conceptualization of a Healthy Attitude Towards Oneself' by Kristin Neff in *Self and Identity*; www.oxfordmuse. com (Conversation, Dining and Dancing) for material from 'The New Conversation' by Theodore Zeldin; Norton for material from *Inventing Human Rights: A History* by Lynn Hunt (Norton, 2007); Oxford University Press for material from *How Are We to Live? Ethics in an Age of Self-Interest* by Peter Singer; Penguin Books Ltd for material from *The Better Angels of Our Nature* by Steven Pinker (Allen Lane, 2011). Copyright © 2011, Steven Pinker; Polity Press and Jeremy P. Tarcher, an imprint of Penguin Group (USA) LLC for material from *The Empathic Civilization: The Race to Global Consciousness in a World in Crisis* by Jeremy Rifkin. Copyright © 2009, Jeremy Rifkin; PuddleDancer Press for material from *Nonviolent Communication: A Language of Life* by Dr Marshall B. Rosenberg (2nd Edition, 2003); Radio Times Online for material from 'Gareth Malone on the Choir: Sing While you Work, Military Wives and Getting Competitive' by Claire Webb, 2012; Random House Group Limited for material from *Twelve Steps to a Compassionate Life* by Karen Armstrong (The Bodley Head); Riverhead Books, an imprint of Penguin Group (USA) LLC for material from *Buddhism Without Beliefs* by Stephen Batchelor. Copyright ©1997, Stephen Batchelor & The Buddhist Ray, Inc,; Zadie Smith for material from 'Generation Why?'. Copyright © 2010, Zadie Smith. First published in New York Review of Books and reproduced by permission of the author c/o Rogers, Coleridge & White Ltd, 20 Powis Mews, London W11 1JN; Souvenir Press for material from *Black Like Me* by John Howard Griffin (Souvenir Press, 2009); Special Broadcasting Service for quoted material in '"Illegals" and the erosion of empathy' by Helen Davidson. Copyright © 2013, SBS; Stanford University Press for material from *Empathic Vision:*

Affect, Trauma, and Contemporary Art by Jill Bennett (Stanford University Press, 2005); The Tanja Howarth Agency for material from *Lowest of the Low* by Günther Wallraff (Methuen, 1998); University of Chicago Press for material from *The Cruel Radiance: Photography and Political Violence* by Susie Linfield (University of Chicago Press, 2010).

INDEX